Hand Book of Synthetic and Herbal COSMETICS

(How to Make Beauty Products)

(With Directory of Machinery & Raw Material Suppliers)

A complete encyclopaedia on Cosmetics (Herbal and Synthetic). The book provides the depth informations regarding to manufacture cosmetics either as an industry or for Home made. The book is covering 42 detailed and exhaustive chapters including various Project Profiles and Suppliers of Plant, Equipments and Machineries for setting up or diversifying the Cosmetics.

Written by

Ankur Kumar

ENGINEERS INDIA RESEARCH INSTITUTE

4449, Nai Sarak, Main Road, Delhi - 110006 (India)
Ph: +91-11-23918117, 23916431, 45120361, 23947058, 64727385
*** E-Mail: eiribooks@yahoo.com & eiriprojects@gmail.com**
***Website: www.eiriindia.org & www.industrialprojectreports.com**

PRINTED & PUBLISHED BY

ENGINEERS INDIA RESEARCH INSTITUTE

4449, Nai Sarak, Main Road, Delhi - 110006 (India)
Ph: +91-11-23918117, 23916431, 45120361, 23947058, 64727385
* E-Mail: eiribooks@yahoo.com & eiriprojects@gmail.com
*Website: www.eiriindia.org & www.industrialprojectreports.com

Sole Distributor:

EIRI PROJECT CONSULTANTS AND PUBLISHERS
4/54 Roop Nagar, Delhi-110007

ISBN: 9788186732212

Printed in New Delhi (INDIA)

2nd Edition

₹ 975/-

Printed & Published by Sudhir Gupta for "Engineers India Research Institute", 4449 Nai Sarak, Main Road, New Delhi -110006

OTHER RELATED BOOKS

SOAPS & DETERGENTS

01 Household Soap. Toilet Soap & Other Soap
02 Profitable Small Scale Manufacture Of Soaps & Detergents
03 Synthetic Detergents With Formulations
04 Modern Technology of Acid Slurry, Surfactants, Soap and Detergents with Formulae

ORGANIC FARMING AND FOOD

01 Hand Book Of Organic Farming And Organic Foods With Vermi-Composting And Neem Products

FISH FARMING & FISHERY PRODUCTS

01 Hand Book Of Fish Farming And Fishery Products

COSMETIC (SYNTHETIC & HERBAL)

01 Cosmetics Processes & Formulations
02 Herbal Cosmetics & Beauty Products With Formulations
03 Profitable Small Scale Manufacture Of Cosmetics (Synthetic & Herbal)
04 Hand Book Of Synthetic & Herbal Cosmetics
05 Technology Of Herbal Cosmetics & Toiletries Products with Formulae

OIL AND FATS

01 Hand Book of Oils, Fats And Derivatives With Refining & Packaging Technology
02 Technology of Oilseeds Processing, Oils & Fats and Refining

ESSENTIAL OILS & AROMATIC

01 Essential Oils Manufacturing & Aromatic Plants
02 Modern Technology Of Essential Oils
03 Technology Of Perfumes, Flavours & Essential Oils
04 Essential Oils Processes & Formulations

PERFUMES AND FLAVOURS

01 Hand Book Of Flavours & Food Colourants Technology
02 Hand Book Of Perfumes & Flavours
03 H.B. Of Perfumes With Formulations
04 Technology Of Perfumes, Flavours & Essential Oils
05 Hand Book Of Flavours Technology

Preface

Cosmetics products are created for application on the body for the purpose of cleansing, beautifying or altering appearance and enhancing attractive features. It is not similar like medicines in addition to it cannot be used to modify the physique function or performance. The cosmetic Industry has witnessed rapid growth over the last couple of decades. Now a day the range of cosmetic and beauty products has widened tremendously. The use of cosmetics has increased exponentially not only among in females but the male population also indulges in their use. A wide range of chemical and natural materials is used in the formulation of cosmetic and toiletry preparations. Cosmetics like creams, gels, face powder, eye makeup, shaving cream, and colognes are used on a daily basis by both women and men. The Indian cosmetic Industry has witnessed rapid growth over the last couple of decades.

Herbal cosmetics in the simple form are the cosmetics which are made ayurvedic base with adding some ayurvedic or medical compounds which contribute some additional specific properties to the herbal cosmetics. Herbal cosmetics include herbal hair oil, herbal shampoos. Herbal tooth paste, herbal tooth powder and herbal face cream.

The Book covers Face Powder, Variations of Face Powder, Toilet Powder, Creams, Vanishing Creams, Foundation Creams, Hand Lotions, After Shaving Lotion s, Deodorants, Lipsticks, Shampoos, Depilatories, Shaving Cream, Cosmetics for Nails, Tooth Powder, Tooth Paste, Mouth Washes, Facial Masks, Cosmetics for Eyes, Cosmetic for Babies, Herbal Cosmetic for the Skin, Hair Shampoos, Anti Dandruff Preparations, Hair Straighteners, Hair Dyes, Bleaches, Colourings and Dye Removers, Oral Herbal Preparations, Project profiles, Suppliers of Machinery & Raw Materials etc.

-Author

Publisher: www.eiriindia.org

CONTENTS AND SUBJECT INDEX

CHAPTERS *PAGE NO.*

PRODUCTION PROBLEMS & RECOMMENDATIONS 1-13

- Duplication of Cosmetics - Perfuming Procedure 1

COSMETICS AND DRUGS 14 -22

- Physical Characteristics of Cosmetics 14
- Comments on these Characteristics 14
- Cosmetic Classification 14

FACE POWDER 23-39

- Properties Desired Discussion of These Properties - Raw Materials Used - Manufacturing Methods - Formulaes 23
- Light Face Powder - With Zinc Oxide 28
- Medium Face Powder - With Purified Kaolin 29
- Medium Face Powder - With Titanium Dioxide 29
- Heavy Face Powder - With Zinc Oxide & Titanium Dioxide 30
- Manufacturing Methods 33
- White Base for Light Powder - With Zinc Oxide 35
- White Base for Medium Powder - With Zinc Oxide 35
- White Base for Medium Powders - With Titanium Dioxide 35
- White Base for Medium Powders - With Zinc Oxide & Titanium Dioxide 36
- Powder Bases 36
- Additional Formulaes 37

VARIATIONS OF FACE POWDERS 40 - 53

- Compacts - Cake Make-Up Powders - Liquid and
- Creams Powders Cosmetic Stockings 40
- Compact Powder Base 43
- Formulaes of Liquid Powders 45
- Formulaes of Cream Powder 48
- Formulaes of Liquid Cosmetic Stocking 50
- Cosmetic Stocking - Light Shade 52
- Colour Base Light 52
- Cosmetic Stocking - Dark Shade 52
- Colour Base Dark 52
- Stick Cosmetic Stocking 53

TOILET POWDERS 54 -58

- Talcum Powder - Dusting Powder -
- After Shave Powder - Baby Powder 54
- Talcum Powders 55
- After-Shave Powder 56
- Body Powder 56
- Baby Powder 57

CREAMS 59-67

- Manufacturing Procedure 59
- Various Formulaes of Cold Cream 60
- Theatrical Cold Cream 65
- Semi-Greaseless Cold Cream 65
- Whitening Cold Cream 66
- Cold Cream 66

VANISHING CREAMS	68-72
- Various Formulaes	68
FOUNDATION CREAMS	73-78
- Various Formulaes of Foundation Cream	73
- Cream Oil Base	75
- Finished Cream	75
- Various Formulaes	76
HAND LOTIONS	79-81
- Varieties-Increased Uses - Formulaes	79
- Various Formulaes	80
- Pineapple Juice Hand Lotion	81
AFTER SHAVING LOTIONS	82-86
- Various Formulaes of Lotion	82
- Dry Skin Lotion	84
- Oily Skin Lotion	84
- Additional Formulaes	85
- After Shave and General Purpose Lotion	86
DEODORANTS	87-93
- General Considerations-Antipersiprants and Deodorants-Labeling Paste Depdorants-Stick	
MASCARA-EYEBROW PENCILS-EYE SHADOWS	94-98
- Eye Shadow	94
- Various Formulaes of Mascara	95

- Various Formulaes of Eye Shadow 96
- Various Formulaes of Make Up Preparations 97
- Various Formulaes of Eyelash 97
- Various Formulaes of EyeBrow 98

LIPSTICS 99-103

- Various Formulaes of Lipstick 101

SHAMPOOS 104-113

- Properties: 105
- "Clear liquid shampoos" 105
- "Baby shampoos" 105
- Sulfonate oil-soapless shampoo - Ingredients Qty. 106
- Miscellaneous shampoos: 106
- "Medicated Dandruff shampoos : 106
- "Soap shampoos : 107
- "Shampoo Additives : 107
- Opaciflers 107
- Solubillzers-Couplers 108
- Thickeners 108
- Conditioning agents 108
- Preservatives 108
- "Shampoo Detergents-Anionic-Fatty alkyl sulfates 109
- "Solid-function shampoos: 109
- "Solid shampoos 110
- "Liquid cream or lotion shmapoos 110
- Powder shampoos 110
- "Jelly (gel) shampoos 110
- "Cream or paste shampoos 111
- Shampoo 111
- Formula for coconut oil shampoos 112
- Formula for vegetable Oil Shampoos 112

- Hair Rinse	113
DEPILATORIES	114-118
- Various Formulaes of Depilatories Powder	114
- Various Formulaes of Depliatories Paste	115
- Various Formulaes of Depilatory Liquid	117
SHAVING CREAM	119-123
- Formulaes of Brushless Shaving Cream	120
COSMETICS FOR THE NAILS	124-127
- Formulaes of Nail Enamels	125
- Formulaes of Nail Polish Removers	126
TOOTH POWDER	128-133
- Various Formulaes of Tooth Powder	128
- Oxygenated Tooth Powder	129
- Antacid Tooth Powder	130
- Sodium Perborate Tooth Powder	130
- Antacid Tooth Powder	130
- Acid Tooth Powder	131
- Foamy Powders	131
- Tooth Powders With Magnesium Peroxide	132
TOOTH PASTES OR DENTAL CREAMS	134-149
- Various Formulaes of Tooth Paste	135
- Inexpensive	138
- High Grade	139
- Acid-Reacting Tooth Paste	139

- Alkaline Tooth Paste 140
- Milk Of Magnesia Tooth Paste 140
- Glycerite of Starch 141
- Soapy Tooth Paste 141
- Magnsia Tooth Paste 144
- U.S. Goverment Tooth Paste Specifications 145

MOUTH WASHES 150-153

- Various Farmulaes of National Formulary Preparation 151
- Alkaline Mouth Wash 152
- Chloro-Phenol Mouth Wash 152
- Resorcin Mouth Wash 153

FACIAL MASKS 154-157

- Acacia Mask 155

COSMETICS FOR THE EYES 158-161

- Various Formulaes of Eye lotions 158
- Various Formulaes of Eye Cream 161

INSECT REPELLING PREPARATIONS 162-164

- Bite Lotions 162
- Insect Bite Lotions 163
- Insect Bite Cream 164

COSMETICS FOR BABIES 165-166

- Baby Powder 165
- Baby Oil 165
- Baby Cream 166

HERBAL COSMETICS FOR THE SKIN 167-183

- Introduction 167
- Equipment used for Herbal Preparations 167
- Cleansing Creams 168
- Various Formulaes of Cleansing Cream 168
- Process of Manufacture 168
- Procedure 170
- Masks 170
- Various Formulaes of Bath 173
- Various Formuaes of Body Lotion 176

HAIR SHAMPOOS 184-198

- Introduction 184
- Types of Shampoos 185
- Various Formulaes of Shampoo 189

ANTI DANDRUFF PREPARATIONS 199-238

- Introduction 199
- Process of Manufacture 201
- Quality Control Aspects 201
- Hair Grooming Preparations 201
- Characteristics of Good Hair Dressing 202
- Various Formulaes of Lotion 203
- Various Formulaes of Liquid Brilliantines 205
- Various Formulaes of Gum Based Hair Dressing 208
- Hair Tonics 210
- Various Formulaes of Hair Tonics 211
- Oil in water Emulsions 215
- Formulations 216
- Various Formulaes of Hair Grooming Preparation 218
- Herbal Cosmetics for the hair 220

- Formula of Herbal hair oil 221
- Herbal Shampoos 222
- Henna hair dye 223
- Applications of Henna 224
- Various Formulaes of Camomile 227
- Depilatories 231
- Various Formulaes of Depilatory 232

HAIR STRAIGHTENERS 239-245

- Introduction 239
- Various Formulaes of Hair straighters 239
- Physical Method of Hair straightening 241

HAIR DYES, BLEACHES, COLOURINGS AND DYE REMOVERS 246-266

- Introduction 246
- Classification of Colouring Agents 246
- Bleaching Agents 248
- Process of Bleaching 249
- Bleaching of hair 249
- Temporary Colourings 250
- Crayons 251
- Various Formulaes of Crayons 251
- Coloured Rinses 251
- Miscellaneous Temporary Colourings 254
- Various Formulaes of Dye 258
- Dye Removers 265

ORAL HERBAL PREPARATONS 267 269

- Tooth Pastes and Tooth Powder 267
- Formula of Tooth Paste 267
- Formula of Tooth Powder 268

Formula of Mouth Wash 268

GOVT. REGULATIONS AND ACTS ON DRUGS AND COSMETICS 270-279

- Drugs and Cosmetics Act 270
- Objective 270
- Synopsis Of Chapter 271
- Section 271
- Section Definitions 272
- Imports of Drugs and Cosmetics 275
- Manufacture Sale And Distribution Of Drug And Cosmetics (Section) 277

BATH PREPARATIONS 280-289

- Introduction 280
- Bath Salts 280
- Various Formulaes of Bath Salts 281
- Bath Oils 282
- Various Formulaes of Bath Oils 283
- Bubble Bath 284
- Characterstics of Bubble Bath 285
- Various Formulaes of Bubble Bath 285
- Procedure 286
- Bath Powders 287
- Various Formulaes of Bath Powders 288

BABY PREPARATIONS 290-306

- Introduction 290
- Emolients used in Baby Preparations 291
- Various Formulaes of Baby Oil 291
- Process of Manufacture 294

- Various Formulaes of Baby Lotion 294
- Various Formulaes of Baby Cream 300
- Various Formulaes of Baby Powder 305

HOME MADE COSMETICS 307-309

- Ingredients 308

HERBAL PREPARATIONS FOR BODY 310-320

- Oatmeal Scrub 310
- Various Types of Bath 310
- Herbal Body Lotion 314
- Various Formulaes of Lotion 314
- Body Massage Cream 315
- Body Massage Oil 316
- Deodorant 317
- Various Formulaes of Deodorant 318

SKIN CLEANSING 321-336

- Ingredients 321
- Moisturising for all Skins 323
- Various Types of Cream 324
- Toning the Skin by Herbal Ways 329
- Herbal Skin Tonics 330
- Home Made Astringents and Skin Tonics 333

HERBAL PREPARATIONS FOR FEET AND HANDS 337-338

- Astringent Foot Freshner 337
- Balm for Corns 337
- Thyme and Rosemary Lotion 337

- Rosemary Jelly 337

HAIR SHAMPOOS AND SETTING 339-342

- Home Made Shampoos 339
- An Energy Recipe 339
- Panama Wood Shampoo 339
- Rum Shampoo 339
- Egg Shampoo 340
- Conditioning Shampoo 340
- Herb Shampoo 340
- Tonic Shampoo 340
- Soapwort and Camomile Shampoo 340
- Hair Styling and Setting Lotions 341

HOW TO LAY OUT A COSMETIC FACTORY 343-348

- Important Details to form a Cosmetic Factory 343

PROJECT PROFILS 349-370

- After Shave Lotion 349
- Face Cream & Body Cream 351
- Herbal Cosmetic 353
- Hair Styling Gel 355
- Herbal Oil 357
- Hair Fixer 359
- Hair Dye in Cream Form 361
- Lipsticks 363
- Nail Polish/Enamel 365
- Petroleum Jelly 367
- Shaving Cream 369

SUPPLIERS OF PLANT AND MACHINERIES 371-386

SUPPLIERS OF RAW MATERIALS 387 401

PACKAGING CRITERIA FOR COSMETICS 402-414

1

PRODUCTION PROBLEMS AND RECOMMENDATIONS

Duplication of Cosmetics – Perfuming Procedure

In Making Cosmetics one should remember that nothing is to be gained by haste. New products should not be placed on the market overnight; batches should not be thrown together hastily.

New products should be tested under all, and particularly the extreme, temperature and humidity conditions they are likely to encounter in the open market. And besides, they should be placed on a shelf on six months. If after six months of testing and shelf life no change is noted in the product, it can be marketed with complete assurance that it will not fail to meet popular approval because of physical or chemical defects.

Of utmost importance is the selection and control of raw materials. Use only the best grades. Since raw materials constitute only a very small percentage of total cost, there is no valid excuse for using inferior grades of materials. Inferior materials save but comparatively little and likely to cause adverse physical and chemical reactions in finished products which will cause rejects and loss or ill will old customers.

All raw materials should be standardized as to quality. Samples from each shipment should be carefully tested and compared with standard specifications. Similarly, a sample from each batch of finished product should be kept for at least two years in order to check returns. Every package should be marked in some way with a laboratory control number, so that when returns occur, the chemist can compare them with production samples and can also refer to batch records for information which will assist him in assigning the reasons for the returns.

In asmuch as the quality of water is variable in different parts of the country, all water used in cosmetic manufacture should be distilled, or purified.

Standards for manufacturing procedure and control of temperature should be established and rigidly adhered to. It is due to the lack of such standards that many manufacturers never produce two successive batches which are uniform in texture and physical properties. Every batch should always be made in exactly the same way.

When new process equipment is purchased, a new set of standards may be established to govern the handling of the new equipment. Sometimes it may be necessary to adjust a formula slightly in order to compensate for differences caused by the use of better, more efficient equipment.

The cosmetic maker should never be completely satisfied with any product. He should keep informed of new raw materials and cosmetic research, of new equipment, of changes in market requirements. Products die of old age or public neglect because manufacturers do not make changes frequently enough to keep their preparations up to date. Perfumes especially are suscetitle to cycles of change in popular taste. Consistencies and types of creams likewise change. Formula changes can be made gradually without disturbing establishes business in the least.

In producing toilet preparations, the chemist or perfumer is usually called upon to make up what is termed "a line". This permits the addition of and elimination of certain products from time to time as the consumers' tastes vary. Since cosmetics lines are in keen competition, they include similar products in most cases. The trade-mark and advertising are the main line of demarcation. This results in duplication or simulation of products except for the perfume characteristic, though even this is also imitated in certain cases.

In order to duplicate competitive products it is essential to have an intimate knowledge of the composition of toiletries. It is often possible to tell what the competitive product is composed of simply by a careful examination. Exact analysis of cosmetics is in most cases impossible and futile.

In imitating a toilet cream, for instance, it may be necessary to establish its emulsion classification. If the cream takes up oil it is a water-in-oil type and very likely a cold cream. If it takes up water, the emulsion is of oil-in-water type. The next operation is to determine which emulsifying agent was used in the original cream. If it is a soap or amine of any kind, a few drops of alcoholic phenolphthalein added to the molten sample of cream will gave a pink colouration. If the sample turns pink and is water-in-oil type of emulsion, the cream is practically certain to be a cold cream made with borax. If the sample does not give an alkaline reaction, it probably is an absorption base cream.

Having determined the general identity of the cream, the percentage of water present may be determined. Deducting this percentage will give the approximate amount of oils, fats and waxes used. If the residue left after evaporate is stickly and tends to drag when rubbed on the skin a hight per centage of beeswax is probable. If it melts quickly on the skin and rubs out easily a high percentage of paraffin, petroleum and mineral oil are indicated. As to the percentage of wax actually employed, inspection of the original cream will provide a clue. A stiff heavy cream will of course contain a high percentage of wax.

These tests are by no means infallible but to the experienced chemist who knows cosmetics, they will be adequate. The next step will be to make a series of samples.

Face powders can be duplicated fairly accurately. a qualititative and quantitative analysis will reveal the relative ratios of inorganic substances present in the sample. An ash determination will give the percent of organic material, and a microscope will serve to identify certain raw materials as well as some of the colors used. Iodine will indicate the presence of starches. Most powders make use of the following substances : titanium oxide, talc, magnesium and calcium, carbonates, magnesium oxide, Zinc stearate, zinc oxide, calcium carbonate, kaolin and colloidal clay. Colors must be matched by comparison, and the perfume will be found the most difficult item to imitate.

Wherever chemists reproduce a skin tonic, or an astringent, they depend a great deal on the taste and physical application of the product. Few skin tonics use ingredients other than a small concentration of glycerin, alcohol, boric acid, acetic acid, witch hazel and distilled water. A comparison of the drying times between the original skin tonic and the duplication will give an idea of the alcohol ratio or better still dropped on a piece of paper exposed to the air will indicate if there is a large percent of glycerin in the product. What has been said of skin tonics can be said also of the solution. The common astringents found in the most preparations an alcohal analysis may be made. Small amount of the tonic of this nature are zinc sulfocarbonate, zinc chloride, tannic acid, aluminium chloride, and alum.

astringents tasting the sample will reveal the strength probably no one has ever successfully analyzed a lipstick other than to give the chemical elements making up its structure. A high acetyl number will indicate the presence of a high percentage of castor oil. Other than it is futile to try to identify the oils, fats and waxes. The best way to duplicate a lipstick is to make many samples until the product gives a similar application, feel, its texture, idelibility, and melting point. Here, as usual, practical experience is far more valuable than chemical theory.

One should be able to judge from the appearance of a hand lotion if it is emulsified, for this type of product then presents a milk-white aspect, and in many cases relies upon a borax-beeswax combination for emulsion stability. Many preparations of this character possess a distinct sheen. This effect usually is obtained by the use of a stearic acid soap concentration, and is heightened by the addition of about ten percent of alcohol and five percent of glycerin, but lotions employing free stearic acid may give a sheen without extra soap, alcohol, or glycerin being present. It is well to remember that sheen is generally destroyed by the addition of even a small amount of mineral oil, and that such an effect can never be obtained unless the wax -oil phase is in a solid or crystalline state at room temperatures.

The next step is to discover the type of gum used for the mucilage base. If the product is stringy as it pours out of the bottle, one can be sure that the mucilage contains karaya. If the preparation is sticky without tasting necessarily of glycerin, quince seed is the probable mucilage base.

Tragcanth can be identified by allowing a small portion of the lotion to evaporate on a watch glass and observing it through a microscope after it dries. A comparison of a known tragcanth mucilage treated in a similar manner will confirm the test. Other gums such locust bean, Irish moss, and gum arabic are less often found in hand lotions, so it is necessary to look for them, before excluding the more common types. Some firms use a mixture of tragcanth and quince seed, but while the majority still employ straight quince seed mucilage in these preparations, aliginates from sea weed are replacing part of the quince seed.

Other ingredients found in the average hand lotion on the market are : boric acid, potassium and ammonium soaps, spermaceti, cetyl alcohol, ethyl alcohol, various glycols and glycol ethers, coconut and mineral oil, diglycol- and mono-glyceryl stearate, and isopropyl alcohol.

What has been said regarding lipsticks and creams, also holds true for hand lotions, viz., a series of samples must be made and the best match chosen. It is best to make this selection after about three weeks have elapsed, for it often takes this time interval for the lotion to age and the sheen to develop.

It will be seen from the foregoing discussion, that common sense based upon empirical experience is just as important in duplicating cosmetics, astechinical skill one knows cosmetic composition one will also acquire knowledge of the materials employed in the manufacture of them and will be familiar with the effects of specific raw materials on the finished products. As greater experience is acquired satisfactory duplicates of standard cosmetics can be made with very few laboratory tests.

The trial and error procedure above outlined is of great importance in running down difficulties and obscure incompatibles which impair the appearance or efficacy of cosmetics from time to time. To the practical cosmetic manufacturer it is of more importance to know how to avoid troubles then to know why the troubles occur. For instance, let us suppose that trouble is encountered with an astringent lotion which upon standing throws down a precipitate. If one is theoretically minded he can make elaborate chemical tests to discover the source of the trouble, but the simplest way to run it down is to make up different samples of the product each of which contains all one of the ingredients. As a rule the offending ingredient will quickly be stopped.

Very often the cosmetic chemist must also possess an intimate knowledge of perfume raw materials and how to compound suitable, lasting odors for toilet articles. In the larger plants this detail is very often in the hands of a specially trained perfumer used in cosmetics have been initated by the perfume raw material houses who devote more time to research in developing new and modern odors than the cosmetic manufacturers do. Properly trained laboratory men make use all of types of perfume raw materials. They realize that perfume specialties result in many cases in more uniform, less troublesome and more successful odors, than result from the use of the so-called pure or natural products often adulterated at the point of production.

The manufacture of perfumes, lotions and colognes, the perfuming of cosmetic ingredients are three entirely different sections of perfumery , each with its highly individual problems.

Consider for instance the difficulties encountered in perfuming face powders. Not only must the perfume be of an attractive odor but it must also be a perfume not adversely affected by the powder itself, which may produce a disagreeable musty odor in combination with certain perfume materials. The well versed perfumer has at his finger tips a variety of little tricks useful in improving the effectiveness of his perfume combinations - such as,, for instance, the use of small additions of peppermint oil, anisic aldehyde, etc.

The best method to perfume powders is to triturate the perfume oil with a comparatively small quantity of precipitated chalk or magnesium carbonate and gradually add this to the powder mixture. Thorough and even mixing is of importance in this operation. Any coloring material used may also be added to the perfume oil.

Terpenes and sesquiterpenes generally resinify under the influence of light and air, while under the same influences alcohols and aldehyde oxidize to odorless acids. Methyl anthranilate, bromstyrol, coumarin and thymol are also changed under the influence of light. More resistant to light are anisic aldehyde, benzyl alcohol, geraniol, indol, phenylethyl alcohol and cinnamic alcohol. Easily affected by light and air are anethol, citral, eugenol, isoeugnol, heliotropin, phenyl acetic aldehyde, terpineol and vanillin.

Attention also should be directed to the fact, known to every well trained perfumer, that the individual ingredients of certain perfume compounds react differently in different mixtures. This is caused by the different chemical reactions of the various ingredients with each other. For instance, methyl anthranilate will retain its characteristic odor in many perfume compounds, especially if these are well fixed with natural resionoids and similar resinious materials. On the other hand it will react with hydroxycitronellal, cinnamic aldehyde, anisic aldehyde and other aldehydes forming so-called Schiff's bases, somé of which are characterized by a deep yellow color. Incidentally, vanillin and also ethyl vanillin may be caused in small quantities in soap perfumes which contain a lferal addition of resinious fixatives, without incurring the danger of discoloration . On the other hand, a mixture of vinillin with eugenol and isoeugnol would soon cause white soap to turn brown or produced dark spots and odor itself to turn definitely unpleasant. Creams based on beeswax with borax or lanolin, etc., are less apt to discolor in combination with perfume oils than do creams emulsified with the help of stronger alkalies.

Many manufacturers of cosmetic preparations pay far too little attention to the matter of perfuming their products, inspite of the fact that the perfume plays so large a part in sales appeal. One happy solution to this problem is offered by the various essential oil houses who put up numerous ready to use—perfumes for specific purposes, such as for face lotions of low alcoholic content, or for creams, powders, brilliantines, suntan preparations, toilet soaps, bath preparations, bath salts, etc. Their use offers many obvious advantages, doing away with the uncertainties of the trial and error method.

The preparation of perfumes and the perfuming of soaps and cosmetics are three quite separate branches of the perfumer's art. The problem that arise in the perfuming of a face powder, for example, are quite different from those encountered in the scenting of a toilet soap or the preparation of a high-grade perfumery extract. One particular cream perfume on the market gives admirable results when used in various types of face cream yet, on its own ie dissolved in alcohol, has by no means an attractive or even a pleasant odor.

A widespread but short-sighted attitude is that which expresses itself in wholesale reduction of perfuming costs, irrespective of quality. Purchasing perfume materials solely on a cheap price basis is usually, in the long run, an expensive policy.

The question that now arises is one of method and procedure. Having perfected a face powder, brillian time, face cream or skin lotion, how should the manufacturer set about perfuming it to the best advantage ? Much depends, of course, upon the individual tendencies of each manufacturer. Some confine their attention to finished compounds, while others like to dilute or modify a basic compound to their own tastes, by utilizing various essential oils, isolates and synthetics. Still others are in a position to employ a perfumer, who may himself carry out a good deal of the compounding from basic raw materials. This means that the extent to which manufacturers are dependent upon the perfumery supply trade for knowledge, experience and inspiration varies from factory to factory. All manufacturers, however, whether they care to admit it or not, are to a very great extent indebted to the specialized researches of the supply trade and many who start off by attempting to make up their own compositions are only too glad, after the novelty of attempted creation has worn off, to put their problems in the hands of a capable supplier.

Extensive investigations and experiments carried out by the leading perfume supply houses have enabled them to market perfume compositions specifically intended for incorporation in the following main groups of toilet preparations and cosmetics : (a) Lotions of low alcohol content; (b) Face creams : (c) Face Powders, talcum powders, body powders; (d) Brilliantines. suntan oils, etc.; (e) Toilet soaps, shaving creams ; (f) Batoh essences (usually of the water-soluble sulfonated oil type); and (g) Bath salts (including combined perfume-color bases).

Many technical writers have over rated the difficulty of compounding perfumes that will dissolve readily in brilliantines of the mineral oil type. Although many published Formulas specify the use of terpeneless oils, on the ground that certain of the terpenes are insoluble in or immiscible with mineral oil, the fact remains that terpenes oils themselves are not always suitable for such incorporation, while some terpenes and resins may quite easily be utilized in brillian time perfumes. For use in compositions intended to be incorporated in mineral oil, linalol, terpineol, benzyl alcohol and esters, geraniol, citronellol, cinnamic alcohol, phenylet alcohol, eugenol, isogrugenol, neroli, amyl cimmamic aldehyde, Lavender oil, spike lavender terpeneless bergamot, ylang ylang, amyl salicylate, ionone, anisaldehyde, and (in traces) heliotropin, synthetic musks, vanillin, Coumarin and styrax are recommended.

When a brilliantine or sun bronze oil is compounded, it should be tested by adding an excessive quantity to an experimental sample of the base. If, after the lapse of a few weeks, the solution remains clear, then the perfume should prove to be quite satisfactory, so far at least as clarity is concerned. Tests of this kind should be as stringent as may be be considered necessary - artificial raising and lowering of the temperatures at which the sample is kept tending to precipitate perfume constituents that might prove unstable in certain products. In general, brilliantines and similar preparations should be perfumed only just sufficiently to mask the fatty odor of the base.

In direct contrast to the somewhat overrated problems connected with the perfuming of oils, is the frequently underestimated difficulty of selecting a really appropriate composition dor use in face powder. Generally speaking, any note that tends to go flat or musty should be avoided in face powder perfuming. On the other hand, cyclopentadecanone and exaltolide help to impart a desirable "lift" to such compositions, while in this connection the use of tiny traces of peppermint oil, anisaldehyde, etc., may also be recorded. It goes without saying that many successful high alcohol perfumes are not nearly so successful when used in face powders. The best method of incorporation is always to make up well-dispersed preliminary batches of both color and perfume, in a portion of the precipitated chalk used or, better still, magnesium carbonate.

Perfumes for face creams must not only be suitable from the odor value and stability points of view; they should also be free from any tendency to irritate the skin or progressively discolor the cream base.

For use in lotions of low alcohol content, perfume compositions must obviously be chosen for their ready solubility in such media. Similarly, for incorporation in bath essences, highly water-soluble perfumes are frequently employed. These latter consist of selected bases embodied in a high-grade neutral finished sulfonated castor oil, and may be obtained in this form most of the well-known perfumery supply houses.

Lipstick perfumes usually have the difficult task to perform of masking the rather pronounced of odor of fats, oils and waxes. Sometimes the perfume is thought to be at fault, when in reality the odor-degeneration is due to the onset of rancidity.

Latterly a good deal attention has been paid to the identification and avoidance of aromatic substances that exhibit a tendency to irritate the skin and give rise to symptoms of dermatitis. Not all authorities agree, however upon published lists of so called irritants, one very well-known expert going so far as to assert that he and a doermatologist co-worker have proved methyl heptin carbonate to be non-irritant.

Other citrus oils, besides bergamot, have been considered by some workers to be unsuitable for indiscriminate use in face cream and lipstick perfumes. The terpenes present in citrus oils have been blamed for cutaneous irritation — notably limonene.

Strongly irritant perfume materials have been listed as follows : Benzylidene acetone, benzaldehyde, phenylacetaldehyde, hydroxycitronellal, eugenol isoeugenol, clove and similar oils, bromdtyol, anisaldehyde ex cresol (not ex anethol) and also the higher aldehydes in general, although the latter are rarely likely to be present in dangerous proportions. Milder irritants have been held to complicate heliotropin, condensation products of hydroxycitronellal, phenol ethers, aceptophenone, citral and — when used in high proportions - diethyl phthalate, sandalwood oil, and methyl cinnamate. Salicylates should also be used with considerable caution.

The other major problem that arises in the perfuming of toilet preparations, and more particularly in the perfuming of face creams and shaving creams, is that of progressive discoloration. Many perfume material have, of course, a characteristic dark color of their own, but that need present no actual problem provided that due allowance is made for it at the outset. What is much more important is the avoidance of those materials which are apt to give rise to progressive discoloration, due to subsequent reactions in the cream base. Unsatisfactory in this connection are vanillin, ethyl vanillin, the eugenol, methyl anthranilate, citral, coumarin (slight yellowing in time), cinnamon leaf and clove opils, lemongrass oil, sage oil etc. Even so, much depends in many cases upon the amount used, the liability to oxidation, the composition of the cream base, and of the perfume itself. Antioxidants retard the discolouration.

2

COSMETICS AND DRUGS

Physical Characteristics of Cosmetics Comments on these Characteristics - Cosmetic Classification

There is, and probably will continue to be, a persistent tendency to attribute medicinal properties to cosmetics. In other cases these preparations are of such a nature that it is difficult to distinguish between a cosmetic and a drug. Some American manufacturers still do not realize that assigning therapeutic properties to a cosmetic brings it under a different section of the 1938 Food, Drug and Cosmetic Act than that which covers cosmetics. Under the Act a product is a cosmetic when it cleanses, beautifies, promotes attractiveness or alters the appearance of the human body. It is a drug, which it cleanses, beautifies, promotes attractiveness or alters the appearance of the human body. It is a drug, which is an inclusive term meaning also a pharmaceutical, a medicine or medicament, a therapeutic treatment, a remedy, when claims are made for its use in the cure, mitigation, treatment, or prevention of diseases, or when it affects the structure or function of the body. Cosmetics that claim medicinal properties must be labeled according to the further provisions of the law. If it is new combination, or uses any new medicinal agent, it must comply with the New Drug Section of this Act. Since the difference between a cosmetic and a drug may be said to exist at the point where a function of the human body is affected, some products are both cosmetics and drugs under the definitions cited above. This is true of items like antiperspirants, sunburn and cheap creams or lotions that claim healing properties, and dandruff liquids used for scalp ailments.

There have also been cases, on the other hand, where food and medicinal products have been offered and advertised with the beauty appeal. An example of a food product being considered a cosmetic occurred some time ago, even before the passage of the Act, when a brand was offered as an internal preparation for improving the complexion. At that time it was a question of excise taxes on cosmetics. In order to make the yeast subject to this tax it was designated as a cosmetic because of its emphasis on the beauty appeal. There are also cases where food suppliers stress the necessity of proper nourishment for personal attractiveness. On borderline products, then, one must be on the alert so as not to overlap and conflict with the various provisions of the Act. If any doubt exists as to claims, it is desirable to secure legal and technical opinions, as well as those of the administrative bosies, or trade associations. It must always be borne in mind that regulations regarding an act or law of this kind are usually necessary. Both the Act and the regulations, therefore, should be consulted very thoroughly.

In this discussions, it is not desirable nor our purpose to pass judgment upon the efficacy of special cosmetics offered as drugs or external medicines. Advertisement feature quite a number of these borderline cosmetics. Among them are vitamin and hormone creams, colloidal sulfur creams, anti-perspirants, astringents, skin lotions or tonics and dentifrices which make strongly to slightly prejudicial medicinal claims. Since advertising also designates a product as a drug or cosmetic, propaganda material must be carefully watched. In some large organizations, any technical statements regarding products must be passed upon or confirmed by the technical men in the laboratory before they are published. This is a sound policy which is often overlooked in many cases where it could be instituted. It does not seem constructive for certain manufacturers in an industry to continue to injure it by emphasizing the medical appeal without due regard to the law. Such a procedure not only antagonizes the regulatory officials but invites criticism from individual medical, dental, and technical men as well as their influential societies.

The Federal Security Agency is on record also against false and misleading names of products. Terms such as food, tonic, grower, restorer, name of a particular organ of the body, revitalizer and eradicator in conjunction with the type of beauty product such as cream, powder, or lotion must be avoided. The endorsement of the cosmetic by some profession, or the claims of the foreign discovery or creation is not permissible. In other words, it is the best policy to stick closely to the letter of the law and regulations. It does seem more reasonable that, if the medicinal appeal is desirable, it should be from the standpoint of the prevention of skin ailments by external medicines, rather than by the curing of such disorders. The use of an antiseptic in a deodorant, hair preparation, lotion or skin astringent can be justified far more consistently than the use of a vitamin or medicament in a cream. This is especially true if it is labeled honestly and if the claims are based upon competent, scientific facts. There is, of course, nothing new in the idea of germicides agents used in the past have not resulted in as effective and servicecable preparations as the newer chemicals now make available.

The discovery of these new bactericides has resulted in impetus to their local application directly to the skin. Even ointments containing the sulfa drugs and penicillin are now said to be producing very favorable result against infections of the cuticle. These ointments are placed on the lesions in a high concentration over small areas to obtain more rapid results than are ordinarily obtained with other treatments. In cases of impetigo, for example, one of the most unsightly facial blemishes, it is said that pencillin thus applied completely readicated the skin disorder within a week and prevented its spread. Since pencillin may be used without serious toxic reaction and may be injected into the muscle dripped into the vein and inhaled as a spray without harm, it may some day be used in cosmetics because of its beautifying properties, although this is not commendable. Other medicinal, less effective ingredients, however, have been used for just such purposes.

In past years germicidal agents were largely associated with strongly odoured chemicals. If they were used for general cleansing purposes tey certainly left a strong scent behind them. Coal tars, phenol, cresol, cresylic acids, pine oil, mercurials, oxyquinoline benzoate and sulfate, chloride of lime or other chlorine containing chemicals were and are generally distasteful smells, they are hardly suitable for use in cosmetics. It is true, however, that are hardly suitable for use in cosmetics. It is true, however, that phenol or carbolic acid and the cresols in small quantities, have been and are being used to some extent in preparations recommended for toilet use.

Germicides have probably been used more generally as preservatives for the preparations themselves than for their germicidal action on the skin. Cosmetics, not only during manufacture, but also during use are often exposed to the action of bacteria and fungi. The development of these organisms under favorable conditions of growth has resulted in spoilage of many types of products. In the past, therefore, preservatives have been used in the cosmetic industry just as food preservatives, like the benzoates, have been used to preserve foods. Special benzoate salts and esters, such as sodium tribenzoate and esters of para hydroxy benzoic acid, have been featured and solid in quantity to toilet goods makers. In this field of preservatives, also, cresol derivatives, substituted phenols and isolates from essential oils with some antiseptic value have been freely offered. All of these products have contributed more or less to the keeping qualities or shelf life of certain cosmetics.

In the field of germicides there has been considerable concentration of germicidal agents having higher phenol coefficients than those most commonly used in the past. The adoption by the U.S.Army and Navy of these newer germicidal agents was revolutinoary and at first developed new problems in the field of germicides and disinfectants. It was found, for example, that the usual, method of testing these for their germ killing value or phenol coefficient fell down in many cases. Some bacteriologists have cotended that this was due the lower concentration of these killing agents which affected the efficiency, especially against S.Aureus, the pus forming organism usually found on the skin. The fact that the Armed Forces have continued to use such germicides, which are made in more concentrated germicidal strength, as to phenol coefficient, indicates that they are working satisfactorily and with little irritation to the skin.

Among the newer germicides which have attracted much attention quite recently is the series of quaternary ammonium compounds. The substituted phenols and substituted methanes have also shown favourable results. Where there is a tendency to assign germicidal properties to specialized cosmetic preparations, it is very probable that these will find uses in the cosmetic field.

The quanternary ammonium compounds are still comparatively new. The first germicides made from this type of germicidal agent. appeared in this country about five years ago. These compounds consist of ammonium compounds of high molecular weight like alkyl-dimethyl-benzyl ammonium chloride or di-isobutyl cresoxy ethoxy ethyl dimethyl benzyl ammonium chloride. Numerous compounds of this type are possible. In general they may be described as non-corrosive, non-staining, odorless, colorless bodies possessing a bitter taste. They are unaffected by salts and are soluble in water as well as a large number of organic solvents. They possess high killing power against bacteria and in the dilutions used for this purpose are both non-irritating and non-toxic. Because their anti-bactericidal properties are reversed by anion active agents, particularly soap, they are referred to as cationic, germicidal agents. They are chemically stable, effective in the presence of organic matter and non-selective. They also possess some fingicidal properties. A large amount of scientific investigation was carried out ' efore certain of these quanternary ammonium compounds were accepted by the council on Pharmacy and Chemistry of the American Medical Association for surgical applications.

Cationic germicidal agents today find application not only in the medicinal field, but are employed for general disinfection, for cleansing public eating and drinking utensils, and in fisheries and on fishing vessels where putrefaction is apt to occur. There are undoubtedly other undeveloped applications, as in the field of certain cosmetics. These compounds will probably find their way into after-shave lotions, hand and skin lotions, hair tonics, deodorants and other cosmetic powders when proper investigations have been completed. They possess the property of adhering effectively to vegetable and animal matter. It may be pointed out that when the hands have been washed with these compounds it is difficult to rinse off the film..As a result the hands are bacteriostatic for an appreciable length of time. The quanternary ammonium compounds are furthermore wetting agents which have the ability of lowering surface and interfacial tension. This imkparts to them the desirable property of more readily removing oily and greasy secretions on the skin when occasion arises.

The sufstitited phenols have increased in use in the

germicidal field in the past years. These are an improvement upon phenol and cresol in some respects. They have greater killing power and may be used in lesser concentration, are less irritating to their skin, though in many cases too irritating for general use, and in most cases are pleasanter in odor though still quite strong. Some of them have good fungicidal properties. It is customary to make finished germicides from these by solublizing them with soaps or wetting in rather strongly alkaline solutions. These germicides are finding increasing uses in hospitals for preparative preparation and cold sterilization of surgical instruments and sick room appliances because of their non-corrosive and less irritating properties. It would require considerable experimentation to incorporate them into cosmetics, but they may find some use in certain of these products.

There have also been marketed and listed in the literature certain substituted methanes which are designated as a "G" Series of germicides. The product known as G-4 is 2,2' dihydroxy 5,5' dichloro diphenyl methane.. Another in this series, G-ii consists of 2,2' dihydroxy 3,5,3',5', hexachlorodiphenyl methane. Besides possessing high phenol coefficients these substituted methanes have excellent fungicidal properties, especially the G-4.

G-4, is a light colored powder, has a slight phenolic odor and does not irritate the skin in the quantity required for use. It is made soluble by the addition of soaps and wetting agents, plus a slight amount of alkali. It is stable and does not readily discolor. G-ii has recently been patented for the production of germicidal soaps in the proportion of from two to three percent in soap base. When incorporated in a milled soap, it imparts germicidal properties that remain effective under conditions of use, cleanses skin with fewer germs after two minutes instead of twenty minutes of ordinary washing and consequently there is less chance of infection in cuts, burns, scratches or blisters. In this regard G-ii is extremely valuable in that there are practically no substance known which will maintain their germicidal properties effectively in soap under these conditions. The use of this germicide in toilet articles containing soap, such as shampoo or shaving cream, will undoubtedly be found feasible because it probably possesses the most desirable of all medicinal properties for such use.

The incorporation of germicides or antiseptics into all types of cosmetics is not easy. Many factors will influence their efficacy. As has already been indicated the pH is of much importance. Unless this can be properly fixed the germicide will not be effective. Then it must remembered that water is necessary to make them germicil or bacteriostatic. Fir this reason, unless exhaustive tests are made in other vehicles, claims for antisepsis should as a rule be make only when there is moisture present. as many parts of the skin are predominantly oily this condition must be considered. All in all it is safer to claim germidical properties only at the time the preparation is applied.

It is not our purpose, as we have said, to encourage the encroachment of cosmetics on the germicial or medicinal field, but there is no questioning the fact that the use of germicides for this purpose has ample justification, more than the use of medicinal ingredients. Personal attractiveness is obtained here by the prevention of unsightly skin conditions. The emphasis on the germicidal or health protective properties of this type of preparation has good appeal and a story of considerable merit can be woven thereabout. It is most certainly more sensible to add germicidal properties to a toilet article, than it is to try to cash in on the addition of some of the products that have been played up in the past.

In classifying cosmetics, it must considered that the consumers of these preparations, most of whom are girls and women, are more concerned with their physical than their chemical charcteristics. The texture, consistency, color, odor, packaging and general appearance are far more important to them than the chemical properties of the ingredienmts or the finished product.

They are definitely impressed by what a cosmetic will do during use. This does not necessarily mean that the chemical technique of making cosmetics is unimportant. It may be pointed out that in many cases it is not at all necessary to duplicate a cosmetic preparation chemically to obtain the same beautifoying effect. It would be most difficult or practically impossible to make this duplication solely through chemical analysis, becauser of the very complex make-up of many cosmetics.

It is, then, in order to comment upon the physical charcteristics. Cosmetics take on various physical forms and may be classified as follows :

1. Emulsions : Cold cream, vanishing cream, liquid cream.
2. Powders: Face powder, talcum powder, tooth powder.
3. Sticks : Lipstick, deodorant stick.
4. Cakes : Rouge compacts, cake make-up.
5. Oils : Brilliantine, hair oild.
6. Mucilages : Wave set, hand lotion.
7. Jellies : Hand jelly, wave set jelly, brilliantine jelly.
8. Suspensions : Liquid powder, cosmetic stockings.
9. Pastes : Tooth paste, dedorant paste, clay packs.
10. Soap : Shampoo soap, shaving soap, toilet soap.
11. Solutions : After-shave lotions, hair sets, astringents lotions.

3

FACE POWDER

Properties Desired - Discussion of These Properties - Raw Materials Used - Manufacturing Methods - Formulas

Of all the cosmetics consumed, face powder undoubtedly leads the list. Not only is this true of women users, but men also like to apply colored talcum powder or some specially compounded powder to the face. This is done either after shaving or to cover up the need of a shave when this operation is dispensed with temporarily. In the olden days it was common practice for women to use a little corn starch or flour on their faces to cover the shine and for some time just plain white face powder enjoyed great popularity. As the art of making this toiletry improved, perfume and color, as well as other improvements were introduced. In this modern day face powders are really products that add very materially to personal attractiveness. Person who are concerned about their looks employ it several time daily. These individual applications are small but the total consumption is great.

Due to misunderstanding and also to competitive, especially negative type of advertising, the use of face powders has come in for some criticism. Common misconceptions which are still heard are that it is harmful because it contains bismuth, lead or mercury, that it produces pimples and blackheads, that it gets into the pores of the skin and clogs them, that due to the content of orris root in particular, it produces an allergy like hay fever, or asthma, and that the use of starch is harmful to the skin.

Face powders as made today, by reputable manufacturers, consist of purified ingredients, approved colors and non-irritating perfumes.

None of these harmful effects is suffered through their use in spite of many daily applications.

In producing a face powder it is of prime importance that woman's requirements be given careful consideration. Probably the first characteristic is the odor. It is second nature for her to smell the powder when it is picked up for examination. The best liked odor must be of such a nature that it blends well with other perfumes and is not too predominant. At the same time it must have lasting qualities in the sealed or opened package and upon the skin. Next, the shade is very important. Many women buy a face powder solely from this standpoint. A large variety of shades are possible with the Federal Security Administration colors designated under F.D. & C. (Food, Drug & Cosmetic) or D. & C. (Drug & Cosmetic). Colors approved by this federal agency, as harmless to the skin. As a rule the powder manufacturers selects water insoluble colors, pigments and lakes to produce the best results.

Besides color and odor, a face powder must possess slip, adhesion, small particle size and covering powder to receive consumer acceptance. It should, furthermore, be fine and soft to the sense of touch and have proper bulking power. Of the various grades of face powder, termed light, medium and heavy, the light and medium with light and medium covering powder are the most popular.

The types of skins which face powder must cover are dry, normal, moderately oily, very oily. Because dry skin secretes very little moisture and no oil, it requires a powder of light covering power. Normal and moderately oily skins, being more shiny due to secretion of oil and moisture, require a powder with more covering power. Very oily skins having a high shine require a powder of heavy covering power.

Special conditions modify somewhat the general rule with respect to the type of powder suitable for a given type of skin. There are many women whose skins are abnormal in spots who should use different powders of different covering power. There are many women whose skins while generally dry yet suffer from oily foreheads, oily noses or oily chins.

Difference in covering power gave rise to the designations light, medium and heavy, which really have nothing to do with the density of the powder. These terms refer to the amount of powder needed to cover the same area of the skin. As the terms are quite common we shall, throughout this chapter, use the descriptions, light for powder with slight covering powder intended for use on dry skins, medium for powder of somewhat more covering power that the light and intended for normal and moderately oily skins, and heavy for powders possessing great covering power intended for use on very oily skins.

In addition to powders of proper covering power a manufacturer must also provide suitable perfumes, an adequate number of popular colors and an attractive package. Intelligent merchandising enables manufacturers to increase the use of face powder by persuading women to buy two colors - one for day and a lighter one for night to offset the effects of artificial lighting.

In order to appreciate the importance of different properties of face powder it must be remembered that its function is to conceal shine and minor skin imperfections. Hence, a primary requisite is covering power. As most of the raw materials possessing this property have it in an excessive degree and are somewhat lumpy tend to drag when when applied to the skin, it becomes necessary to make the utilize another material which will act as a vehicle or diluent for the covering agent and at the same time make possible easy and smooth application to the skin. This function is supplied by talc. Next, it is necessary to make the powder sufficiently adhesive so that it will remain on the skin for a reasonable length of time. This requirement is supplied by calcium, magnesium and zinc stearates and sometimes by the addition of an oil. Finally face powder must have as ingredient which acts as a binder for the color and perfume, and which will facilitate the distribution of both through the batch during the manufacturing operation. These functions are supplied by magnesium carbonate and precipitated chalk.

Hence, all the face powders must possess the following :

(a) Covering Power.
(b) Slip.
(c) Adhesiveness.
(d) Absorption.
(e) Color and Perfume.

The various weights of face powder are differentiated from each other mainly by the percentage of covering agent present in the formula. Talcum and face powders can be made of any pure white, chemically inert powder that is sufficiently fine and possesses one or more of the above properties. The materials commonly used, grouped according to function are as follows : Where a material has more than one property it is listed twice:

Covering Power : Titanium dioxide, zinc oxide, zinc sulfide, lithopone, kaolin (colloidal), calcium sulfate, magnesium oxide, starch.

Slip : Talc, starch, metallic soaps.

Adhesiveness : Calcium, magnesium and zinc stearate, starch, and colloidal clay (purified kaolin).

Absorption : Precipitated chalk, magnesium carbonate, starch, purified kaolin.

The materials listed above constitute the bulk of the face powder on the market. The principal materials are zinc oxide, titanium dioxide, talc, kaolin, the stearates, starch and chalk.

Rice starch, while it is a constituent of many leading French powders, is not favored in this country because it emphasizes the light hair on the lips and cheeks by clinging to them and also because in absorbing moisture the starch particles swell. It does, however, impart to the face a smooth "peachy" effect so sought after in these days when powder is dusted instead of being rubbed on the face with the puff, and it must be admitted the rice starch is as yet the only single material possessing all the properties of face powder. Used alone it is a fairly good light powder, but the insuperable drawbacks of rice and all other starches make it undesirable to use too much. Precipitated chalk imparts the same "peachy" texture, and is not harmful, but ordinary grades do not spread or adhere evenly. There are, however, certain grades of processed chalk which have considerable slip, some covering power and adhesiveness that could be used in face powder in fairly considerable proportions.

Although barium sulfate is used internally in X-ray work, there is some apprehension among chemists that its constant use in face powder might be dangerous in view of the known toxicity of the other related barium salts. High grade lithopone, which aroused criticism on the same score recently, was shown by a long series of clinical studies to be definitely non-toxic.

Bismuth compounds are used in Europe, but as they darken upon exposure to light it is difficult to see any reason for their use in face powder. The most widely used face powder materials are : zinc oxide, purified kaolin, talc, the metallic stearates - particularly zinc stearate - precipitated chalk and magnesium carbonate. Titanium dioxide is a more recent addition. It possesses much greater dry covering power than zinc oxide besides being extremely fine, white and chemically inert. Any insoluble, inert, white, powder of about 200 mesh, having proper properties may be used in the proportion to obtain the desired effect.

With a better understanding of the reasons for different weights of face powder and a more thorough comprehension of the functions of the ingredients from which it is compounded, we pass to the development of formulas. The formulas presented were developed after considerable research and wide acceptance has demonstrated their soundness. It will be observed that in the composite tables the same ingredients are used, and the only differences are in the proportions of the ingredients, especially of the covering agent. It is mainly in this property that face powders differ. Hence, these formulas, when blended, will serve as standards of perfect balance in respect to the different degrees of covering power, of slip, adhesiveness and absorption. The manufacturer is at liberty to match these powders with any combination of materials with which he elects to experiment. It will be observed that the constant factors in each formula are covering agent, adhesive agent, absorbent agent. The variable factor is talc, which fluctuates with each formula depending upon the amount of color and perfume introduced. The functions of each material are designated as follows :

(a) Covering agent
(b) Slip
(c) Adhesive agent
(d) Absorbing agent
(e) Perfume
(f) Colors

Light Face Powder
With Zinc Oxide

FORMULAS FOR POPULAR SHADES

Materials	White	Peach	Rachel	Natural	Flesh	Ocshre	Suntan
(a) Zinc oxide	18.00	18.00	18.00	18.00	18.00	18.00	18.00
(b) Talc	69.00	67.52	68.00	68.06	68.64	64.84	58.69
(c) Zinc stearate	6.00	6.00	6.00	6.00	6.00	6.00	6.00
(d) Precipitated chalk	6.00	6.00	6.00	6.00	6.00	6.00	6.00
(e) Perfume	1.00	1.00	1.00	1.00	1.00	1.00	1.00
(f) Ochre		1.44	1.00	0.88	0.33	4.09	8.89
Brilliant pink lake		0.44	0.00	0.06	0.03	0.07	0.35
Burnt sienna		0.00	0.00	0.00	0.00	0.00	1.07
	100.0	100.0	100.0	100.0	100.0	100.0	100.0

Medium Face Powder With Purified Kaolin

FORMULAS FOR POPULAR SHADES

Materials	White	Peach	Rachel	Natural	Flesh	Ocshre	Suntan
(a) Titanium dioxide	4.00	4.00	4.00	4.00	4.00	4.00	4.00
(b) Purified Kaolin	20.00	20.00	20.00	20.00	20.00	20.00	20.00
(c) Talc	66.00	64.52	65.00	65.06	65.64	61.84	55.69
(d) Magnesium Stearate	3.00	3.00	3.00	3.00	3.00	3.00	3.00
(e) Magnesium Carbonate	6.00	6.00	6.00	6.00	6.00	6.00	6.00
(f) Perfume	1.00	1.00	1.00	1.00	1.00	1.00	1.00
(g) Ochre		1.44	1.00	0.88	0.33	4.09	8.89
Brilliant pink lake		0.44	0.00	0.06	0.03	0.07	0.35
Burnt sienna		0.00	0.00	0.00	0.00	0.00	1.07
	100.0	100.0	100.0	100.0	100.0	100.0	100.0

Throughout the given formulas all the quantities are stated as percentages. The shades produced will vary depending upon the concentration of color employed.

Medium Face Powder With Titanium Dioxide

FORMULAS FOR POPULAR SHADES

Materials	White	Peach	Rachel	Natural	Flesh	Ocshre	Suntan
(a) Titanium Dioxide	5.21	5.21	5.21	5.21	5.21	5.21	5.21
(b) Talc	82.79	81.31	81.79	81.85	82.43	78.63	72.48
(c) Zinc stearate	5.00	5.00	5.00	5.00	5.00	5.00	5.00
(d) Precipitated chalk	6.00	6.00	6.00	6.00	6.00	6.00	6.00
(e) Perfume	1.00	1.00	1.00	1.00	1.00	1.00	1.00
(f) Ochre		1.44	1.00	0.88	0.33	4.09	8.89
Brilliant pink lake		0.44	0.00	0.06	0.03	0.07	0.35
Burnt sienna		0.00	0.00	0.00	0.00	0.00	1.07
	100.0	100.0	100.0	100.0	100.0	100.0	100.0

Heavy Face Powder
With Zinc Oxide & Titanium Dioxide

FORMULAS FOR POPULAR SHADES

Materials	White	Peach	Rachel	Natural	Flesh	Ocshre	Suntan
(a) Titanium dioxide	3.00	3.00	3.00	3.00	3.00	3.00	3.00
(b) Zinc Oxide	20.00	20.00	20.00	20.00	20.00	20.00	20.00
(c) Talc	66.00	64.52	65.00	65.06	65.64	61.84	55.69
(d) Zinc Stearate	4.00	4.00	4.00	4.00	4.00	4.00	4.00(e)
Precipitated Chalk	6.00	6.00	6.00	6.00	6.00	6.00	6.00
(f) Perfume	1.00	1.00	1.00	1.00	1.00	1.00	1.00
(g) Ochre		1.44	1.00	0.88	0.33	4.09	8.89
Brilliant pink lake		0.44	0.00	0.06	0.03	0.07	0.35
Burnt sienna		0.00	0.00	0.00	0.00	0.00	1.07
	100.0	100.0	100.0	100.0	100.0	100.0	100.0

The colors given above are very popular ones. Each experimenter will have to adjust them to suit his own wishes because the results obtained in making up the above formulas will depend upon the strength and purity of the colors employed. There are so many variations of ochre, for instance, that two manufacturers using the same powder formula, but different ochres, are quite likely to get very different shades. There are some excellent standardized synthetic ochres on the market which are five or six times as strong as natural ochre.

It is best to purchase a fairly large quantity of colors at one time. This insures uniformity over a considerable period of time. With the indicated colors ; ochre, brilliant lake pink, and burnt sienna one can produce virtually all face powder shades exceptingof course the fads like orchid and green. As already stated, a large variety of approved colors is available.

Using the above tinted powders the cosmetic experimenter can match almost any shade he wishes to duplicate. For instance, a little of the ochre added to the rachel will produce a dark rachel. Beige and all the other pink-tan variants can likewise be produced by careful blending of two or more shades.

Certain facts are to be derived from a study of the above formulas.

1. The ingredients, with the expansion of talc, are constant for all shades.

2. Chalk is a constant factor throughout all shades and weights.

3. The amount of color necessary to produce a given shade never varies regardless of the weight of the powder.

4. It will be observed that light powder contains slightly more zinc stearate than medium, and medium slightly less than heavy ; the reason being more oily less adhesivenes is required to make powder adhere.

5. It will be noted that the amount of talc is fairly constant throughout all formulas which employ zinc oxide as a covering medium. This is desirable condition because it provides for a heavy powder with substatially as much slip as a light powder. Many of the heavy face powders on the market lack slip because the increased amount of zinc oxide necessarily employed to secure greater covering power diminishes appreciably the percentage of talc in the formulas.

In making heavy powder we avoided this pit fall by providing for increased covering power by combining a smaller percentage of zinc oxide with titanium dioxide. In this way all the formulas given possess substantially the same amount of slip in spite of the fact that they vary widely in covering power. The substitution in whole or in part of titanium dioxide for zinc oxide in the heavy formulas makes it possible to obtain the same covering power which a higher percentage of zinc oxide would give without losing any of the necessary slip. Experience has shown that heavy powders containing a high percentage of zinc oxide have a tendency to cake. This is avoided in the heavy face powder given above which goes on an easily as a light powder.

However, titanium dioxide has about five times the covering power of zinc oxide, a fact which makes it possible to secure equivalent covering power by using considerably less of it. Because of the possibility that it may not hold the color as well as zinc oxide when the powder is in contact with the secretions of the face, it is desirable to mix it with zinc oxide.

The use if titanium dioxide presents some problems. It does not dry tint as readily as zinc sulfide or zinc oxide, hence, it is recommended that the titanium dioxide be added to the chalk in making the color base, and that it be well milled.

Some manufacturers add mineral oil or cold cream to face powder, but it is difficult to say that these additions serve any useful purpose excepting when the formula is so badly unbalanced that powder will not cling to the face. The addition of cols cream is superfluous because the winter content soon evaporates, leaving only the oil.

Some authorities state that magnesium carbonate is more absorbent than precipitated chalk and holds the perfume better. The usual proportions of magnesium carbonate to precipitated chalk, when both are used in the same formula, are magnesium carbonate 4 to 2 of precipitated chalk. If any experimenter wishes to adjust the above formulas he may add 4% of magnesium carbonate and reduce the chalk to 2%. When both are employed it is customary to mix the perfume oils with the magnesium carbonate and the colors with the chalk.

It is inadvisable to increase the stearate above the indicated quantities because excessive amounts tend to increase the transparency of the powder after it has been applied.

It must be recommended that only the finest, whitest grade of the highest quality raw materials should be used in making face powder.

Many face powders of different qualities can be made from the same formula by using different grades of raw materials. For example, any of the above powder formulas made with cheap talc will be decidedly inferior to the same formulas in which the finest, whitest grade of talc is employed, and, what is more important, the inferior materials being off color, usually grayish, will not tint as well as the better quality materials. Therefore, to produce best results the following grades of raw materials are recommended :

Zinc oxide........................ Finest, white grade.
Talc................................ Finest white, 99% through 200 mesh.
Zinc stearate..................... Whitest grade made from triple pressed
.... stearic acid and odor free.
Magnesium carbonate .... Lightest, whitest grade.
Titanium dioxide............... Finest white 200 mesh or better.

It is obvious that since it is necessary to mix several materials to secure the various properties necessary for face powder, present day products are mixtures lacking in true homogeneity. This could be overcome by precipitating the ingredients upon each other instead of mixing them, but unfortunately no practical precipitation apparatus is built small enough for the requirement of face powder.

MANUFACTURING METHODS :

Mix the perfume compound with a part of the magnesium carbonate or the chalk in an enameled white pail or suitable vessel. When the oil is absorbed rub the mixture through a hand sieve with a stiff bristle brush or run it through a power brush sifter until the perfume is uniformly distributed. Mix the colors in the same way with the rest of the magnesium carbonate or chalk. Continue mixing until a portion rubbed out on a white paper shows no colour flecks. Keep a sample for matching successive batches.

Then weigh out and put the rest of the raw materials into a mixer, add the perfume and the colour bases, and mix until uniform. Take a sample and rub it out on white paper. It should, if properly blended, show no colour flecks and should merge with the matching sample without any line of demarcation. Continue mixing until this result is achieved. Finally sift the powder so as to secure at least a 160 mesh product. In order to save cleaning the sieves, some manufacturers prefer to sift all materials first before mixing.

In addition to sifting and bolting face powders, certain terms like air floated, micronized and air-spun have been used to describe the fineness of particle size and the process by which this conditioned is obtained. This property results, not only from sifting, but also from subsequent processing as well. In air floating, the finished product is passed through a mill equipped with a fan, cyclone and dust arrester to air separate the coarser particles which cannot be blown or floated to a predetermined height, until they are sufficiently fine. A micronizer is a mill that will grind all the powder particles to a desired micron size, a micron being 0.001 mm. or about 0.00004 in. By the air spinning process the powder is whriled around by a purified, continuous air stream under great pressure in a closed, cylinderical, specially constructed metal vessel. This causes the powder particles to be knocked against one another at high speeds, estimated at over a thousand miles per hour, by this attrition the particles are reduced in size and the desired bulk is reached. At this point the smaller particles are permitted to flow from the cylinder through the use of the centrifugal force principle, while the larger ones cannot make their exit until they are divided finely enough.

The advantages of processes like these are that not only is a finer powder obtained but more uniform distribution of perfume and colour is afforded and greater flufiness is obtained. Some firms go even step further and age the finished powder for several weeks in air tight bins before filling it.

By another method it is common practice to subdevide the manufacture of powder into two operations, first the preparation of white powder base, which is perfumed and stored in air tight bins to age and mellow the perfume. During this process it will permeate every particle of the base material. The second operation embraces the manufacture of colour bases of which sufficient quantities are made up at one time for several batches. This procedure speeds up the operation of making face powder and aids in securing uniformity of successive batches. The white powder base may be made up as follows :

WHITE BASE FOR LIGHT POWDERS
With Zinc Oxide

Zinc Oxide	22.83%
Talc	67.63
Zinc Stearate	6.26
Precipitated Chalk or Magnesium Carbonate	2.25
Perfume	1.04
	100.00

WHITE BASE FOR MEDIUM POWDERS
With Zinc Oxide

Zinc Oxide	26.04%
Talc	65.46
Zinc Stearate	5.21
Precipitated Chalk or Magnesium Carbonate	2.25
Perfume	1.04
	100.00

WHITE BASE FOR MEDIUM POWDERS
With Titanium Dioxide

Titanium Dioxide	5.43%
Talc	86.07
Zinc Stearate	5.21
Precipitated Chalk or Magnesium Carbonate	2.25
Perfume	1.04
	100.00

WHITE BASE FOR MEDIUM POWDERS
With Zinc Oxide & Titanium Dioxide

Titanium Dioxide	3.00%
Zinc Oxide	21.25
Talc	68.29
Zinc Stearate	4.17
Precipitated Chalk or Magnesium Carbonate	2.25
Perfume	1.04
	100.00

In comparing the percentages of the individual materials in the foregoing bases with the percentages of the same materials in the table of powder formulas previously recorded, it will be observed that the percentages are somewhat higher in the bases. This is due, of course, to the omission of some of the chalk and the colours. However, when colour base is added the percentage formula will be found to correspond with these formulas.

The following colour bases will give satisfactory shades. The use of more or less of the base will give shades to suit individual taste.

POWDER BASES

Peach (Also called nude, natural)-

Precipitated Chalk	59.0%
Golden Ochre	40.0
Brilliant Pink Lake	1.0
	100.00

Use 5 parts and 95 parts white powder.

Rachel -

Precipitated Chalk	75.0%
Golden Ochre	25.0
	100.00

Use 4 parts and 96 parts white powder.

Flesh -

Precipitated Chalk	90.0%
Golden Ochre	9.5
Brilliant Pink Lake	1.0
	100.00

Use 4 parts and 96 parts white powder.

Naturelle -

Precipitated Chalk	75.0%
Golden Ochre	24.0
Brilliant Pink lake	1.0
	100.00

Use 4 parts and 96 parts white powder.

Ochre -

Precipitated Chalk	54.0%
Golden Ochre	43.0
Brilliant Pink Lake	3.0
	100.00

Use 8 parts and 92 parts white powder.

Suntan -

Precipitated Chalk	36.0%
Golden Ochre	58.0
Brilliant Pink Lake	6.0
	100.00

Use 9 parts and 91 parts white powder.

Additional Formulaes

In cases where it is desired to have greater latitude than is afforded by the formulas outlined in the formula tables presented, others selected from the literature are given. The colours and perfumes are omitted as these vary materially.

Talc	40.0	56.0
Colloidal clay	20.0	20.0
Zinc Oxide	20.0	10.0
Zinc stearate	.....	10.0
Precipitated Chalk	15.0	......
Magnesium Carbonate	5.0	4.0
Talc	75	......

Zinc Oxide	20	......
Zinc Stearate	5	......
Talc	60.0	80.0
Zinc Oxide	10.0	15.0
Zinc Stearate	20.0	4.0
Magnesium Carbonate	10.0	1.0

Talc	69.0	82.79
Zinc Oxide	18.0	......
Titanium Dioxide	......	5.21
Zinc Stearate	6.0	5.0
Precipitated Chalk	7.0	7.0

Talc	74.5	30.5
Zinc Oxide	10.0	20.0
Titanium Dioxide	3.5	5.0
Collodial Clay	......	40.0
Precipitated Chalk	5.0	......
Magnesium Stearate	......	5.0
Zinc Stearate	7.0	......

Talc	40.0	15.0
Collodial clay	45.0	25.0
Titanium Dioxide	4.0	5.0
Magnesium Stearate	6.0	10.0
Precipitated Chalk	......	45.0

Talc	20.0	38.0	40.0
Collodial Clay	20.0	10.0	10.0
Zinc Oxide	15.0	12.0	18.0
Magnesium Stearate	5.0	13.0	7.0
Magnesium Carbonate	10.0	2.0	5.0
Precipitated chalk	30.0	25.0	20.0

Talc	15.0	67.0
Collodial clay	35.0	20.0
Titanium Dioxide	10.0	4.0
Magnesium Stearate	5.0	3.0
Magnesium Carbonate	5.0	6.0
Rice Starch	30.0	......

Talc	52.5	67.0
Collodial Clay	15.0	......
Titanium Dioxide	......	3.0
Zinc Oxide	12.0	20.0
Zinc Stearate	7.0	4.0
Magnesium Carbonate	2.5	......
Precipitated Chalk	11.0	6.0

Talc	51.5	51.5
Titanium Dioxide	3.0	5.0
Zinc Oxide	12.0	12.0

Collodial Clay	13.0	11.0
Magnesium Carbonate	2.5	2.5
Precipitated Clay	11.0	11.0
Zinc Stearate	7.0	7.0

Talc	31.5	46.8
Collodial Clay	31.5	18.0
Zinc Oxide	20.0	13.5
Titanium Dioxide	......	4.5
Zinc Stearate	8.0	8.1
Precipitated Chalk	6.0	4.5
Magnesium Carbonate	1.0	4.5
Mineral Oil	2.0	0.1

4

VARIATIONS OF FACE POWDERS

Compacts - Cake Make-Up Powders - Liquid and Creams Powders - Cosmetic Stockings

Since compact powders, cake make-up powders, cream powders and liquid powders are closely allied to face powders in composition, we choose to discuss them at this point rather than under make-up cosmetics. Cosmetic stockings, also, closely stimulate liquid powders so it will be more advantageous to include them in our consideration of liquid powders.

We have emphasized that slip, adhesion, covering power, colour and odor are important properties of a consumer acceptable face powder. This is equally true of compact powder which in the last analysis is a face powder that has been compacted into a tablet. The processes used to make compacts are closely allied to that of tablet making in the pharmaceutical field. It may be pointed out at this point that the methods of making cake rouge and compact powder are essentially the same, since rouge is merely a more highly coloured tablet of compact powder. The same equipment suffices for making either product.

There are three common processes used for tableting face powders. These are wet compression method. I the dry compussion method and the wet molding method. The last of these is seldom used.

The manufacture of compacts is largely vested in private brand houses who are able to invest in the special, costly equipment necessary to produce the tablets in large quantities. Unles a cosmetic house has large output it is advisable to have these products made by these private labels plants and filled into the cases bearing their own trademark and of their own design. Cases made of metal, plastics and paper together with the necessary pufffor application are available from numerous manufacturers or in smaller quantity directly from the compact makers. Only in a few cases do these manufacturers market a compact through the regular channels to the consumer. On the other hand, the exact methods by which they make these cosmetics are guarded as a trade secret and specific information as to formulation and processing is not very available.

A brief outline of the three methods, however, is in order.

By the wet compression method the powdered ingredients are mixed, until uniform just as a face powder is made. Powders in the fine state will not compress into a tablet so further processing to form granules is necessary. The powder base is, therefore, wet down with a liquid and binder and thoroughly mixed in a suitable mixer until stiff pasty mass is formed. This is granulated by working it while damp through about a one-eighth inch mesh wire screen tacked over a frame through a specially built granulator. The wet granules are spread on trays and dried. these dried granules are then compressed by a tablet or compact press.

In the dry compression method the powder base, colour and perfume are milled by a pulverizer or ball mill. The milled powder is then moistened with the binding solution and thoroughly mixed until it is granular. The granules are then compressed and the finished cakes are allowed to dry in a drying cabinet at about 140°F.

The wet casting process consists of making a wet, heavy paste of all ingredients. The paste is poured or pressed by rolling into lubricated nickel molds, in which the cakes are allowed to dry. Just before putting the molds into the dryer, dextrin or gum arabic adhesive is painted over the surface of the rouge cakes and glass, porcelain or metal plates, properly shaped, are pressed down on the glued surface to the cakes. When the cakes are dry they adhere to the plates.

A compact must neither be too hard nor too soft. The powder must come off easily on the puff and the cake must not get hard and shiny. The basic materials are the same as those for face powder; talc, kaolin, collodial clay, bentonite, zinc oxide, titanium dioxide, precipitated chalk, magnesium carbonate, and the stearates of zinc, aluminium and magnesium. The colours are mineral pigments, lakes and other D & C colours similar to those used for face powder. The stearates make good binders and spreading agents. Talc should be limited to 50% as more will cause the cakes to crack. The binding solution should me made up in quantities and kept at standard viscosity. This requires a preservative. The binding solution is a mucilage made from these materials: gelatin, gum tragacanth, gum acacia, gum karaya, methyl cellulose, quince seed, rosin, Irish moss and gum tragcanth. Ocasionally lanolin dissolved in ether is added.

A typical binding solution formula is as follows :

Gum tragcanth mucilage (2%)	20.0%
Quince seed mucilage (2%)	10.0
Gelatin mucilage (3%)	10.0
Rosin tincture	1.0
Water	58.8
Methyl p-hydroxy benzoate	0.2
	100.00

A typical binding solution formula is as follows :

Talc (300 mesh)	40.0%
Zinc Oxide	20.0
Zinc Stearate	6.0
Rice Starch	10.0
Magnesium Carbonate	3.0
Collodial Clay	10.0
Colour Pigment	10.5
Perfume	0.5
	100.00

To make a finished compact from these mix all ingredients of the base formula together and run through a pulverizer, or a ball mill. Moisten the base powder with a sufficient quantity of the binding solution to make a suitable granulation for the type of process being followed. Compress and dry the cakes.

Other formulas for base powder follows :

Talc California	42 lbs.
China Clay	15 lbs.
Zinc Oxide	7½ lbs.
Zinc Stearate	7½ lbs.
Gum Arabic mucilage Q.S. to granual perfume	7½ lbs.
Lake Colour	

COMPACT POWDER BASE NO. 1

Kaolin	40 lbs.
Talc	40 lbs.
Magnesium Carbonate	10 lbs.
Rice Starch	10 lbs.
Perfume	10 oz.
Anhydrous Lanolin	3 oz.
Ether	2 fl.oz.
	100 lbs.

Mix the powderes materials in a mixer together with proper amount of lake colours. Granulate with the lanolin ether solution and binding solution.

More recently cake make-up, also designated as pan-cake make-up, a registered name, by the originator of this product, has had large customer acceptance. It has gained a firm foothold as a new cosmetic because it possesses advantages not found in other preparations. The use of cake make-up produces a flat, smooth, enduring finish to the skin that cannot be acquired by any other cosmetic. At the same time it conceals minor skin imperfections. Variations of these two results as regards water repellence, adherence to the skin for a long period, and masking ability are possible.

In the manufacture and formulation of cake make-up it should first of all be stressed that great care must be excercised to keep formulas and processing standardized. Unless the mixing operations, drying temperatures and fineness of the powders are kept uniform an inferior product will result. Colours should be very carefully watched. In U.S. Patent 2,101,843 the methods of manufacturing a patented product are described in detail. Other information as to the emulsifying agent, ratio of pigment and powders and similar limits are described in this patent.

The composition of cake make-up varies. The powders consist of those usually found in face powders like talc, chalk, kaolin, collodial clay, titanium dioxide and zinc oxide. These are used in addition to light or heavy mineral oils, vegetable oils, pigments, perfumes, water, humectants like glycerol and glycols, binding and emulsifying agents.

The finished cake should be so formulated that it will come off easily with a moistened applicator or sponge, as an emulsion or by some other medium and lay on the skin uniformly. Some products are then blended into the skin while moist by rubbing with the fingers or cleaning tissues while others are permitted to dry on the skin and the excess powder is brushed off. The film produced in either case, should not "draw" the skin through too rapid drying out, stay on during a normal day, repel the moisture caused by perspiring, and be readily removed by washing with soap and water.

In order to obtain these desirable properties, a few comments regarding the mineral earths used are enlightening. Titanium dioxide and zinc oxide impart covering and masking properties to the cake. Kaolin and collodial clay helps as binder in compressing but if used too large amounts cause the absorption of too much water, causing the film to pile up and become uneven. Chalk regulates the ease of brushing off or blending with the skin. Talc is more or less a stable filler but care must be used in its selection and use or too much shine will be imparted. It is necessary for the cosmetic chemist to use a combination of these powders, in such a way, that the effect desired is obtained in proportioning these mixed earths and other powders ordinarily used in face powders.

As to the ingredients used in the formulas, the pigments should be selected so that they do not "bleed" during perspiration. Many manufacturers prefer approved water insoluble lakes and mineral pigments. By a combination of these desired shades may be reached. The oils may be either light or heavy mineral oils and vegetable oils. They are added to produce the desired amount of oiliness. Mineral oils are stable but vegetable oils should be stabilized with an anti-oxidant or rancidity is apt to occur. Numerous emulsifying agents, such as used in creams and lotions, are available. Care must be used in their selection and just the right amount should be added to the mixed powders so as not to over dry the skin by degreasing it.

The method of manufacture is not unlike that used for compacts. In the patent mentioned the powders are mixed. The water oil emulsion and humectant are added to form a paste which is passed through a roller mixer to obtain greater homogeneity.This paste is then granulated and pressed into cakes. Variations of this method are used, the object being to obtain a uniform granular material to feed to the compression machine that will form a cake that is neither too friable nor too dense. The use of gum mucilages as binders influences this condition to a great extent. The lubricating property of the granulation in the compression press must also be given consideration.

Liquid and cream powders often called "night whites" are used for evening wear to offset the glare of electric lights. These preparations are applied to face, neck and arms because of their high opacity they serve to blend the colours of skin which is exposed only in evening dress.

NO. 1 Liquid Powder

Collodial Clay	18.0%
Titanium Dioxide	2.0

Glycerin	8.0
Water	71.5
Perfume	0.5
	100.0

NO. 2 Liquid Powder

Collodial Clay	8.0%
Precipitated Chalk	5.0
Zinc Oxide	10.0
Glycerin	5.0
Alcohol	5.0
Orange Flower Water	67.0
	100.0

NO. 3 Liquid Powder

Talc	10.0%
Collodial Clay	5.0
Titanium Dioxide	5.0
Glycerin	10.0
Rose Water	64.0
Alcohol	5.5
Perfume	0.5
	100.0

NO. 4 Liquid Powder

Collodial Zinc Oxide	6.0%
Pecipitated Chalk	8.0
Collodial Clay	3.0
Zinc Stearate	2.0
Glycerin	3.0
Witch Hazel	10.0
Orange Flower Water	68.0
	100.0

NO. 5 Liquid Powder

Titanium Dioxide	5.0%
Precipitated Chalk	8.0
Collodial Clay	5.0
Glycerin	3.0
Rose Water	79.0
	100.0

NO. 6 Liquid Powder

Collodial Zinc Oxide	8.0%
Collodial Clay	5.0
Precipitated Chalk, heavy	6.0
Glycerin	5.0
Witch Hazel	10.0
Orange Flower Water	66.0
	100.0

NO. 7 Liquid Powder

Heavy Mineral Oil	45 lbs.
in which is dissolved by agitation and heat	
Magnesium Oleate	2 lbs.
Titanium Dioxide	20 lbs.
Chalk Light	3 lbs.
Talc	5 lbs.
Perfume	3 oz.
Red Iron Oxide	6 oz.
Light Ochre	3 oz.

Variations of these last two and Sienna and burnt under may be used. Stir the other ingredients into the oil solution of magnesium oleate. Stir while filling.

In addition to the materials included in these formulas barium sulfate bismuth subnitrate, bismuth subcarbonate, lithopone and similar materials are sometimes employed. It cannot be said that they have any advantage over the materials specified. Some manufacturers add a small amount of starch or saponin in order to make the powder adhere better and also to make the suspension more stable. The addition of thickeners or adhesives must be made with caution because the product should not be made sticky, nor should it require an undue of time to dry.

The manufacturing methods for liquid face powder and similar suspensions, are so simple they require but passing mention. The powdered ingredients and colour, if any is used, are mixed together in a powder mixer. The liquid ingredients are blended in a suitable tank which preferably is equipped with a mechanical agitator in motion. After all the powders have been added the mass is stirred for about half an hour longer. The finished liquid powder is then filled, agitating during the filling operation, in order to assure uniform distribution of the powder in the liquid phase of the preparation, until the filling tank is emptied.

NO. 8 Cream Powder

Vanishing Cream	70.0%
Talc	24.0
Titanium Dioxide	5.5
Perfume	0.5
	100.0

NO. 9 Cream Powder

Glyceryl Monostearate	10.0%
Glycerin	3.0
Heavy Mineral Oil	5.0
Spermaceti	5.0
Stearic Acid	2.0
Caustic Potash U.S.P.	0.1
Water	48.4
Perfume	0.5
Titanium Dioxide	6.0
Talc	20.0
	100.0

Dissolve the caustic potash in water then add all the rest of the ingredients with the exception of the perfume, but include the colour. Bring the mixture to a boil with constant stirring. Continue stirring until all of the materials have melted and have become homogeneous. Shut off the heat and continue stirring until mass is cooled, then add the perfume. Run the mass through a roller or ointment mill if the colour does not come out uniformly.

NO. 10 Cream Powder

Glycerin	42.0%
Stearic Acid	10.0
White Face Powder	42.0
Distilled Water	4.0
Potassium Hydroxide U.S.P	1.5
Perfume	0.5
	100.0

Colour to suit.

Dissolve the Potassium Hydroxide in water, melt the stearic acid and add the caustic solution. Mix until saponification is complete. Heat the glycerin; add the face powder and colour and mix until all lumps have disappeared. Then incorporate the first mixture, add the perfume and mix again. Run the product through an ointment mill to assure smoothness and uniformity of colour distribution. Lake colours are best for this type of product.

While cosmetic stockings are hardly face powders, their similarity to liquid face powder is so close that for purposes of expediency they may be best discussed at this point. Leg make-up differs from facial make-up in that face powders seek to impart a matural appearance to the skin while cosmatic stocking seek to give to the bare legs the artificial texture-like appearance of women's hose.

The requirements, then, of these products are that of colour simulate that of the popular shades of women's hose, that when applied it resembles the texture of sheer stockings, that the colour does not come off easily with water nor by rubbing against clothing, that it goes on smoothly and uniformly and that it adheres lastingly.

An excellent discussion of these cosmetics appeared in a recent article by Kalish* which warrants inclusion in this work. He states :

Probably the simplest type of cosmetic stocking is an aqueous dye solution. A combination of acceptable dyes is dissolved in water and the solution applied to the legs. The skin is stained and the colour can be removed by soap and water, but not easily by water alone. A certain amount of alcohol is usually included in the solution to make drying more rapid. Some glycerin, sorbitol, propylene glycol, or pentanediol should be included for the emollient effect upon the skin as well as to impart a slight luster. Finally, a little wetting agent must be present to assure even deposition of colour. Preparations of this type have one serious disadvantage, namely, they do not adequately hide tha natural texture of the skin and blemishes remain visible.

NO. 1 LIQUID COSMETIC STOCKING

Dye	2.0%
Wetting Agent	1.0
Glycerin	4.0
Alcohol	10.0
Water	83.0
	100.0

Liquid powder types of cosmetic stockings are the most popular, and, in our opinion, the most generally satisfactory. They contain about 20 per cent of pigment mixture suspended in a liquid medium, usually with some gum or resinous material to act as a binder.

Colour is given by insoluble pigments of the harmless earth colour group and lakes made from certified dyes. These must be extended by the addition of white materials with a certain amount of covering power. This covering power is necessary to hide minor blemishes and irregularities in skin texture, yet a heavily powdered appearance, from too much covering power, must not result. Zinc oxide and titanium dioxide, used sparingly, will gave desired opacity. Precipitated chalk, because of its smaller covering power, may be used in relatively larger proportions. Zinc stearate is useful in assisting adhesion. Collodial clay, and especially Bentonite, assist in keeping the pigments in suspension for a longer time, making application that much easier. Talc will supply a certain amount of luster to the mixture, premitting better simulation of silk texture.

Water is the primary suspending medium for the powder mixture, but it should be modified by the addition of some alcohol to facilitate drying. Furthermore, the addition of a little glycerin or other humectant liquid serves to prevent the powder from flaking off the legs. Again, the addition of a little wetting agent assists in assuring uniform spread of colour on application. Finally, a fixative of some type must be added to make the powder adhere firmly to the skin surface. Gums must be used cautiously, since they may cause the powder to cake into a hard mass at the bottom of the bottle. A very low viscosity methyl cellulose should be useful for this purpose. More valuable, as being less water-soluble, are certain substances, such as alkaline shellac, borate esters including those of the glycols and sorbitol, dispersed casien, etc. The use of latex is desirable.

In addition to the insoluble pigments, it seems a good idea to add a very small amount of dye of the same shade, soluble in the medium used. This will not only tint the liquid, but will also very slightly stain the skin. In this way, an effect similar to that in lipsticks will result, where top colour from the pigments may eventually be rubbed off, with the undertone of dye still imparting colour.

NO. 2 LIQUID COSMETIC STOCKING

Precipitated Chalk	10.0%
Talc	5.0
Titanium Dioxide	3.0
Bentonite	2.0
Alcohol	8.0
Glycerin	3.0
Wetting Agent	0.5
Methyl Cellulose	0.5
Water	68.0
Dye and Pigment	Q.S.
	100.0

NO. 3 LIQUID COSMETIC STOCKING

Collodial Clay	10.0%
Precipitated Chalk	10.0
Talc	5.0
Alcohol	5.0
Sorbitol	5.0
Soluble Casein	3.0
Water	62.0
Dye and Pigment	Q.S.
	100.0

COSMETIC STOCKING

LIGHT SHADE

Colour Light Base (see below)	131 lbs.
Carbitol	33 lbs. 4 oz.
Cetyl Alcohol # 1	20 lbs.
Wetting Agent	16 lbs. 8 oz.
Benzoic Acid Ester	1 lb. 2 oz.
Perfume	1 lb. 5 oz.
Water	100 gals.
	100.0

Colour Base Light

Titanium Dioxide	250 lbs.
Sun Tan C 33-007	50 lbs.
Brown # 1	5 lbs.
Brown # 1076	5 lbs.
Umber A-8534	5 lbs.
	315 lbs.

Premix and grind colours in a micronizer before using in above.

COSMETIC STOCKING

Dark Shade

Titanium Dioxide	7 lbs. 12 oz.
Colour Base Dark (see below)	42 lbs. 12 oz.
Carbitol	13 lbs. 4 oz.
Cetyl Alcohol # 1	8 lbs.
Wetting Agent	6 lbs. 8 oz.
Benzoic Acid Ester	8 oz.
Perfume	8 oz.
Water	43 gals.

Color Base Dark

Titanium Dioxide	250 lbs.
Sun Tan C 33-007	50 lbs.
Brown # 1	15 lbs.
Umber A 8534	15 lbs.
Brown # 1076	5 lbs.
	335 lbs.

Premix and grind colours in a micronizer before using in above.

The soluble casein is made by dispersing one pound of casein in one gallon of water with the help of 2 ounces of triethanolamine.

Cream leg make-up is used to a limited extend. Creams can be readily smoothed out to make a uniform coating that will be very adherent. The best type of base to use is a vanishing cream containing adequate pigment to do a good covering and tinting job. For ease in spreading, the cream should be rather soft, and to prevent rolling, enough humectant must be present. A very little oil will add to the luster. Talc and titanium dioxide, both inert, are the most appropriate pigments and extenders to use along with the colouring material.

Finally, leg make-up has been made available in stick form. A composition of this type consists of a wax-oil mixture along with a large amount of pigment. It has the advantage of ease of application and considerable staying powers, so that even swimming will not readily remove the preparation. The base mixture must not have too high a melting point, or it will not rub out easily, yet must melt low enough to spread well. The base will provide the texture effect, so that pigments are necessary only for colour and hiding power. In this, as in all other mixtures, pigments must be milled very fine so that no colour streaks will show.

STICK COSMETIC STOCKING

Petrolatum	45.0%
Ozokerite	15.0
Soft Amorphous Wax	10.0
Deodorized Cocoa Butter	5.0
Titanium Dioxide	20.0
Colour	5.0
	100.0

5

TOILET POWDERS

Talcum Powder - Dusting Powder - After-Shave Powder - Baby Powder

Toilet Powders comprise talcum powder, dusting powder - also termed body powder or after-bath powder - after-shave powder and baby powder. The aggregate sale of these cosmetics is undoubtedly larger in ton volume than that of face powder because they are used more extravagantly and over larger surfaces of the body than face powders.

Of these toilet powders, the most important is talcum powder. This is dispensed from lithographed cans, glass containers, paper, or paper and plastic packages with shaker-tops. As the name implies, it consists mostly of talc, sometimes mixed with other ingredients. These may be the same as those used and discussed under face powders, though not in the same large proportions because users of talcum powder look for the slip, peculiar to talc. Only the purest grades of talc are used for high grade preparations. Some manufacturers use the less pure grades and sell large packages for a small price, basing their appeal upon economy. Perfume helps very materially to promote the sales of talcum powder and colour is of some value though the white and natural shades sell in largest volume. In some cases medication, like boric acid and camphor, is added. If medicinal claims are included, this makes the powder a drug and not a cosmetic.

Closely allied to talcum powder are dusting powder. These have about the same composition as talcum powder. The dusting or body powders are sold in flat, round, oval or angular metal, plastic or paper cans, usually with a puff to apply the powder to a person. After-shave powder consists of talc to which has been added the colour and some other mineral ingredients to make it go on smoothly, cling to the face with less sheen and more nearly match the colour of men's flesh than straight talcum does. Baby or nursery powder is iusually less heavily perfumed than other toilet powder and without colour. Boric acid is a favourite adition not only to baby powder but to all toilet powders because of its soothing slightly antiseptic properties.

The same general methods of mixing the ingredients together as described under face powders are employed in making toilet powders. In most cases it is easier to obtain a uniform blend in less time. This is because toilet powders are not as complicated as face powders.

The following formulas are satisfactory. It should be pointed out again that, since talcum, body and after-shave powders are so closely related, it is possible to designate any of these formulas by any one of the three names if it is so desired.

TALCUM POWDERS

No. 1

Talc	71.0%
Precipitated Chalk	20.0
Zinc Stearate	3.0
Boric Acid	5.0
Perfume	1.0
	100.0

No. 2

Talc	54.0%
Precipitated Chalk	40.0
Zinc Stearate	3.0
Boric Acid	2.0
Perfume	1.0
	100.0

No. 3

Talc	79.0%
Magnesium Carbonate	15.0

Boric Acid	3.0
Magnesium Stearate	2.0
Perfume	1.0
	100.0

No. 4

Talc	19.0%
Calcium Carbonate	60.0
Rice Starch	15.0
Boric Acid	5.0
Perfume	1.0
	100.0

After-Shave Powder

No. 5

Talc	71.5%
Titanium Dioxide	3.0
Zinc Stearate	4.0
Precipitated Chalk	20.0
Golden Ochre	0.5
Perfume	1.0
	100.0

Body Powders

No. 6

Talc	50.0%
Kaolin	30.0
Boric Acid	2.0
Precipitated Chalk	17.0
Perfume	1.0
	100.0

No. 7

Talc	50.0%
Precipitated Chalk	25.0
Magnesium Carbonate	20.0
Zinc Searate	2.0
Boric Acid	2.0
Perfume	1.0
	100.0

No. 8

Talc	68.0%
Precipitated Chalk	15.0
Collodial Clay	5.0
Boric Acid	3.0
Magnesium Stearate	3.0
Magnesium Carbonate	5.0
Pefume	1.0
	100.0

No. 9

Talc	70.0%
Kaolin	13.0
Magnesium Stearate	8.0
Precipitated Chalk	5.0
Magnesium Carbonate	3.0
Pefume	1.0
	100.0

No. 10

Talc	70.0%
Collodial Clay	11.0
Precipitated Chalk	10.0
Zinc Stearate	5.0
Boric Acid	6.0
Perfume	0.25
	100.0

BABY POWDERS

No. 11

Talc	63.63%
Kaolin	20.0
Zinc Stearate	5.0
Precipitated Chalk	5.0
Boric Acid	6.0
Oxyquinoline Benzoate	0.12
Perfume	0.25
	100.0

No. 12

Talc	66.75%
Magnesium Carbonate	5.0
Collodial Clay	10.0

Magnesium Stearate	5.0
Boric Acid	10.0
Titanium Dioxide	3.0
Pefume	0.25
	100.0

No. 13

Talc	54.0%
Kaolin	20.0
Zinc Stearate	5.0
Precipitated Chalk	11.0
Boric Acid	10.0
	100.0

There are other cosmetics which could be designated as toilet powders, such as deodorant powders, foot powders, tooth powders, hair powders and suntan preventive powder. As these have special properties, however, we will discuss them as we consider the function of these specialized preparations.

6

CREAMS

The manufacturing procedure for making cold creams is as follows:

Dissolve the borax in hot water. Melt the various waxes together and add fatty substances like lanolin, lard, petrolatum, if desired, and run into the oils, keeping the temperature at about 70^{0}C. Pour in the borax solution at the same temperature with constant stirring. Mix without heat for about one hour and one half. When cool (about 45^0 - 50^{0}C.) add the perfume.

It is a necessary precaution in making cold creams, to have the molten fats and water solution at the same temperature before mixing them, because the addition of cold water to hot waxes is likely to result in partial solidification of some of the wax, in the form of minute particles that will impart grittiness, an unpleasant defect, when applied to the skin.

In making variations of the usual cold cream with triethanolamine, melt the waxes, fats and oils together, bringing the temperature to about 80^{0}C. Then into a separate kettle put the water, glycerin and triethanolamine and bring the solution almost to the boiling point. Add the melted fats to the triethanolamine solution. Stir rapidly until an emulsion forms and when the temperature drops to about 45^{0}C., add the perfume.

When making cold cream, containing lanolin absorption base, melt the waxes, add the absorption base to the mineral oil and bring the temperature of the mixture to about 80°C. Then slowly add water heated to the same temperature, stirring until throughouly emulsified. When cool, add the perfume.

The manufacture of cold cream containing glyceryl monostearate is very simple. All the ingredients in the formula are put into a kettle and heated to the boiling point with constant stirring until all of the glyceryl monostearate has melted. Stirring is continued until cool enough to perfume.

The consistency of any of the following formulas can be adjusted by increasing or decreasing the wax content. Although it is not indicated, the keeping qualities of all creams containing vegetable oils is assured by the addition of 0.15% of a good preservative, such as methyl or propyl parahydroxybenzoate. Borax also exerts a preservative action but only a very mild one. In all cases mineral oil of 66-75 viscosity (Saybolt) can be substituted for vegetable oils.

VARIOUS FORMULAES FOLLOW :

NO. 1 COLD CREAM

White Beeswax	7.0%
Paraffin	10.0
Ceresin	3.0
White Mineral Oil (65 - 75)	44.0
Borax	1.0
Water	34.5
Perfume	0.5
	100.0

No. 2

Spermaceti	5.0%
White Beeswax	15.0
White Mineral Oil (65 - 75)	55.0
Borax	0.8
Distilled Water	23.7
Perfume	0.5
	100.0

No. 3

White Beeswax	20.0%
White Mineral Oil (65 - 75)	50.0
Distilled Water	28.8
Borax	0.7
Perfume	0.5
	100.0

No. 4

White Beeswax	20.0%
White Mineral Oil (65 - 75)	50.0
Rose Water	29.5
Borax	0.5
	100.0

No. 5

Spermaceti	8.0%
White Beeswax	12.0
White Mineral Oil (65 - 75)	55.0
Distilled Water	23.5
Borax	1.0
Perfume	0.5
	100.0

No. 6

Spermaceti	5.0%
White Beeswax	15.0
Lanolin	3.0
Peanut Oil, Refined	51.7
Distilled Water	24.0
Borax	0.8
Perfume	0.5
	100.0

No. 7

White Beeswax	22.0%
White Mineral Oil (65 -75)	50.8
Distilled Water	26.0
Borax	0.8
Perfume	0.4
	100.0

No. 8

White Beeswax	15.0%
Benzoinated Lard	50.0
Lanolin	9.0
Distilled Water	24.5
Borax	1.0
Perfume	0.5
	100.0

No. 9

White Beeswax	15.0%
White Petrolatum	10.0
Sesame Oil	20.0
Almond Oil	20.0
Borax	1.0
Rose Water	34.0
	100.0

No. 10

Spermaceti	10.0%
White Beeswax	12.0
Almond Oil	56.0
Borax	1.0
Rose Water	21.0
	100.0

No. 11

Sesame Oil	42.5%
Lanolin	4.5
White Beeswax	15.5
Spermaceti	6.0
Borax	1.0
Water	30.0
Perfume	0.5
	100.0

No. 12

Lanolin Absorption Base	20.0%
White Mineral Oil (65 - 75)	54.0

Water	24.5
White Beeswax	15.0
Perfume	0.5
	100.0

No. 13

Paraffin	6.0%
White Beeswax	12.0
White Mineral Oil (65 - 75)	54.0
Stearic Acid	1.0
Borax	1.0
Water	25.5
Perfume	0.5
	100.0

No. 14

Beeswax	25.0%
Mineral Oil	25.0
Water	48.75
Borax	1.25
	100.0

No. 15

Beeswax	25.0%
Mineral Oil	37.5
Water	36.25
Borax	1.25
	100.0

No. 16

Beeswax	16.67%
Mineral Oil	33.33
Water	49.17
Borax	0.83
	100.0

No. 17

Beeswax	14.28%
Mineral Oil	57.14
Water	27.87
Borax	0.71
	100.0

No. 18

Beeswax	25.0%
Mineral Oil	50.0
Water	23.75
Borax	1.25
	100.0

No. 19

Beeswax	20.0%
Mineral Oil	40.0
Water	39.0
Borax	1.0
	100.0

No. 20

Beeswax	16.67%
Mineral Oil	50.0
Water	32.5
Borax	0.83
	100.0

No. 21

Beeswax	14.28%
Mineral Oil	42.84
Water	42.13
Borax	0.75
	100.0

NO. 22 COLD CREAM 905

Protegin X	20.0%
White Wax	4.0
Ceresin	10.0
Mineral Oil	10.0
Glycerin	5.0
Water	51.0
	100.0

In making a cream solely from beeswax, mineral oil, water,and borax, the following general factors should be considered: Borax should not be less than 5 per cent of the beeswax used; not more than 8 per cent depending upon the acid number of the beeswax. As the proportion of beeswax increases, the cream becomes harder.

Mineral oil, in relationship to water, has a stiffening, rather than a softening effect upon the cream as the proportion is increased. Above 60 per cent of mineral oil, the cream shows signs of instability.

Increase of water softens the cream until the product becomes definitely liquid. When water is too low, the cream may be of the water-in-oil type rather than the customary oil-in-water. Increasing amounts of water seem to lead to finer grained and more lustrous creams. A good balance seems to be reached when water and oil are present in approximately equal amounts but good products result when the water-oil ratio varies from 1:2 to 2:1

NO. 23 THEATRICAL COLD CREAM

Beeswax	15.0%
White Paraffin Oil	60.0
Rose Water	24.0
Borax	1.0
	100.0

To make this, melt the wax, add the paraffin oil and continue to heat with constant stirring until they are well mixed. Use indirect heat to avoid overheating. Dissolve the borax in the rose water with the aid of heat and while still warm gradually add to the melted wax and oil, stirring constantly until cold. If desired distilled water may be used in place of the rose water and any desired perfume added.

NO. 24 SEMI-GREASELESS COLD CREAM

Beeswax	15.0%
Spermaceti	1.5
White Petrolatum	9.0
White Paraffin Oil	46.0
Cocoanut Oil	1.5
Powdered Borax	0.5

Powdered White Castile Soap	0.5
Water	26.0
	100.0

Melt the solids by indirect heat, add the oils and stir well. Dissolve the soap and borax in the water by means of heat and while still hot add the solution gradually with constant stirring to the wax and oil mixture. Continue to heat for five minutes, stirring all the time, then remove from the fire and stir until cold. As with other creams, this one may be made heavier by adding more wax.

NO. 25 WHITENING COLD CREAM

White Petrolatum	74.0%
Beeswax	12.0
Spermaceti	4.0
Titanium Dioxide	10.0
	100.0

Heat oil and waxes to 140ºF. in agitator. Dissolve borax and Ultramarine in hot water and adjust temperature to 140ºF. in jacket kettle. Pour water solution into wax, melt and agitate for one hour. Draw out little from bottom of the kettle to asssure proper mix. Fill at once.

NO. 26 COLD CREAM

White Rose Mineral Oil	110 lbs.
Paraffin (Refined M.P. 133ºF.)	15 lbs.
Spermaceti (Block)	12½ lbs.
Water	55 lbs.
Borax (gran.)	36 oz.
Ultramarine	30 grains
Cold Cream Perfume	22 oz.

Melt the wax with the spermaceti and petrolatum as usual and while cooling rub up with the titanium dioxide, mixing evenly. Dissolve the oils in the alcohol and stir into the mixture. Pass through an ointment or roller mill before filling.

The above formulas, while typical, do not include all the variations of cold creams that are possible. Many other combinations may be made. In some cases, borax is omittedand the beeswax and oil are melted together, cooled to the point at which solidification begins and warm water is added by beating it into the mixture. Such creams are not as white, of as high luster, nor of as smooth a texture as those containing borax. they are also less stable.

Cold creams made with borax are far superior to those without it, since the emulsion is whiter, smoother, and more stable. Creams of this type are oil-in-water in character if enough water (about 30 per cent or more) is present. Borax in excess of the amount required for neutralization makes the cream more alkaline without contributing to appearance or stability, while too little borax does not lead to the desired smooth cream.

7

VANISHING CREAMS

Vanishing cream is usually filled cold, utilizing the a plunger or auger typr filler which will permit the cream to be filled from the bottom of the jar upward, thus eliminating all danger of air pockets. The container into which it is packed should be equipped with a very tight seal to prevent evaporation. It is also customary in certain plants to fill the cream just above the melting point when it is semi-liquid. In such cases the temperature must be carefully controlled and a filler be used that will readily handle thick liquids. A moving belt for cooling the packsges is advisable and when the cream has cooled the tops must be carefully watched so as to prevent an unsightly appearance. It is the custom when these creams are filled hot to scrape the tops of jars with a specially designed scraper before the caps are applied.

It may be mentioned that by increasing the stearic acid content of vanishing cream to 30% or more, rolling massage creams can be made. Also, as discussed in the chapter on cleansing cream, rubbing massage creams can be made by incorporating glycerite of starch with light vanishing cream. Although preservatives are not included in all the following formulas, it is desirable to add 0.1% in cases where mold growth may develop.

No. 1

Stearic Acid	24.0%
Water	64.0
Glycerin	10.51
Potassium Hydroxide	0.99
Perfume	0.5
	100.0

Melt the stearic acid, preferably by indirect heat. Dissolve the potassium hydroxide in the water, add glycerin and heat to 185⁰F. and slowly add to melted stearic acid with constant stirring. Perfume at 105⁰F.

No. 2

Stearic Acid xxx	17.0%
Sodium Carbonate	0.5
Potassium Hydroxide	0.5
Glycerin	6.0
Water	71.0
Alcohol	4.5
Perfume	0.5
	100.0

Melt the stearic acid. Make a solution of the alkalies in the water, add the glycerin. Then add the solution with steady agitation to the melted fats, continue stirring until emulsification has taken place. Continue stirring until temperature has dropped to about 105⁰F. Dissolve the perfume in the alcohol and stir this in. Allow the batch to stand aside for a day before filling.

No. 3

Stearic Acid xxx	22.0%
Cocoa Butter	1.0
Potassium Hydroxide	0.9
Mineral Oil	2.0
Distilled Water	63.6
Glycerin	10.0
Perfume	0.5
	100.0

Dissolve the alkali in the water, add glycerine. melt the stearic acid and cocoa butter, add the mineral oil and then add the alkali solution. Continue stirring until emulsified. Perfume at 105⁰F.

No. 4

Stearic Acid xxx	14.0%
Cocoa Butter	4.0

Glycerine	8.0
Potassium Hydroxide	0.65
Borax	0.25
Perfume	0.5
Water	72.6
	100.0

Melt the stearic acid and cocoa butter, bring the temperature to 175°F. Dissolve the alkalies in water, add the glycerin and heat to 185°F. and add the glycerine and heat to 185°C. and add this to the stearic acid mixture. Mix for about two hours and perfume.

No. 5

Glyceryl Monostearate	10.0%
Stearic Acid xxx	3.0
White Mineral Oil	3.0
Potassium Hydroxide	0.1
Spermaceti	5.0
Titanium Dioxide	2.0
Water	72.4
Glycerin	4.0
Perfume	0.5
	100.0

Put all the ingredients into a melting kettle and bring to the boiling point with continuous stirring. When the glycerol monostearate has melted, strain the solution, and continue the stirring until the temperature has dropped to 105°F. Then add the perfume.

No. 6

Stearic Acid xxx	20.0%
Cetyl Alcohol	1.0
Potassium Carbonate	2.0
Borax	2.0
Glycerine	8.0
Alcohol	6.0
Water	60.5
Perfume	0.5
	100.0

Melt the stearic acid and cetyl alcohol together. Dissolve the alkalies in the water, add glycerin. Add this solution to the melted fats with continuous stirring. When the temperature has dropped to about 40^{0}C. add the perfume dissolved in the alcohol.

No. 7

Stearic Acid xxx	19.0%
Glycerin	6.5
Potassium Hydroxide	0.9
Water	65.6
Gum Tragacanth Powder	1.0
Alcohol	6.3
Methyl Parahydroxybenzoate	0.2
Perfume	0.5
	100.0

Mix perfume, alcohol, preservative and the tragacanth with half of the water. Heat the rest of the water, dissolve the alkali in it and add the glycerin. Melt the stearic acid and mix in the alkali solution. When emulsified, heat the tragacanth solution slightly and add with steady mixing.

No. 8

Triethanolamine	2.0%
Stearic Acid xxx	17.0
Lanolin	1.0
Borax	4.0
Glycerin	5.0
Water	70.5
Perfume	0.5
	100.0

Melt the lanolin and stearic acid. make a hot solution of the borax, triethanolamine, glycerine and the water. Add the alkali solution to the stearic acid and stir until emulsification has taken place. When the temperature drops to about 40^{0}C. add the perfume.

No. 9

Stearic Acid xxx	18.0%
Benzoinated Lard	2.0
Cocoa Butter	2.0
Strong Ammonia Solution	1.0
Water	70.5
Glycerin	6.5
Perfume	0.5
	100.0

Melt the stearic acid, lard, and cocoa butter. Mix the ammonia with the water; add glycerin and heat to 85°C. and stir it into the melted fats. Perfume at 40°C.

No. 10

Stearic Acid xxx	25.0%
Spermaceti	5.0
Amino Glycol	1.5
Water	60.5
Glycerin	8.0
	100.0

Melt the stearic acid and spermaceti. Make a hot solution (165°F.) of the amino glycol, the water and the glycerin. Add the alkaline solution slowly to the stearic acid. Mix at the same temperature and stir until emulsified. Perfume at 105°F.

8

FOUNDATION CREAMS

Foundation creams are not unlike vanishing creams. They usually contain pigemnts ground into these creams with a roll paint mill or ointment mill. Two typical formulas are :

No. 1 Foundation Cream

Tegin	12 lbs.
Mineral Oil	2 lbs.
Glycerin	5 lbs.
Spermaceti	5 lbs.
Titanium Dioxide	3 lbs.
Water Dist	72.9 lbs.
Oil Pink Colour	Q.S.
	100.0

No. 2 Foundation Cream

Tegin	12 lbs.
Mineral Oil	2 lbs.
Glycerin	5 lbs.
Spermaceti	5 lbs.
Aluminium Silicate	5 lbs.
Water Dist	70 lbs.
Oil Pink Colour	Q.S.
	100.0

In making liquid creams, more dificulty is encountered than with solid creams. Breaking of the emulsion is the main trouble, but change in consistency and viscosity may also appear as the product ages. The use of gum mucilages and other ingredients in formulas is apt to produce unpredictable changes. The testing of these creams by heat and cold over a period of weeks is desirable to guard against subsequent criticism. At least two weeks' test in a temperature control oven at 100^0F. and in refrigerator at just below freezing (32°F.). is desirable. Then, too, it is good policy to reverse the samples and to pursue other tests, like exposure to light, as conditions may indicate.

The actual procedure for manufacturing liquid creams varies considerably and is largely governed by the type of emulsifying agent used. The stability of an emulsion is also dependent upon this emulsifying agent and how it is employed. With these details in mind, we will consider liquid emulsions by classifying them according to the emulsifying them according to the emulsifying agents used rather than by their intended uses.

As a preliminary statement, it should be emphasized that it is a wise policy first to work out any method of emulsification in small laboratory lots, before making large batches. From these laboratory samples, in which standardized procedure is carefully charted, one should gradually work up to the desired sized batch. The operations which are particularly important are the quantities of water, oil, thickener if used, and emulsifying agent to be used, the order in which these materials are handled to make an emulsion, the type, speed, and time of mixer and mixing operation, purity of the raw materials used, temperature at which the emulsion is made and the pH of the finished cream. Careful and standardized procedured of these points are necessary for the making of an acceptable, stable emulsion.

In order to examine the manufacturing details of making emulsions, it is more convenient to refer to specific formulas. By so doing we can more accurately and concretely develop the modus operandi. As already stated, these liquid emulsions will be classified according to the emulsifying agents used, like soap emulsions, amine emulsions, polyhydric alcohol ester emulsions and others.

The old type almond cream or lotion still meets with favour in certain directions even though it does not incorporate the more modern emulsifying agent. It is not only more difficult to make, but also less stable than liquid emulsions made by other methods.

A typical formula follows

No. 1

PART I CREAM OIL BASE

6½	lbs.	Beeswax
16½	lbs.	Spermaceti (refined)
68	lbs.	Almond Oil (Sesame Oil or Peanut Oil may be substituted)
20	lbs.	Water Distilled
$1^1/_8$	lbs.	Borax

PART II FISISHED CREAM

50	lbs.	Cream Oil Base (Part I above)
10	lbs.	Neutral White Soap
150	lbs.	Water Distilled Perfume

To put a cream of this type together, a cream oil base as #1 is first prepared. This is done by dissolving the borax in the water which is heated to about 150°F. to facilitate solution. The beeswax, spermaceti and vegetable oil are then melted together by indirect heat and the borax solution is stirred in gradually at 140°F. until the mass is homogeneous when cooled. Then the mixture is drawn into suitable covered containers and either transferred directly to the emulsifying mixer or permitted to stand for future further manipulation.

To make the finished cream the required quantity of cream oil base is transferred to a suitable emulsifying mixer. As intimate agitation is important, a covered variable three speed cake type mixer in which the pan revolves as well as the stirring arms is very adaptable. The soap in powdered form is added to the cream oil base and mixed in until tthe mix is form. The water which has been heated to about 140°F. is then added very slowly, in a constant thin stream. If it is not taken up by the mass rapidly enough to form an emulsion, the addition of water is interrupted and mixing continues until the water is incorporated properly. When about two-thirds of the water has been added the mixer is changed to intermediate speed to prevent slopping over and the water addition and mixing continued until all water is used up. The perfume is nor added very slowly. The mixer is then changed to the low speed and mixing continued until the liquid cream reaches room temperature. It is finally passed through colloid mill or homogenizer, stored for 24 hours, tested for quality and filled.

A variation of this method may be illustrated by another formula. This consists of five steps :

No 2

Step No. I

Melt together at 150°F.

10 lbs. Spermaceti
1¼ lbs. Beeswax
2½ lbs. Stearic Acid xxx
10 lbs. Almond Oil or other suitable refined vegetable oil, e.g. Peach Kernel or Raisin Seed
4 oz. Perfume

Step No. II

Dissolve by Heat

11¼ lbs. Castile Soap Powder
100 lbs. Distilled Water

Step No. III

Dissolve by Heat

5 lbs. Gum Tragacanth and
3 lbs. Benzoic Acid in
320 lbs. Water Distilled (When Cool Add)
12½ lbs. Glycerine
2 gals. Alcohol S.D. 39 B

Step No. IV

Dissolve

2½ lbs. Borax in

40 lbs. Water, hot distilled

Step No. V

To make the finished cream add # II to # I, then add # IV to this and finally add # III. This nust be done in a suitable, efficient emulsifier. Emulsification is continued until the mass is emulsified and then the cream is passed through a colloid mill or homogenizer to assure a more stable emulsion. It is then ready for bottling.

Liquid creams may be made much more easily with emulsifying agents which contain an amino group like triethanolamine (TEA) and amino glycol which are most frequently used for liquid cosmetic creams.

In order to illustrate the method, which has been found most convenient for liquid creams made with TEA, we will again use an almond type cream as our guide. In this formula it is possible, however, to make numerous substitutions for the peanut oil indicated. This may be replaced by any suitable vegetable oil, mineral oil, partially by lanolin or beeswax, spremaceti, ceresin, cetyl alcohol or isopropyl esters of the fatty acids. It is permissible to add gum, mucilages or solutions, preservatives and other lotion ingredients like glycerin or propylene glycol. The purpose of this formula, which is very simple one, is to point out a method used in making emulsions with TEA.

No. 3

I

9 lbs. Stearic Acid xxx
3 lbs. Triethanolamine
400 lbs. Water Distilled
1 lbs. Borax

II

70 lbs. Peanut Oil refined

1½ lbs. Perfume

To make the emulsion heat #I by indirect heat at 140°F. until the stearic acid melts and is neutralized by the TEA. Then add this to the peanut oil-perfume mixture # II, which has been heated to about 130°F. Mix vigorously with a suitable mechanical agitator and continue agitation until the emulsion reaches 5°F. above room temperature. Strain to storage tank and fill the next morning.

9

HAND LOTIONS

Varieties-Increased Uses-Formulaes

Care and a certain amount of skill are required in making hand lotions. All formulas should be carefully compounded and thoroughly shelf tested before placing them on the market. Typical hand lotion formulas are present with directions for making them.

No. 1

Stearic Acid	3.15%
Glycerin	6.0
Potassium Hydroxide	0.15
Water	79.3
Alcohol S.D.	8.5
Perfume	0.5
Quince Seed	2.25
Preservative	0.15
	100.0

Dissolve the potassium hydroxide in one-third of the water and add the glcerin. Bring the rest of the water to a temperature of 80^{0}C.; add the quince seed and soak for six hours and strain through muslin. Melt the stearic acid, dissolve the perfume in the alcohol; add to the hot potassium hydroxide solution the melted stearic acid and boil for a minute. Allow the temperature to drop to about 70^{0}C. and then stir it into the quince see mucilage. Stir occasionally until cool, then slowly add the alcohol, preservative and perfume. Note : a clear mucilage is obtained if it is made cold by soaking the seeds or the gum, as the case may be, overnight. In this case the preservative should be dissolved in the water first.

No. 2

Gum Tragacanth (# I ribbons)	6	lbs.
Tincture Benzoin Sumatra (25 oz. per gal.)	2	gals.
Glycerin C.P.	40	lbs.
Boric Acid	14	lbs.
Alcohol S.D. 39-B	$9^1/_8$	lbs.
Water Distilled	77	gals.
Perfume	3	lbs.
	94	gallons

To make this formula make a mucilage of the gum tragacanth with 50 gals of the water. Make upthe tincture of benzoin. Both mucilage and tincture must be strained or filtered well. Dissolve the boric acid in the rest of the water (hot) in the mixing tank. Add the mucilage, then the alcohol in which the perfume has been dissolved. While stirring in well add the tincture. Mix well, strain again and fill when cool.

No. 3

Gum Tragacanth (# I ribbons)	6	lbs.
Glycerin C.P.	40	lbs.
Boric Acid	6	lbs.
Borax	3	lbs.
Alcohol (S.D. 39-B)	11	gals.
Perfume	3	lbs.
F.D.C. Red #1 (Ponceau 3 R)	¼	oz.
Water Distilled	85	gals

Follow method under # 2 except for addition of tincture of benzoin.

No. 4

Stearic Acid	1.5%
Soap, powdered neutral white	1.0
Alcohol S.D. 39-B	4.0
Glycerin	5.9
Borax	2.5
Gum Karaya	1.5
Water	82.95
Perfume	0.5
Preservative	0.15
	100.0

Mix the gum karaya with alcohol and stir into half the water (warm). When dissolved strain through muslin. (Note : The purer the grade of gum employed, the quicker will it dissolve and the higher will its viscosity be.) Heat the rest of the water and dissolve in it the borax, add the soap, glycerin and melted stearic acid and agitate until cool. Then add the mucilage, preservative and the perfume.

NO. 5 PINEAPPLE JUICE HAND LOTION

3% Mucilage of Irish Moss	37.0%
Glycerin	10.0
Alcohol	15.0
Boric Acid	0.5
Tr. of Benzoin	0.5
Pineapple Juice	36.8
Methyl Parahydroxybenzoate	0.2
	100.0

The above preparation may be perfumed to suit. Pineapple juice is an excellent hand cleanser. The Irish moss mucilage is made by soaking 3% of cleaned Irish moss in 97% by weight of water. After soaking overnight drain off the mucialge and add the required quantity to the above formula. The procedure is similar to the preceeding formulas. Up to 5% of powdered soap can be added.

10

AFTER SHAVING LOTIONS

The popularity of lotions for the use of men during shaving operations continues to increase. While they are often termed after-shave lotions, the use of electric razors particularly has brought into prominence pre-shaving lotions. Then too, purveyors of lotions and liquid creams recommend their products for use during or after shaving. The purposes of a shaving lotion are various. They may be used for their usual emollient effect, to produce an astringent effect to soften the beard, to allay irritation, for the styptic properties to check the flow of blood from razor scratches and for their antiseptic properties. Then too, many shavers enjoy the cooling and refreshing feeling of applying an after shaving lotion. In this respect they prefer one with a bite obtained with substances like capsicum or cantharides or with high alcoholic content. In other cases they like the odour during and after application. Of the various odors used lilac,lavender, bay rum, fougere royal or odors having a lift are most acceptable.

In many cases shaving lotions are nothing more than toilet waters with another name but in view of the properties desired as listed above, it is good judgement to add ingredients other than those that make toilet water as a shaving lotion.

As a cue for the making of various types of shaving lotions, these formulas are cited :

No. 1

Alcohol	20.0%
Zinc Sulfate	0.5
Glycerin	5.0
Benzocaine	0.2

Perfume	0.3
Water	74.0
	100.0

Dissolve benzocaine and perfume in alcohol, add glycerine. Dissolve zinc sulfate in water and add to above. Mix and filter.

No. 2 General Purpose Lotion

Oxyquinoline Sulfate	0.5%
Lecithin	1.0
Sodium Lauryl Sulfate	1.0
Tincture of Benzoin	5.0
Alcohol 39-A	17.0
Chloro-thymol	0.1
Menthol	0.2
Glycerin	10.0
Chloroform	6.0
Rose Water or Witch Hazel	59.2
	100.0

Mix the chloroform and the glycerin and dissolve the lecithin in it. Dissolve the oxyquinoline sulfate in water and the chlorothymol, sodium lauryl sulfate and menthol in the alcohol. Add the tincture of benzoin. Add the various solutions to the rose water and mix.

NO. 3 GENERAL PURPOSE LOTION

Boric Acid	2.3%
Menthol	0.05
Glycerin	2.0
Alcohol 39-A	8.0
Witch Hazel	87.15
Perfume	0.5
	100.0

Same as No. 2.

No. 4

Oxyquinoline Sulfate	0.5%
Alcohol 39-A	8.0
Glycerin	4.0
Water	87.0
Bay Oil	0.5
	100.0

Dissolve the oxyquinoline sulfate in the water; mix the glycerine, the oil of bay, the alcohol. Add to the water, mix throughly, allow to stand for 24 hours and filter.

NO. 5 DRY SKIN LOTION

Glycerin	10.0%
Gum Tragacanth Powder	1.5
Lavender Oil	0.5
Menthol	0.1
Alcohol 39-A	10.0
Rose Water	20.0
Methyl p-hydroxybenzoate	0.1
Witch Hazel	57.8
	100.0

Mix the gum tragacanth powder with half the alcohol, add preservative and add the witch hazel. Dissolve the menthol and lavender oil in the rest of the alcohol, add the glycerine. Mix this with the rose water; then add the witch hazel-tragacanth solution. Allow to stand two days and filter.

NO. 6 OILY SKIN LOTION

Tincture of benzoin	3.0%
Alum Powder	2.0
Glycerin	3.0
Alcohol 39-A	8.0
Witch Hazel	40.0
Rose Water	43.95
Menthol	0.05
	100.0

Dissolve the alum in the rose water. Dissolve the menthol in alcohol, add tincture of benzoin and glycerine. Mix the two and add witch hazel.

NO. 7 DRY SKIN LOTION

Boric Acid	2.0%
Alcohol 39-A	6.0
Glycerin	10.0
Tincture Benzoin	2.5

Witch Hazel	40.0
Rose Water	43.95
Menthol	0.05
	100.0

Dissolve the alum in the rose water. Dissolve the menthol in alcohol, add tincture of benzoin and glycerine. Mix the two and add witch hazel, glycerin and alcohol mixture. Allow to stand 24 hours and filter.

ADDITIONAL FORMULAES

No. 8

Witch Hazel	15.0%
Alcohol	10.0
Alum	0.5
Menthol	0.05
Ethyl Aminobenzoate	0.05
Boric Acid	1.0
Glycerin	5.0
Water	68.4
	100.0

No. 9

Alcohol	10.0%
Zinc Sulfate	0.8
Ethyl Aminobenzoate	0.1
Citric Acid	1.0
Sorbitol 85%	5.0
Water	83.1C
	100.0

No. 10

Alcohol 39-B	65 gal.
Water Distilled	37 gal.
Glycerine	1 gal.
Sodium Aluminium Sulfate	8 oz.
Perfume	28 oz.

No. 11

Isopropyl Alcohol (deodorized with odor neutralizer)	30 gal.
Witch Hazel	20 gal.
Water Distilled	62 gal.

G-4	8 oz.
Perfume	32 oz.

NO. 12 AFTER SHAVE AND GENERAL PURPOSE LOTION

Borax	10 oz.
Pentaphen (Sharples)	10 oz.
Glycerine	150 lbs.
Alcohol S.D. 40	50 gal.
Water Distilled	50 gal.
Perfume	25 oz.

No. 13

Boric Acid	2.0 oz.
Menthol	0.05 oz.
Glycerine	2.0 lbs.
Alcohol 39-B	8.0 gal.
Witch hazel	88.0 gal.
Perfume	0.5 oz.
Oxyquinoline Sulfate	0.5 lbs

11

DEODORANTS

General Considerations-Antiperspirants and Deodorants-Labelling-Paste Depdorants-Stick Deodorants-Cream Deodorants

Body odor or B.O. has probably been more forcibly called to our attention as a social evil, through soap advertising than in the field of cosmetics. Then too, soap advertisers recognized the fact that men as well as women have B.O. It has an error to assume that objectionable body odors are peculiar to women folk. Men also are unfortunate enough to be afflicted with this characteristic.

In order better to understand the causes underlying body odor, it is of interest briefly to delve into the sweat gland structures of the skin. These are classified in various ways by physiologists. Sweat glands occur in large numbers in all parts of the skin. Certain authorities specify glands in the skin under two types. Thus sweat glands are said to be those with but a single layer of cells (eccrine glands) an there are those with a multiple layer of cells (apocrine glands) like sebaceous glands. In the sweat glands, only secretions are elinated and in the multiple layer glands, a part, at least, of the cells enter into the composition of the secretory matter. It is a function of sweat glands to regulate body heat by evaporation of perspiration from the surface of the skin and also the amount of warm blood sent through the skin. It is estimated that nearly 90% of body heat loss takes place through the skin. As the external temperature rises, the secretions of the sweat glands increase, more evaporation occurs and a lowering of the temperature takes place. If the temperature is lowered, these sweet glands contract, the blood vessels are constricted and diminish the flow of blood through the skin. Thus the body heat control system is practically automatic. While it has been supposed that sweat glands occur only with hair follicles, this is not true. On portions of the body like the palms of the hands or soles of the feet, we perspire very freely due to the presence of sweat glands as an accompanying skin organ. Two types of sweat glands then are present, i.e., those with hairy and those with non-hairy ducts. they empty through sweat pores to the skin.

In the process of perspiration, certain peculiarities occur. Some individuals secrete sweat which is of offensive odor and in certain cases it is considerably coloured . In many cases certain persons perspire locally and freely during all seasons. This condition is termed hyperidrosis. For example we frequently shake hands with people whose palms are always moist, even when they are not under nerve strain or again we meet persons who complain of constant annoying perspiration of the feet. The secretions from the sweat glands consist largely of water with some salt. Very slight quantities of material prone to decompose into malodorous products are also present.

The correction through cosmetics of conditions which cause body odor is carried out by two methods, i.e., deodorants and antiperspirants. Since the latter are drugs and not cosmetics, a discussion of the action of these need not be dwelt upon in great detail. The principal upon which antiperspirants act is to contract the sweat pores by strong astringent action so that perspiration is not freely exuded. The two ingredients most commonly used for this purpose are aluminum chloride and aluminum sulfate. The former is used most generally in liquid preparations and the latter in creams. As a matter of fact, antiperspirants occur most generally as liquids or creams containing 10% to 15% of these aluminum salts. Since they are quite strongly acidic in reaction it is not possible to incorporate them into the usual cream unless the accessory ingredients are acid stable. As a guide as to how these prepartions are made, we present three typical formulas.

No. 1 LIQUID ANTIPERSPIRANT

Aluminum chloride	130
Urea	30
Distilled Water	840

Dissolve the aluminum chloride and urea in the water and filter. The use of a filter press is recommended, but filtration through paper with the aid of diatomaceous earth (Kieselgur) will do. The solution should not come in contact with metal, especially not with iron.

No. 2 ANTIPERSPIRANT CREAM

(Vanishing Cream Type)

a. Acid-stable glyceryl-monostearate	170
b. Spermaceti	90
c. Glycerin	39
d. Distilled Water	380
e. Preservative	1
f. Aluminine sulfate	150
g.Distilled Water	150
h.Titanium dioxide	20

Dissolve (f) in (g), then stir (h) into the solution. Heat (c) (d) (e) in the mixing kettle at 90^{0}C.

Heat (a) (b) also to 90^{0}C.and introduce into the water phase with fairly vigorous agitation. Stir untill the emulsion is well formed and cooled to 40^{0}C, then add gradully the mixture of (f) (g) (h).

No. 3 GENERAL TYPE FORMULA FOR ANTIPERSPIRANT CREAM

(Absorption Base Type)

a. Absorption base	240
b. Aluminum sulfate	150
c. Distilled Water	600
d. Titanium dioxide	10

Dissolve (b) in (c), add (d). Add this mixture gradually to (a) while stirring, with both phases at 50^{0}C. Stir until 25^{0}C is reached, pass through an ointment mill.

This type of cream can be adjusted for consistency by addition of waxes like spermaceti or ozokerite. The great advantage of an absorbtion base cream is that it will not dry out and harden. But its formulation and handling have to be carefully worked out to give a product which holds up satisfactorily.

It will be observed that no perfume is included in these formulas as this is not necessary in this type of preparation.

Deodorants on the other hand are considered as cosmetics. Their purpose is to remove the offensive odoor of sweat which as it is deposited upon the skin under favorable conditions, such as moisture and warmth, underegoes decomposition and chemical changes. This may become offensive even in spite of bathing and hygiene. Body odor also is referred to as bromidrosis (fetid or foul smelling perspiration).

It is the desire of every person to rid himself of this objectionable body odor. Body odor cannot be altogether eliminated by frequent bathing because persipiration, being continuous and leaving a constant deposit on the skin, may become malodorous in a period of four to six hours after a bath. Some persons are affected with bromidrosis or fetid perspiration because of physiological conditions. Persons affected with certain diseases develop a characteristic odor and it has been observed that emotional reactions such as fear and anger increse the flow of perspiration and intensify its odor.

Although the ancients used perfume, especially sandalwood and musk, to conceal body odor, perfumes cannot be said to be effective because the odoriferous products of perspiration are extremely difficult to conceal permanently unless so much of the perfume is used that it also becomes objectionable to such an extent that their nature is changed and hence they acquire an objectionable odor, which is in some cases worse than the odor of perspiration.

The normal body exudes from one of three quarts of perspiration a day. The water content of this perpiration evaporates immediately, depositing waste matter on the surface of the skin which rapidly undergoes changes through bacterial and chemical action. Consequently a deodorant should conceal these conditions in order to prevent the formation of decomposition products, it should neutralize body odors, it should possess a pleasant odor and be non-irritating and non-toxic.

There are two types of deodorants. One is intended merely to deodorize perspiration without restricting its flow and the other is designed to deodorize and prevent decomposition through bacteria inhibiting action. These types take the forms of liquids, pastes, powders, compacts and sticks. It is obvious, of course, that the liquid and the paste types are best suited for restrictives deodorants because they will exert more lasting astringent action. The dry types are best suited only for deodorizing purposes. Although many of the powders and sticks on the market contain astringents it is quite probable that they exert very little astringent action because the astringents contained in them cannot readily penetrate into ducts leading to the sweat glands.

Before compounding a deodorant it is necessary first to deside what type it shall be and second to determine its specific use. Although doedorants are generally used for arm pits, many are also used for deodorizing sanitary napkins. Obviously a deodorant of the latter type should not be astringent and hence the use of materials like aluminum chloride is precluded.

As no one chemical possesses all the properties for an effective deodorant it is customary to utilize two or more to produce a product that has the requisite properties. A deodorant may be antiseptic; it may be (depending upon the use to which it is to be put) astringent; or it may be both. Among the materials used are boric acid, benzoic acid, oxyquinoline sulfate, formaldehyde, zinc salicylate, zinc sulfocarbolate, alumnol, alumnol, aluminum acetate, aluminum chloride, alum, tannoform, hexamethyleneteramine, thymol, aluminum sulfate, methyl p-hydroxybenzoate, propyl-p-hydroxy benzote, quaternary ammonium compounds and others.

Each of these chemicals has one or more properties which makes it useful in one type of deodorant or the other. Oxyquinoline sulfate is said to be an excellent ingredient because it is not only a powerful antiseptic but it is an excellent deodorant besides being non-toxic and non-irritating. When the deodorant is also to be an astringent it is necessary to be discriminating in regard to the type of astringent selected and the amount used in the formula because some astringents are likely to be a harsh. Having compounded a suitable formula, it is essential to obtain a perfume that will not be incompatible with other ingredients.

To restrict or to prevent perspiration in one part of the body usually does not cause injury because it will not interfere greatly with the total normal perspiration exuded by the body . The perspiration which would normally be evaporated at the treated area is diverted to some other part of the body.

From the above description of the methods by which body odor may be controlled it is evident that deodorants act by neutralizing the odors after secretion while antiperspirnts restrict the flow of the perspiration itself. Under the Federal Food, Drug and Cosmetic Act, those that restrict perspiration effect the function of the body and hence are defined as a drug. This means they must be labelled as such and state the active ingredients. On the other hand substances which merely neutralize the odor and remove it from the surface of the skin are cosmetics. Care then must be made in these borderline products not to make usage claims to conflict with the statute and its regulations. Improper labelling will result in a libel. Another item that should be watched closely is the action of certain deodorant ingredients on clothing. Various types of cloth should be tested against them and if weakend or acted upon proper caution remarks should appear on the labels.

Aluminum chloride is probably more widely used in astringent deodorants than any other chemical. It is a powerful astringent with excellent deodorizing properties. Oxyquinoline sulfate is a very good ingredient, being both antiseptic and deodorant.

The following formulas illustrate various types of liquid deodorants. The first three illustrate the use of the two most commonly used materials, namely aluminum chloride and alum.

No.1 DEODORANT LIQUID

Aluminum chloride	15.0%
Water	81.4
Glycrin	3.0
Propyl parahydroxy benzoate	0.1
Perfume	0.5
	100.0

11

MASCARA-EYEBROW PENCILS-EYE SHADOWS

EYE SHADOW is an important item im make up. The three popular colours are blue, brown, and green. This preparation is applied on the eyelids and around the eyes to accentuate their brilliance.

Eyebrow pencil are hard crayons, usually black, and are used for darkening the eyebrows and for simulating eyebrow growth when none is evident.

Mascara is used for the eyelashes and as a rule is applied with a brush. Mascara is popular in make-up cosmetics, and will be discussed in detail.

In making mascara, care must be exercised in selecting the colour and the other basic constituents. The colour must be harmless and intense in shade. A number of types of lampblack may be used for black. For brown shades, burnt umber, or synthetic ochre with or without the addition of a trace of lampblack will give suitable shades. Such colors are sometimes offered to the trade in paste form.

There are three types of mascara: liquid, cream and cake. Liquid mascara must be a permanent suspension of coloring matter, usually in a light mucilaginous vehicle. Gum acacia, tragacanth, karaya, and gelatin are useful for the mucilage. Gelatin increases the ability of the mascara to cling to the lashes.

An emulsion of glyceryl monostearate and water, combined with color, is effective. Methyl cellulose is also useful.

Cream mascaras usually consist of an emulsion of glyceryl monostearate and water, stiffened to the proper consistency by the use of waxes or gums. Another type consists of pigment milled into a mixture of vegetable or mineral oil and wax.

The most popular type of mascara is the cake form. Sometimes this was made of mild toilet soap, sometimes with beeswax and petrolatum added. This type has the disadvantage of smarting the eyes if not carefully used.

One ot the best mascara bases is glyceryl monostearate. But mascara made only of glyceryl monostearate and pigment is unsuitable because no coloring will adhere to the moist brush when it is rubbed on the cake. To avoid this, the surface tension of the material must be lowered with triethanolamine. Triethanolamine can be combined with cetyl alcohol, stearic acid or other fatty acids such as oleic or ricinoleic. About 50% of the base should consist of triethanolmine soaps, the rest of petrolatum and waxes.

NO. 1 MASCARA

Mild toilet soap base	100 lbs.
Zinc oxide.	1 lb.
Petrolatum (cream)	2 lbs.
Gum tragacanth solution (1$^{1/14}$ lbs. gum to25 lbs. hot water)	24 lbs.
Black shade	20 lbs. D & C Black # 1
	20 lbs. Logwood Ext.
Brown shade	20 lbs. D&C Brown #1
	1 lb. D&C Black #1
	10 lbs. Logwood Ext.
Blonde shade	24 lbs. D&C Brown # 1

Mill, plod and shape in same manner as toilet soap is made.

No.2 MASCARA

Glyceryl monostearate	10.0%
Triethanolamine	3.0
Stearic acid	15.0
Petrolatum	20.0
Gelatin	2.0
Water	17.0
Beeswax	25.0
Prepared lampblack	8.0
	100.0

Soak the gelatin in hot water. Melt the beeswax, stearic acid, petrolatum and glyceryl monostearate, stir in the lampblack thoroughly. Add the trietanolamine to the gelatin suspension and then add the mixture to the melted mass. Stir well. Any type of mascara can be made from this base, the beeswax being the regulator by varying which any degree of consistency can be obtained.

No.3 EYE SHADOW

Eye shadow Base

White petrolatum, short fibre, soft	70.75%
Cetyl alchol	3.0
Lanolin	10.5
White beeswax	5.25
Spermaceti	10.5
	100.0

NO. 4 EYE SHADOW BLUE

White beeswax	2.25%
Spermaceti	4.5
Lanolin	4.5
White petrolatum, short fibre, soft	42.65
Ultramarine	15.28
Zinc oxide	30.57
Perfume	0.25
	100.0

Mix the coluor with the zinc oxide; add the petrolatum to make a mass and grind it through an ointment mil. Melt the beeswax, spermaceti and lanolin. Add the coluor base and the perfume.

No. 5 MAKE-UP PREPARATIONS

BROWN

Beeswax	2.25%
Spermaceti	4.5
Lanolin	4.5
White petrolatum, short fibre, soft	41.5
Zinc oxide	26.9
Burnt umber	20.0
Perfume	0.5
	100.0

Mix the petrolatum, zinc oxide, and burnt umber and run it through an ointment mill. Melt the other ingredients; add the color base and perfume

No. 6 GREEN

Beeswaxi	3.36%
Spermaceti	6.72
Lanolin	6.72
Petrolatum, short fibre, soft	43.75
Chrome oxide	15.0
Zinc oxide	24.2
Perfume	0.25
	100.0

Mix the green pigment with the zinc oxide ; add the petrolatum and run it through an ointment mill. Melt the other ingredients: add the color base. perfume and mix.

NO. 7 EYELASH AND EYEBROW POMADE

Peach kernel oil	18.0%
Parafifn	11.0
Petrolatum	70.3
Menthyl p-hydroxybenzoate	0.2
Perfume	0.5
	100.0

No. 8 EYELASHLUX

Benzoinated lard	50 parts
Stearic acid XXX	20 parts
Beeswax	5 parts
Liquid petrolatum	30 parts
Castor oil	5 parts
	100.0

Make base by melting together.
For black add 10 oz. lampblack per 25 lbs. of base.
For brown add 8 oz. burnt umber per 25 lbs. of base.

To incorporate colors melt the base and rub color very smooth with sufficient molten base to wet color well. Add slowly to molten base, pour into molds. If packaged in tubes thin to proper consistency with castor oil.

No. 9 EYEBROW PENCIL

Yellow wax	10.0%
Parafifn	30.0
Cocoa butter	30.0
Petrolatum	20.0
Carbon black	10.0
	100.0

NO. 10 EYEBROW PENCIL BASE

Soft parafifn	40.0%
Hard parafifn	42.0
Colour,as desired	18.0
	100.0

13

LIPSTICS

The manufacture of lipsticks does not involve an intricate procedure. The usual modus operandi for the various formulas presented may be outlined in a few simple steps. These are:

I. Dissolve the bromo acid, the castor oil or other solvent in a suitable jacketed kettle at 160^0 F. by slow agitation.

II. In another kettle heat the other oils, fats or waxes with indirect heat at not too high a temperature. Mix in the pigment colors thoroghly .

III. Add II to I and mix the mass continuously.

IV. Run Mixture III through a jacketed paint or hopper mill several times to disperse the colour, so it is homogeneous while keeping the temperature sufficiently high so as to prevent crystallization of the waxes.

V. When the mass is about 5% -10% above the congealing point, pour it into the molds and chilli quickly.

VI. Remove the cast sticks from the molds, fit into the holders, flame with a suitable gas flame to produce a glossy surface and complete the packaging.

The above steps in the manufacture of lipsticks may be varied and simplified to fit certain compositions of formulas but even though using short cuts the procedure is not modified greatly . It involvs considerable manual labour. To overcome this, certain refinments in the casting and flaing have been evolved by large volume producers. Instead of using the usual hand molds, rotary machines holding specially designed molds have been devised. This cuts down materially upon labor. Still other improvements have been made in the mixing operations. After the colours have been milled into the fatty base and remelted, any air remaining in the mass is removed through vacum. This aids in preventing holes in the finished lipstick after they are molded and flamed. In still other cases the flaming operation is carried out with infra red lamps instead of a direct flame.

In order to determine the thickness and uniformity of the film applied to the lips by a lipsticks, a better method of measurment than the common practice of rubbing the lipstick on the arm is desirable.

It is obvious that in making a comparisom of film thickness the "ärm" method is in accurate because it is not possible to apply lipstick by hand with uniform pressure. The stick which has been applied with the heaviest pressure will show the thickest or heaviest film. Another variable factor is the difference in the diameter; the widest mark will be made by the thickest stick. Another variable is the shape of the end of the stick. A round one will make a mark of certain width; a pointed one another ; a chisel shaped still another.

Realizing these variables, Seil and Chilson set up an apparatus to make an accurate comparison of lipstick films, eliminating as many of the variables as was humanly possible to do so by the means available in a laboratory. To eliminate the variable due to differences in shape of points and in differing diameters, they used as a holder a glass tube four inches long and having an internal diameter of three-eight inch. Into this glass tube they inserted a plug of cotton which fitted snugly but not immovably. Then they melted the lipstick samples and cast them in short pieces of glass tubing so that they would get samples that would fit the first glass tube in which they were to be held. After inserting the lipstick sample into the holder made of glass tubing as described, the end of the lipstick was squared off, and then they weighted the holder and the sample it contained under carefully controlled conditions to determine its precise weight.

This holder was transferred to a clamp affixed to an ordinary iron laboratory table stand, and the clamp was lowered untill the end of the holder containing the lipstick sample was within and eighth inch of a flat piece of chromium plated steel about six by ten inches in size . At this point they had a sample of lipstick held vertically above a polished chromium plated surface (tile or glass would do as well) with the exposed, squared end of the lipstick pointed downward.

Then they prepared slides consisting of very heavy transparent cellulose stitched to white bond cardboard, which was ruled in uniform parallel lines. One of these slides was placed under the lipstick holder, and held at a predetermined point. Now a glass rod having a series of rubber corks at one end to serve as weights was accurately weighed and thrust into the lipstick sample holder. The weight of this rod forced the lipstick sample into contact with the transparent cellulose and held it there at uniform, unvarying pressure. Then the paper slide was drawn under the lipstick sample for a definite distance and this procedure was continued untill the desired area had been covered, the lines or marks not being allowed to overlap.

After this, the lipstick hoder was carefully removed without directly touching it with the hands, so that its weight would not be influenced by moisture, and it was weighed again. The difference between the weight of the holder before the slide was drawn under it and its weight after drawing, represented the weight of the film on the paper.

By using transparent paper a visual record was obtained of the uniformity of the film under constant pressure and it was possible to make a direct comparison of colour characteristics. Sticks that tend to make a smeary, crumby mark could be instantly compared with those that made uniform line. The same process revealed defects in the stick due to varying hardness. In some of those tested, the line at one point was wide and smooth and at another narrow and irregular. Such conditions were due, of course, to poor control of manufacturing and casting processes.

By having sevral sample holders in the same clamp a comparison of several different sticks can be made at the same time. By passing the finished slide through ammonia vapor the colour will devlop quickly and if it contains any fluorescein derivatives, a colour comparison can readily be made. It is felt that this method, while not absolutely fool-proof, is accurate enough for comparative purposes because any errors in the method will be reflected in all samples in the same degree.

No. 1 LIPSTICK MEDIUM

Petrolatum amber	7,257 gms.
Paraffin 140^0 M.P	2,608 gms.
Ceresin	1,502 gms.

Carnauba wax	368 gms.
Geranium lake	1,360 gms.
Maroon lake	425 gms.

No. 2 LIPSTICKS LIGHT

White petrolatum	$8^{1/2}$ lbs.
Paraffin 140° M.P	$4^{1/4}$ lbs.
Ceresin pure	$1^{1/4}$ lbs.
Carnauba waw	6 oz.
Anhydrous lanolin	$1^{1/4}$ lbs.
Brilliant lake	$4^{1/4}$ oz.
Geranium lake	$9^{1/2}$ oz.
Vermilion toner	2 oz. 375 grs.
Paratoner B.	1 oz.
Perfume QS	

Grind the above in paint mill, then mold.

No. 3 LIPSTICK DARK

Amber petrolatum	$9^{1/4}$ lbs.
Paraffin 140° M.P	$2^{1/2}$ lbs.
Ozokerite	$1^{1/4}$ lbs.
Caranauba wax	6 oz.
Geranium lake	2 lbs.
Paratoner B	$6^{1/2}$ oz.
Maroon lake	$9^{1/2}$ oz.
Perfume QS	

No.4 LIPSTICK INDELIBLE

Anhydrous lanolin	27.210 gms.
Beeswax	57.210 gms.
Castor oil	6,600 cc.
Bromo acid	0.880 gms.
Perfume QS	

Dissolve bromo in castor oil then add to melted fats. Then mold

No. 5 LIPSTICK FORMULA, GREASY TYPE

Castor oil	12.100 gms.
Spermaceti	1.000 gms.
Beeswax white	1.000 gms.
Parafffin 140^{0}M.P.	.700 gms.
Colour	1.000 gms.
Special paste bromo	3.000 gms.

This stick has 172^{0}F. melting point.

No. 6 LIPSTICK TANTALUS

Bromo acid	24 oz.
Cosmetic red	4 oz.
Brilliant red	52 oz.
Castor oil	100 oz.
Beeswax	99 oz.
Paraffin (M.P.128^0)	80oz.
Petrolatum (White)	332 oz.
Mineral oil	30 oz.

14

SHAMPOOS

Shampoo is a preparation of a surfactant (ie, surface-active material) in suitable from liquid, solid or powder which when used will remove surface grease, dirt and skin debris from the hairshaft and scalp without affecting adversely the hair, scalp or health of the user

The shampoos are available both in solid and liquid form. But the powedr form is most common, and in their preparations, the main difference lies in the varying proportions of soap. But it is necessary to have the other bases in its place to check the clotting of hair. Saponine and sulphonated lorol (trade mark for a group of straight chain normal even-numbered carbon alcohols ranging from C -8 to C - 18 and including mixtures of these) are the common ingredients in all shampoos to increase lather and avoid the precipitation of lime from hard water. The alkaline bases like dry sodium carbonate Na_2CO_3 and sesquicarbonate ($Na_2CO_3 . NaHCO_3 . 2H_2O$), saponify the grease, which is washed away while rinising .... Generally, shampoos are cleansing water solutions or suspensions of cleansing agents mixed with such ingredients which may improve the performance. Mainly, synthetic detergents are used, though sometimes soap is also used. But synthetic detergents are more effective, and in a good shampoo soap has no place. The following additives are incoroporated : thickeners, opacifiers, conditioners, lime-soap dispersants, seqestrants, solubilizing and coupling agents, bacteriocide and fungicide materials, perfume, colour etc.

There are clear liquid shampoos, liquid cream or lotion products, cream or paste shampoos, jelly products, powders, and even solid shampoos in tablet and leaf form. In respect to functions, there are all-purpose shampoos as well as special shampoos for dry hair, oily hair tinted and bleached hair. There are also special conditioning shampoos, dandruff shampoos, hair colouring shampoos, as well as special shampoos for babies and chidre. There have been even egg. beer and coffee shampoos.

The primary function of a shampoo is that of cleansing the hair of accumulated sebum, scalp debris and residues of hair grooming preparations. Although any detergent can do this job, cleansing should be selective and preserve a quantity of the natural oil that coats the hair and above all, the scalp.

Properties:

A shampoo must not only clean, but must also beautify the hair giving a soft, lustrous and manageable effect. It must contain ingredients to enrich and nourish the hair and the scalp, removing surface oil, dirt and skin debris. It must also produce rich lather both in hard and soft water, should be covenient to use and not leave residue on the hair. It must be non-toxic, non-irritating, and should not permanently damage sensitive eye tissue in case of accidental occurrence into the eye.

"Clear liquid shampoos"

Are relatively straight-forward water solutions of one or more shampoo detergents or soap, together with other ingredients. In a clear liquid shampoo, it is important that the base detergents or soap have good water solubility and a relatively low cloud point. Solubilizing agents are sometimes used to improve and maintain clarity and to aid the solubility of various additives. Thickeners, such as alkylolamides, are usually employed to increase viscosity.

"Baby shampoos"

Are based upon detergents which provide the so-called "no eye sting" feature. The imidazoline-type (cyclomidium type) amphoteric detergent has been recommended for this purpose. Unique sulfosuccininc acid esters have also been suggested.

SULFONATE OIL-SOAPLESS SHAMPOO

Ingredients	Qty.
Sulfonated castor oil (100%basis	125
Sulfonated olive (100% basis)	125
Sulfonated cocanut oil (100% basis)	125
Polyethylene glycol 1000	10
Morpholine	10
Water	10
Perfume	600

Firt three ingredients, are mixed together and heated to 104^0 F. It is the moropholine and the polyethlene glycol 1000, follwed by the water. Perfume is added after cooling.

Miscellaneous shampoos :

Innumerable shampoos containing such strange ingredients as beer, egg. coffee, malt, etc, have been marketed since many years. The major claim for such products usually in special conditioning, but the success has generally been poor and short lived at best. It should be emphasized that under the regulations of the U.S. Food and Drug Administration, a shampooing. It can contain less egg and then be labelled "plus egg". in a subordinate position and in smallar type. In any case, it must contain at least 2% egg; any less is insignificant.

"Pressure-dispensed aerosol shampoos have been marketed but with little success".

Colour shampoos are discussed under hair colouring and bleaching.

"Medicated Dandruff shampoos :

Medicated shampoos recomended for the control and correction of dandruff. Today a number of medicated dandruff shampoos enjoy a reputation for appreciable effectivnessd. One such product, obtainable only by prescription, is a shampoo in the form of a 2.5% suspension of selenium disulphide in a detergent base. Another contains zinc pyridinethione (zinc -2 - pyridinethiol - 1 - oxide), as the antidandruff ingredient and sodium alkyl glyceryl ether sulfonate as the base detergent. A wide range and assortment of other antidandruff ingredients are used in shampoo. These include bacteriostatic compounds such as hexachlorophene, heavy metals such as cadimium sulphide and tellurium oxide, hydroxyquinolines, biphenamine hydrochloride (2-diethylmino) ethyl 2-hydroxy-3-biphenamine hydrochloride) (2-diethylamino) ethyl2-hydroxy-3biphenylcarboxylate hydrochloride), a polyvinyl pyrolidone-iodene complex quaternized polythionates, allantoin, and many others.

"Soap shampoos. :

Soap offers an apperciably advantage over synthetic detergents in respect to the manageability and condition of the hair following shampoos.

Moderen soap shampoos are generally based upon alkanolamine soaps rather than the soda or potash soaps that were once used. The alkanolamine soaps are preapared by reacting the amine with the appropriate fatty acid. In the preparation of soap-based shampoos, generally mono or triethanolamine is reacted with a mixture of coconut fatty acid and oleic acid. Solubilizing-coupling agents are included to achieve and maintain clarity.

"Shampoo Additives :

Beside from the detergent-cleaning ingredients employed in shampoos, many other materials are used to achieve specific forms and functions, or to improve certain properties.

(1) Opacifiers

Are used to tender transparent shampoos opaque. There are usually waxlike materials which are relatively insoluble, but readily dispersible in the shampoo. It is important that they should not have appreciable deleterious effect on shampoo properties, such as lather formation. Some opacifiers solidify or crystallize in such a manner that they give the product a shimmering, pearlescent effect. Generally, esters such as glycol and glyceryl stearates are used. Higher alcohols, such as stearyl and cetyl alcohol, stearate soaps, and waxy alkylamides also find application.

(2) Solubilizers-Couplers

Are valuble adjuncts to clear shampoos. They are used to solubilize poorly soluble ingredients, such as perfume oils, preservatives, and bacteriocide and emollient additives. Ethyl alcohol and, on occasion, isopropyl alcohol, have been used for this pupose as have been glycerol, propylene glycol, and diethylene glycerol, propylene glycol, and diethylene glycol monoethyl ether. Surfactants with hydrotropic properties are also of interest as solubilizers.

(3) Thickeners

Are used to increase the viscosity of liquid shampoos and to provide the desired consistency in get and cream shampoos. As noted earlier, the alkyloamides are particularly recommended. In the case of sodium lauryl sulfate shampoos, addition of inorganic saltls will form the consistency of cream shampoos. It has been shown , however , that too much electrolyte causes softening . Sodium stearate and stearic amides are excellent thickeners for cream shampoos; polyvinyl alcohol, methylcellulose, and sodium alginate have also been suggested.

(4) Conditioning agents

Are used in shampoos to improve the manageability and the so-called "finish"of the hair. Various oils, fatty alcohols, glycol esters, humectants, and protein derivatives are used to improve conditioning. Lanolin has found widespread use as a hair conditioner, particularly in cream and liquid cream shampoos. Lanolin oil and derivatives have also been recommended and have been the subject of considerable investigation. As noted earlier, selection of the base detergents is an important factor in hair conditioning. Moreover several types of surfactants, including alkyloamides, fatty amine oxides, fatty acid-peptide condensates, and cationic-anionic complexes are considered to contribute to hair conditioning.

(5) Preservatives

"Are necessary in surfactant-based shampoos since these products are capable of supporting mould and bacteria growth .Typical shampoo preservatives are methyl and propyl parabens (i,e, p-hydroxybenzoates) and p-chlorometacresol. Formaldehyde and dehydroacetic acid salts have also been recommended. Phenylmecuric salts are used in very dilute concentrations, where regulations permit the use of such components.

"Shampoo Detergents- Anionic-Fatty alkyl sulfates

Are unquestionably the most important synthetic detergents used in shampoos. The primary alkyl sulfates are the detergent workhouses of the shampoo industry. They are sulfuric acid esters prepared from fatty alcohols by sulfation with chlorsulfonic acid or sulfuric acid. The alcohol are usually prepared by catalytic hydrogenation or by sodium reduction of the corresponding fatty acids. The primary alkyl sulfate mostly used in shampoos is the so-called lauryl sulfate which contains a mixture of C10 to C18 compounds with C12 compound predominating. Various salts of lauryl sulfate are available including sodium,

Potassium, calcium, zinc, ammonium , magnesium, as well as mono, di and triethanolamine. Although dry forms are avilable, the lauryl sulfates are generally sold as paste or as water solutions. Lauryl sulfates with metallic cations are generally offered as 30% active water solutions or as pastes with up to 2.5% free alcohol and 1-11.5% inorganic salt. The alkanolmine salts, because of the much larger cation, will contain more active ingredient on a total solid basis, but actually no more on a fat content basis. The various salts differ rather markedly in their properties, Particularly in respect to colour, cloud point, and viscosity. The viscosity of the sodium salt is especially affected by inorganic salt content. Since there is some danger of hydrolysis, the fatty alkyl sulfates may be buffered on the alkaline side by the manufacture.

Concentrations of lauryl sulfates in shampoos generally range from about 7 to 15% on anhydrous basis.

Oxo-process alcoholes produced by the Fischer-Tropsch oxidation of paraffins are also sulfated and find some application in shampoos. The so-called tridecyl alcohol sulfate in its properties.

Fatty alkyl ether sulfates, fatty monoglyceride sulfate, fatty acid-peptide condensates, fatty acid-sarcosine condensates, sulfosuccinic acid esters,

sodium N-coconut acid-N-methyllaurate, Isethionates, Alkylaranesulfonic acids are discussed in the similar manner as above.

"Special-function shampoos:

Are disscussed at length below. Generally, the special function or feature is exclusive of the product from and is achieved by choice of detergent and/or incorporation of special additives.

"Solid shampoos

Consist of either detergent or soap pressed into a bar or tablet shape. In another type, the detergent is dried or pressed as a thin sheet or leaf.

"Liquid cream or lotion shampoos

Are opaque, viscous, liquid sharnpoos which have the appearnce of cosmatic skin lotions. They are not emulsions in the pure sense, but contain generous concentrations of suspended opacifiers such as glycol stearates. Less soluble detergents with high cloud points are generally used in this type of product and relatively heavy viscosities are usually required in order to maintain long-term suspension of the opacifier.

Powder shampoos

Are of two types. One type is simply powdered detergent which is dissolved in water before use. The other is the so-called "dry"shampoo consisting of mixtures of oil-absorbing powders, such as fuller's earth, starch, kaolin, talc, and the like. This product is simply spread through the hair and then brushed out after it has absorbed surface oil from the hair.

"Jelly (gel) shampoos

Are very similar to clear liquids but tend to be more cocentrated. Heavy viscosity is generally achieved by using relatively high concentrations of alkyloamide, soap, or synthetic gum.

"Cream or paste shampoos

Are not unlike the liquid cream products except that they have a firm, paste like consistency which is achieved by the incorporation of relatively insoluble fatty ingredients. Such as sodium stearate, and by the use of electrolytes which serve to salt out some of the base detergents. Here again less soluble detergents are employed.

(1) SHAMPOO

Ingredients	Qty.
Sulphonated olive oil	16.0
Sulphonated caster oil	16.0
Water	68.0
Colour	qs.
Perfume	qs.
	100.00

(2) SHAMPOO

Ingredients	Qty.
Sulphonated castor oil	77.0
Mineral oil (light grade)	3.0
Oleyl alcohol	3.0
Glycerin	3.0
Water (distilled)	14.0
	100.00

(3) SHAMPOO

Ingredients	Qty.
Dry shampoo (powder)	40
Fullers'earth	20
Borax	5
Sodium sesquicarbonate	20
Starch	15
Total	100

FORMULA FOR COCONUT OIL SHAMPOOS

Ingredients	I	II	III	IV	V	VI
Coconut oil	16%	37%	21%	21%	20%	14%
Potassium Hydroxide (85%)	4	29	4.1	1.1	4.1	6
Water	80	5	54	68.7	54.03	57
Glycerol	-	29	-	-	-	12
Perfume	-	q.s.	0.5	1.0	1.0	0.5
Olive Oil	-	-	3	9.9	4	-
Sodium Hydroxide, (95%)	-	-	1.9	4.4	1.87	0.5
Ethyl alchol	-	-	15	2.8	15	-
Ethylene diamine tetraacetic acid (EDTA)	-	-	0.5	-	-	-
Palm oil	-	-	-	5.1	-	-
Oleic acid	-	-	-	-	-	10

FORMULA FOR VEGETABLE OIL SHAMPOOS

Ingredients	I	II	III
Coconut Oil	15%	70%	-
Palm Oil	5	-	-
Potassium hydroxide, 90%	3	q.s. to pH 9.0	14.5%
Sodium hydroxide 90%	1	-	-
Ethyl alcohol	7	-	37
Water	69	q.s. 100	-
Coconut fatty acids	-	14	-
Stearic acid	-	14	-
Glycerol	-	2	6
Perfume	-	0.5	-
Olive oil	-	-	34
Corn oil	-	-	8.5
Sodium lauryl sulfate	-	3	-

HAIR RINSE

Ingredients	% by wt
Triton x-400 concentrate	2.3
Cetyl alcohol	0.3
Potassium chloride	0.8
Water	96 .6

The pH of the formulation is 4.4. These cream rinses should be diluted for use at the rate of 1 spoon to 8 oz. of water.

Approximately 1/2 of the water is heated to 180°F. Cetyl alcohol is added and stirred slowly until molten. Slow speed agitation is used during the entire manufacturing process. Care should be taken to prevent the incorporation of air into the product.

Triton x-400 is heated to 170°F and added to the water slowly. Then the temperature of the mixture is reduced to 150°F and agitated slowly for at least 1/2 hr.to insure uniformity and maximum emulsion stability. The temperature is further reduced to 120°F.

The potassium chloride is dissoved in the balance of the water and heated to 120°F. Then this solution slowly added to the Triton x-400 cetyl alcohol emulsion. The heat source is removed and the batch is agitated slowly for an additional hour, or untill the mixture gels. Colouring agents and perfumes solubilized in Triton x-400 may then be added.

15

DEPILATORIES

The usual types of chemical depilatories are represented by the following typical formulas.

No.1 DEPILATORY POWDER

Titanium dioxide	23.0%
Barium sulfate	35.0
Wheat starch	40.0
Menthol	0.2
Perfume	1.8

Dissolve the menthol in the perfume oil; rub it up with a little of the starch. Sift the titanium dioxide and barium sulfide into the mixer. Mix and sift in the remainder of the starch, then sift in the menthol-perfume mixture. Mix the entire batch for about half an hour and then fill containers.

No.2 DEPILATORY POWDER

Barium sulfide	28.0%
Pulverized neutral soap	5.0
Wheat starch	40.0
Rose geranium perfume	1.8
Zinc oxide	25.0
Benzocaine	0.2
	100.0

Mix the benzocaine and perfume and rub it up with a little of the starch. Sift the barium sulfide and the zinc oxide and the remainder of the starch into the mixer and mix. Add the pulverized soap and the perfume mixture. Close the mixer and mix for about half an hour. Fill at once.

No. 3 DEPILATORY POWDER

Strontium sulfide	35.0%
Corn starch	35.0
Talc	28.0
Menthol	0.2

Perfume	1.8
	100.0

Make by same method as Formula No. 1

No. 4 DEPILATORY POWDER

Strontium sulfide	25.0%
Barium sulfide	10.0
Corn starch	35.0
Calcium carbonate	28.0
Perfume	2.0
	100.0

Mix as above.

No. 5 DEPILATORY POWDER

Barium sulfide	15.0%
Strontium sulfide	20.0
Talc	14.0
Calcium carbonate	24.0
Corn starch	25.0
Lavender oil	2.0
	100.0

Proceed as with the previous formulas.

No. 6 DEPILATORY PASTE

Strontium sulfide	30.0%
Corn starch	15.0
Precipitated chalk	15.0
Glycerin	10.0
Water	29.0
Perfume	1.0
	100.0

Add the glycerin to the water. Mix in the strontium sulfide. When solution has been effected mix and sift in the precipited chalk and the starch, then add the perfume. Mix thoroughly untill a smooth paste is obtained. The consistency of this paste can be regulated by means of the starch and chalk mixture.

No. 7 DEPILATORY PASTE

Strontium sulfide	15.0%
Barium sulfide	15.0
Talc	10.0
Corn strach	20.0
Glycerin	18.0
Water	20.0
Perfume	2.0
	100.0

Mix the barium and strontium sulfides with the water and glycerin. Mix the starch and the talc; sift the dry materials into the sulfide solution. Mix well and add the perfume.

No.8 DEPILATORY PASTE

Fresh sulfurated lime	25.0%
Colloidal clay	5.0
Corn starch	15.0
Precipited chalk	35.0
Glycerin	19.0
Perfume	1.0
	100.0

Make the sulfurated lime as follows: Take 16 parts of quick lime, 25 parts of sublimed sulfur, 1500 parts of water. Add a small quantity of the water to the lime sufficient to slake it. Boil the remainder of the water. Mix the slaked lime and sulfur and gradually add the boiled water. Then boil this mixture with frequent agitation untill a sufficient amount of water has been driven off by evaporation to make the mixture equal a thousand parts. Keep the mixture at the boiling point for an hour, adding whatever water may be lost in order to do this. Then allow the mixture to stand untill cool and strain it. This will give a solution which will be clear brownish red in colour. Take the amount of sulfurated lime of the formula, mix in the glycerin. Sift and add the dry materials untill a paste of the proper consistency is formed. Add the perfume.

No. 9 DEPILATORY POWDER

Barium sulfide (light gray)	10 lbs.
Venetian red	1 lb.
Sodium bicarbonate	9 oz.
Terra alba	100 lbs.
Perfume	8 oz.

No. 10 DEPILATORY POWDER

Barium sulfide	20 lbs.
Zinc oxide	20 lbs.
Soap neutral powder	1 lb.
Glycerin	1 lb.
Talc	80 lbs.
Perfume	3/4 lb.

No. 11 DEPILATORY LIQUIDS

Sodium sulfide	9.0%
Glycerin	10.0
Water	78.5
Alcohol	2.0
Perfume	0.5
	100.0

Dissolve the sodium sulfide in half of the water; add the glycerin and mix. Add the remainder of the water and finally add the perfume, dissolved in the alcohol. Mix well and filter. The strength of this depilatory can be increased by increasing the percentage of sodium sulfide but in no case should it exceed 10%.

No. 12

Sodium sulfide	10.0%
Starch	10.0
Glycerin	10.0
Water	67.0
Alcohol	2.5
Perfume	0.5
	100.0

Dissolve the sodium sulfide in half the water. Make a paste with the glycerin and the starch and add this to the sulfide solution, then add the remainder of the water and the perfume dissolved in the alcohol. Mix thoroughly. In this formula the starch is optional. Some prefer to omit it.

16

SHAVING CREAMS

The equipment required to make no-lather cream is quite simple. It consists of a steam-jacketed kettle made either from tinned copper, aluminium, glass-lined steel or stainless steel. This is required to hold and heat the stearic acid and other oils. A lye tank made from either black iron or stainless steel is required for the lye. The agitating kettle consists preferably of a stainless steel, steam-jacketed kettle equipped with a slow moving agitator. There is furthermore required the necessary measuring vessels and scales to measure and weigh out the ingredients. Laboratory testing equipment should be available and,of course, collapsible tube or jar filling and closing equipment is necessary for packaging the product. In cases where large quantities are produced, cartoning machinery is desirable.

A few comments should be made regarding the steam-jacketed agitator kettle. While stainless steel is best, tinned copper or glass-lined steel may be used to prevent discoloration of the cream. The kettle should be so built that the bottom outlet of the kettle is flush with the inside, or just slightly above the bottom of the dome or cone if the bottom is conical or dome shaped. This opening should not be smaller than 2 1/2 inches. The agitator should move slowly, not over 10 R.P.M. It should be of strong, stout construction, be made of the same materials as the kettle itself and be of such design as to mix the cream well when it is stiff and to difficult consistency to stir. If it is desired to accelerate the cooling of the batch, the jacket of the kettle may be equipped to circulate cold water, which should enter from the bottom and flow out at the top. This arrangement makes it possible to cool a lot of cream over night while stirring and fill it the day after it is made. In this regard it is again to be emphasized that the agitator should be of the slow motion type, for long time rapid mixing is apt to aerate the cream.

As was indicated above many combinations of the ingredients mentioned are possible to make brushless shaving creams. These may be varied to suit the chemist's ideas and to give advertising materials to sell the finished products. It is not possible to set forth all the formulas which may be devised. Of these numerous combinations, therefore, we will consider only a few typical ones.

The brushless shaving cream of the earlier type is made by the following formula :

Stearic acid (triple pressed)	13 lbs.
Coconut oil (cochin)	2 lbs. 13 oz.
Caustic potash lye 38^0 B	3 lbs. 6 oz.
Glycerin	12 lbs. 8 oz.
Boric acid (crystals)	2 lbs.
Water (soft or distilled)	60 lbs.
Perfume	3 oz.

The method of procedure in manufacturing brushless shaving cream by this formula is first to break the stearic acid into pieces and mele it together with the coconut oil by indirect heat in a separate kettle.

The boric acid is dissolved in about a gallon of water, heated to near the boiling point. When the solutionn is clear, the glycerin is added.

The rest of the water and the caustic potash lye are poured into the mixing kettle and heated to 140^0 to 150^0 F. The hot boric acid solution is poured in on top of the water and temperature is maintained at around 150^0 .

The stearic acid-coconut oil mixture is now run into the kettle on top of the water-lye-glycerin solution through a strainer with the agitator runing. After all of the stearic acid is added, the agitation continues untill the mass is smooth.

Continue the stirring for several hours or a better procedure is to turn the cold water into the jacket of the cream mixing kettle and stir over night untill the cream is cold. Then the perfume is added and stirring is continued to distribute it properly. When the cream is completely cold it should be examined for consistency, after which it may be filled into jars or tubes as desired.

A brushless shaving cream made with lanolin has the following composition :

Stearic acid (triple pressed)	25 lbs.
Anhydrous lanolin	3 lbs.
Alcohol (S.D. 3A)	2 lbs.
Triethanolamine	3/4 lb.
Borax	1/2 lb.
Glycerin	3 lbs.
Water (distilled or softened)	70 lbs.
Perfume	4 oz.

The modus operandi for this formula is first to melt the stearic acid and lanolin by indirect heat in the melting kettle. Pour the water into the mixing kettle and when heated dissolve the borax in a portion thereof. Add the borax solution and the triethanolamine to the hot water in the mixer. This has been heated to about 150^{0}F.

With the agitator runing pour the stearic acid-lanolin mixture slowly into the mixing kettle; stir untill smooth and the white emulsion has formed. Continue the stirring untill the mass cools, then add the glycerin, alcohol and perfume.

Another brushless shaving cream made with triethanolamine is formulated as follows ;

1

Stearic acid (triple pressed)	240 lbs.
Beeswax	80 lbs.
Mineral oil	40 lbs.

Melt these ingredients in a separate kettle at about 160^{0}F.

2

Triethanolamine	15 lbs.
Water (distilled or softened)	1210 lbs.
Borax	8 lbs.
Sulfonated castor oil	4 lbs.
Glycerin	48 lbs.

Pour these together in the mixing kettle and heat to 150° F., being sure that the borax is all dissolved by agitating the liquid well.

With the agitator running, pour the stearic acid mixture into the liquid in the mixer in a slow steady stream. Agitate for several hours untill the mass is perfectly smooth. Withdraw a sample, cool and examine for consistency. A pH reading at this point should show the cream to be acid, runing between 6.6 and 6.8. This pH may be adjusted by small additions of mineral acid if required or more triethanolamine if too acid.

When the cream is of the proper consistency, turn the cold water into the jacket and agitate over night. In the morning add about 5 pounds of suitable perfume and continue mixing untill the perfume is uniformly distributed.

It is advisable in making up this formula that a close check of all weights be made. If the cream is too stiff hot water may be added in the mixer to thin to the proper consistency.

No. 3 BRUSHLESS SHAVING CREAM

Stearic acid	13 lbs.
Coconut oil	2 lbs. 13 oz.
Water distilled	7 gals.
Potash lye 38° B.	3 lbs. oz.
Borax	6 oz.
Carbitol	6 1/2 pints
Glycerin USP	1/2 gal.
Boric acid crystals USP	2 lbs.
Perfumfe	3 oz.

Melt the stearic acid and coconut oil and strain through cloth into a clean kettle. Dissolve boric acid, potassium carbonate, borax, glycerin and carbitol in water. Have both solutions at 85° C. Pour the water solution in the mixer first. Then add the stearic acid very slowly while stirring. Start the mixer in a low speed and when the cream starts to get thick, put in high speed untill the cream is white, smooth and cool. Then add perfume and mix for a moment.

No. 4 BRUSHLESS SHAVING CREAM

Stearic acid	15 lbs.
Beeswax	5 lbs.
Mineral oil	2 1/4 lbs.
Sulfonated castor oil	4 oz.
Triethanolamine	15 oz.
Water	78 lbs.
Borax	8 oz.
Glycerin	3 lbs.

Brushless shaving creams are apt to undergo changes as they age. As has already been indicated, atmospheric conditions, especially extreme heat and extreme cold contribute greatly to these variations. For these reasons it is advisable to take samples of the filled tubes from each batch. These should be kept under extreme heat and extreme cold in the laboratory for a period of weeks and then checked for consistency at room temperature. While the creams hold up more satisfactorily on the acid side, it frequently happens that certain peculiarities in raw materials may cause a difference in the cream as it ages. Constant, careful investigation is necessary to produce a completely satisfactory product.

While the formula referred to above are merely types, it is possible to alter them in many directions. This may be done, for example, by using olive oil instead of coconut oil, glyceryl monostearate instead of lanolin, other amines, like amino methyl propanol, instead of triethanolamine, solubilized mineral oil instead of the regular cold cream type of minral oil. Then too, a wetting agent may be added to increase the spreading power of the cream on the face, and possibly its rinsing qualities. Or certain germicidal substances may be partly replaced by witch hazel. These are just a few of the many suggestions for giving these creams distinctive properties and characteristics. These additions and variations may affect the consistency of the cream very materially . For this reason any samples which are made up should be carefully studied in the laboratory before going into actual production .

The popularity of brushless shaving creams, or no-lather shaving creams is still increasing . For this reason they deserve close attention and study by those interested in producing shaving products.

17

COSMETICS FOR THE NAILS

The majority of nail polishes consist of a base, like triacetyl cellulose of nitrocelloulose, a resin, a plasticizer, a solvent, a dye or pigment and a suitable perfume. A few words as to the function of these ingredients are of interest.

If nitrocellulose were used alone the film of enamel would crack, not spread evenly and not adhere properly to the nail. It is for this reason that the resins, plasticizers and solvents are introduced. The more common natural resins used are shellac, benzoin, dammer, sandrac and ester gums. Plastic resins like polyvinyl and polystyrene derivatives also give satisfactory results. These resins aid in the formation of the film and the adhesion thereof to the nail. The plasticizers consist most generally of high boiling liquids like the high boiling glycol esters, tricresyl phosphate, triphenyl phosphate, dibutyl phthalate and castor oil. Camphor, a solid, is also used. Their function is to preserve the flexibility and adhesive power of the film. The solvents thin out and disperse the fingernail enamels. They shoud be of such a character that the lacquer sets in about a minute or a minute and a half after aplication. Acetone, alcohol, amyl acetate, ethyl acetate, amyl formate and ethyl propionate are used in combination or alone as solvents. It is important that the phenomena known as "blushing " be prevented in the polish by cooling the nail surface below the atmosphere's dew point. Too rapid drying also is to be avoided or an uneven film will be produed.

The selection and blending of the pigments is most important. About a dozen basic colours make up the large array of shades for fingernail enamels. These must comply with the terms of the Food, Drug and Cosmetic Act, should disperse well, be resistant to light, alkali such as is found in kitchen cleaning and dishwashing compounds, be non-staining and produce a good gloss. Colours that have an affinity for one another must be used to prevent separation. Insoluble lake colours with a small percentage (about 5%) of titanium dioxide are preferred. The mineral colour like iron oxide, the ochres, siennas, lampblack and ultramarine are useful for blending purposes. Here again it is to be pointed out that unless the volume of nail polish sales is large it is a wise policy to purchase the finished product from a private brand house rather than gamble with an untried product.

Perfume is not necessary in nail enamels but add to its finer qualities. It is used mainly to counteract the unpleasant odor of the solvents used. About 1% is the proper quatity to use and here again a compound should be used that is miscible with the ingredients and one which does not discolour and dull the shades of the finished enamel.

To devolop a suitable nail enamel, lacquer or polish, then, certain requirements are necessary. The glossing materials, resins, plasticizers, solvents, pigments and perfumes must be properly balanced to meet these requirments. These are proper flow to produce a glossy, even film, no stickiness to the finished film, proper adhering qualities and no cracking or peeling of the film after application. It must also not develop blush or clouding, it must be light proof, resistant to soapy and slightly alkaline water, it must not dry out the fingernails, the colours must be non-staining and the shades must be uniform and popular.

To formulate such a polish requires considerable research and testing. As new ingredients come into the market improvements are constantly being made. Just to indicate the approximate composition of nail enamels four formulas are presented:

No. 1

Nitro cellulose (1/2 Second Vis)	10.0%
Ethyl acetate	50.0
Butyl acetate	20.0
Diethyl phthalate	15.0
Camphor	4.5
Colour (dye)	0.5
	100.0

Dissolve the nitro cellulose and the camphor in the ethyl acetate. Add the rest of ingredients. Perfume and colour as desired.

No.2

Celluloid clear	25.0%
Acetone	125.0
Amyl acetate	125.0
Oil pink	0.2
Rhodamine B	0.01

No.3[1]

1/2 Sec. viscosity nitrocellulose dry	10%
Anhydrous methyl alcohol	85
Ethylene glycol monomethyl ether	15
	100

No.4 [2]

Glycerin	0.5%
Purified sulfuric ether	4.65
Zinc oxide	15.0
Acetone	19.0
Amyl acetate	18.0
Buty alcohol	22.0
Pure celluloid	20.0
Olive oil	0.5
Ultramarine	0.15
Lavender oil	0.2
	100.0

Nail polish removers consist of a single solvent like acetone or combinations of solvents of which the following are typical:

Nail Polish Removers

No. 5

Butyl stearate	60.0%
Ethyl acetate	40.0
	100.0

No. 6

Butyl stearate	35.0%
Isopropyl alcohol	65.0
	100.0

No. 7

Castor oil	10.0%
Dibutyl	40.0
Ethyl acetate	50.0
	100.0

No.8

Glycol ethyl ether	97.0%
Peanut oil	2.5
Perfume	0.5
	100.0

No. 9

Glycol ethyl ether	46.0%
Ethyl acetate	15.0
Paraffin	5.5
Beeswax	6.5
Stearic acid	20.0
Triethanolamine	6.0
Perfume	1.0
	100.0

18

TOOTH POWDER

There are various classes of tooth powders on the market. These comprise the most common or foaming, abrasive type, those that contain charcol, the medicated type and the dissolving type. Two common formulas for foaming type of tooth powder are as follows:

No. 1

Precipitated chalk, dense	160 lbs.
Calcium sulfate (chrysalba)	20 lbs.
Neutral white soap powder	30 lbs.
Saccharine	5 oz.
Flavor	3 lbs.

No. 2

Precipitated chalk, dense	44 lbs.
Precipitated chalk, light	20 lbs.
Silica air-floated (000 grade)	25 lbs.
Zinc chloride	1 lb.
Castile soap powder	5 lbs.
Borax	5 lbs.
Saccharine (soluble)	4 oz.
Flavor	1 lb.

A tooth powder which contains charcoal may be made by this formula:

No. 3

Ground wilow charcoal	100 lbs.
Precipitated chalk, dense	90 lbs.
Neutral white soap powder	30 lbs.
Saccharine	6 oz.
Flavor	4 lbs.

There are many variations of medicated tooth powders possible, but the most popular ones on the market today are those that base their claims on their peroxide content. Formulas for this type are as follows:

No. 4

Precipitated chalk, light	100 lbs.
Precipitated chalk, dense	100 lbs.
Powdered sugar	10 lbs.
Sodium perborate	25 lbs.
Flavor	4 lbs.

No. 5

Precipitated chalk, dense	150 lbs.
Magnesium carbonate	25 lbs.
Saccharine	5 oz.
Flavor	4 lbs.
Calcium peroxide	25 lbs.

The dissolving types of tooth powders consist of combinations of entirely water soluble substances like borax, salt, sodium bicarbonate and sodium perborate. Sodium perborate which was used in the pure state several yeare ago has been quite generally criticized because it is claimed to be deleterious when used in the mouth.

Since this tooth powder field is one in which many formulas may be devised, additional composition of these products are presented.

No.6 OXYGENATED TOOTH POWDER

Tricalcium phosphate	35.0%
Precipitated chalk	40.15
Pulverized neutral white soap	10.0
Sodium perborate	14.0
Flavor (oil of wintergreen)	0.75
Saccharine	0.1
	100.0

No. 7 ANTACID TOOTH POWDER

Purified zinc peroxide	10.0%
Precipitated chalk	46.0
Tricalcium phosphate	20.0
Bicarbonate of soda	6.5
Pulverized neutral soap	6.0
Confectioner's XXXX sugar	11.0
Flavor to suit	0.5
	100.0

No. 8 SODIUM PERBORATE TOOTH POWDER

Magnesium carbonate	24.0%
Precipitated chalk	35.0
Sodium perborate	14.5
Sodium bicarbonate	13.95
Soap	4.0
Sugar	7.5
Methyl salicylate	0.75
Menthol	0.1
Oil of cinnamon	0.2
	100.0

No. 9 ANTACID TOOTH POWDER

Sodium perborate	10.0%
Precipitated chalk	66.0
Tricalcium phosphate	12.0
Soap	3.5
Sugar	8.0
Flavor	0.5
	100.0

No.10 ANTACID TOOTH POWDER

Precipitated chalk	48.0%
Magnesium hydroxide	6.5
Tricalcium phosphate	9.5
Soap, powdered neutral white	6.75
Talc	19.0
Sugar	9.5
Flavor	0.75
	100.0

No. 11 ACID TOOTH POWDER

Cream of tartar	24.0%
Milk sugar	18.0
Calcium sulfate	47.25
Titanium dioxide	10.0
Flavor	0.75
	100.0

No. 12 ACID TOOTH POWDER

Tartric acid	2.0%
Sodium benzoate	4.0
Calcium sulfate	25.0
Talc	42.0
Colloidal clay	25.1
Honey	1.0
Colour	0.1
Flavor	0.8
	100.0

No. 13 FOAMY POWDERS

Powdered precipitated chalk	65.0%
Powdered sepia	4.5

Powdered castile soap	18.3
Powdered orris	9.0
Saccharine	0.2
Oil of wintergreen	3.0
	100.0

No. 14

Precipitated chalk	63.0%
Powdered myrrh	5.5
Powdered sugar	21.0
White castile soap	10.5
Oil of wintergreen	Sufficient
	100.0

TOOTH POWDERS WITH MAGNESIUM PEROXIDE

No. 15

Magnesium peroxide 30%	25.0%
Precipitated chalk	50.0
Precipitated magnesium carbonate	15.0
Bentonite	10.0
	100.0

No.16

Magnesium peroxide 30%	25.0%
Silica gel	10.0
Precipitated chalk	50.0
Soap powder	10.0
Milk sugar	5.0
	100.0

The modus operandi for tooth powders is comparatively simple. The procedure is first to pre-mix the flavor, colour, sweetener and other ingredients present in small quantities into a portion of the chalk or other abrasive by rubbing the liquids in by hand and then through a sieve or preferably through a small pre-mixer equipped with a brush sieve. This mixture is then screened and blended in a larger mixer into which the rest of the powdered ingredients have been added. The agitator is run untill the mass is uniform, when it is run into storage and filled by the common types of dry filling equipment.

19

TOOTH PASTES OR DENTAL CREAMS

Tooth pastes or dental creams are not so simply compounded as dental powders. Unless the manufacturing operations are carefully carried out, later defects are apt to appear in the finished product during shelf life. It is quite common knowledge that tooth pastes are bad actors and often deteriorate for some unknown cause. Any tooth paste manufacturer will verify this, for such occurrences come up when least expected. The making of these products, then, requires most careful attention. The mixers, ointment mill and filling equipment should all be adapted to the particular product being made. Consistencies of tooth pastes vary very materially, so a mixer for one type of paste may not be adapted for another. Even after mixing is uniform, it is very desirable to pass the product through an ointment mill to mill out the lumps or undistributed materials and produce a more homogeneous and smoother product. The equipment required is a jacketed or tin-lined stainless steel kettle to prepare various mucilages and glycerite of starch, tanks to hold the flavors, a properly designed mixer and an ointment mill. All this equipment should be made from materials that will not affect the colour or taste, like tin-lined copper, glass lining or stainless steel. Not only does this prevent the discoloration of the paste, but small quantities of heavy metal like iron and copper are apt to affect the taste of the product adversely. We have already referred to this in discussing collapsible tubes, wherein we pointed out that these have resulted in some discoloration and off flavor. The facility with which the mixer and other equipment can be cleaned should also play an important place in its selection. In addition to this, proper type tube filling equipment to package the material is required.

The composition of tooth pastes varies considerably. They can be classified in different ways, but the simplest method to classify them for our purpose is according to their foaming or lathering ability. We can, by this method, put them into three classes, those with no foaming properties, those with slight foaming properties and those with high foaming qualities. The amount of foam produced during use is, of course, dependent upon the amount and kind of wetting agent or soap used in the product. A typical formula for a tooth paste made without soap or faoaming ability follows:

FORMULA 1

Simple syrup USP	5 lbs.
Mineral oil, heavy	5 1/2 lbs.
Glycerite of starch USP	111 1/2 lbs.
Precipitated chalk, light	83 lbs.
Magnesium carbonate	2 lbs.
Calcium sulfate	5 lbs.
Milk of magnesia USP	36 lbs.
Saccharine	2 1/2 oz.
Gum tragagcanth	2 oz.
Flavor	4 oz.

As a premise to all directions in making tooth paste, it is pointed out that all the tooth paste ingredients which we will consider, and this applies particulary to liquid ingredients, are taken by weight and not by volume for the obvious season that temperature changes will increase and decrease the volume of liquids.

The formula which we have selected may be classed as a milk of magnesia type of dental cream. It includes more ingredients than are usually found in a tooth paste and has been particularly selected for this reason. The steps in putting this formula together follow this procedure:

1. The simple syrup, glycerite of starch and milk of magnesia are prepared before hand. It is good policy to make these up in sufficient quantities to take care of as many batches as conditions dictate. These are all made according to the USP XI directions or variations may be desirable in the making of the milk of magnesia by more facile methods than those outlined in the Pharmacopoeia.

2. The gum tragacanth is mixed with part of the hot water employed in making glycerite of starch, and is filtered into this as the glycerite is cooling. To blend the ingredients, the simple syrup, mineral oil, glycerite of starch, milk of magnesia and flavor are weighed and put into the mixer. The saccharine is pre-mixed with the calcium sulfate. This mixture is first added to the liquids while the agitator is running. Then the rest of the

abrasives are gradually added and the mixing is continued untill the mass is homogenous. It is then passed through an ointment mill, after standing over night, run to the storage tank which feeds directly to the filling machine, tested for consistency and other properties, and filled.

It is quite simple to convert this formula into a foaming type of tooth paste by the addition of alkyl or alkyl aryl sulfate by merely replacing a part of the chalk with these wetting agents. These may be incorporated anywhere from one per cent to five per cent, depending upon the amount of lathering quality desired. The in-corporation of wetting agents in dental creams does not offer the same difficulty as the addition of soap.

Two formulas for tooth paste made with medium quantities of soap follow:

FORMULA 1

1. Make up a mucilage paste in a glass-lined or stainless steel jacketed kettle, equipped with a mixer by charging it with 75 1/2 lbs. glycerin USP, start the agitator and gradually add in small quantities 4 1/2 pounds powdered Irish moss, ground to pass at least 120 mesh. Continue to mix at room temperature untill the mass is uniform. This takes about half an hour. Turn the heat onto the jacket and heat to 212 degrees F., with the mixer running untill all the Irish moss is dispersed.

Dissolve 6 1/2 oz. solube saccharine and any colour if desired in two pounds of distilled, hot water. Stir this well with a paddle and add to the glycerin-Irish moss mixture above.

Add 25 pounds distilled water and keep the temperature at 212 degrees F. Continue the mixing, shut off the heat and agitate while cooling. Cool down to about 120 degrees F. and strain off the mucilage through a muslin cloth or suitable filter.

2. Make up a soap mixture by following these directions: First dissolve 7 3/4 pounds sodium carbonate USP in 47 1/2 pounds of distilled water by heating to about 180 degrees F. Melt 7 3/4 pounds stearic acid XXX in a glass-lined vessel.

Transfer the sodium carbonate solution to a suitable mixer and add the molten stearic acid in a thin steady stream, stirring the soap well, but slowly to prevent aerating it too much. Continue the mixing until it is uniform, keeping the soap hot. Then with the agitator running, gradually add 12 pounds 13 ounces of neutral white soap and when the soap mixture is uniform and smooth, it is ready for use.

3. Transfer the strained mucilage base to a pony or other suitable type mixer. Add the soap mixture and stir the two together. With the mixer running, gradually add 116 1/2 pounds light precipitated chalk. Reduce the speed of the mixer and add 307 pounds of water distilled. Continue to mix untill the mass is homogeneous, scraping down the sides of the mixer and the agitator blades occasionaly. When uniform, remove the finished paste to tubes or small tanks. Let it stand over night and the next morning pass it through an ointment mill, after which the product may be examined for consistency and other characteristics. Then fill it.

FORMULA 2

1. In a tinned-copper, jacketed kettle heat a mixture of 20 pounds of propylene glycol and 51 1/2 pounds of glucose (sweetose type) to about 220 degrees F. Dissolve 4 ounes of salt in 8 1/4 pounds of distilled water and then stir in 9 pounds redried starch. Stir well to wet the starch and add this mixture gradually to the hot glycol-glucose mix, continuing the agitation with a wooden paddle if it is so desired. Continue to heat at boiling temperature untill the mass is transparent and smooth.

2. Make an Irish moss mucilage by adding 6 pounds of Irish moss, picked free from extraneous material, in 384 pounds of boiling hot distilled water. Stir well to extract the moss and permit the temperature to drop to about 100 degrees F. Strain the mucilage through a muslin cloth and dissolve 12 ounces of benzoic acid therein. Bring the yield up to exactly 360 pounds with cold distilled water. This batch represents sufficient Irish moss mucilage for five batches of tooth paste.

3. Transfer 72 pounds of Irish moss mucilage into a suitable mixer. Add the glycol-glucose solution above while it is still warm and sift in while agitating:

Neutral white soap .... 13 3/4 lbs.
Benzoic acid .... 3 1/4 lbs.

Saccharine .... 1/2 lb.

Stir untill smooth and add the flavor. If menthol is used be sure to dissolve it in the flavoring oils before addin. About 4 pounds of flavor are used for a batch this size. Continue the mixing, then add gradually in 25 pound lots, stirring between additions.

Light precipitated chalk .... 115 lbs.
Calcium sulfate (chrysalba)............. 8 1/2 lbs.

When this has all been mixed in, finally add 45 pounds magnesium hydroxide paste (hydro magma paste) ; mix untill uniform after all the ingredients have been added. This takes about one-half an hour. Let stand over night and then cool and fill.

It will be noted that the above formula contains no glycerin. If it is desired to use this, glycerin may be used in amount equal to the sum of the weight of the propylene glycol and glucose indicated. The methods of making are exactly the same.

A tooth paste with a high soap content and containing no water has the following composition:

Neutral white soap .... 96 1/2 lbs.
Light precipitated chalk .... 82 lbs.
Alcohol specially denatured 31-A. (20 lbs. neutral white soap not over 5% moisture and 100 lbs. glycerin added to 100 gallons ethyl alcohol.)
Glycerin USP .... 80 1/2 lbs.
Benzoic acid .... 35 oz.

To put together this type of dental cream, first make an essence of the alcohol, glycerin, benzoic acid and flavor. Charge into a mixer, preferably covered, the soap and the chalk and blend them by mixing. Add the essence gradually to this soap-chalk mixture and continue stirring untill the mass is smooth. Cool the paste and fill as soon as possible.

No. 1 INEXPENSIVE

Precipitated chalk, light 44.0%
Colloidal clay 3.0
Gum tragacanth mucilage (2%) 3.0
Glucose 4.0

Glycerin	15.0
Water	30.3
Flavor	0.5
Methyl parahydroxybenzoate	0.2
	100.0

Put hot water, glucose and mucilage into a hot mixer. Sift the dry ingredients and slowly add them to the liquids while mixing. Mix untill smooth paste is obtained, then run through an ointment mill or a roller mill. Add preservative and flavor.

No.2 HIGH GRADE

Precipitated chalk, light	46.0%
Powdered gum tragacanth	1.0
Pulverized neutral white soap	4.1
Glycerin	24.5
Water	18.7
Powdered soluble saccharine	0.1
Methyl parahydroxybenzoate	0.1
Flavor	0.5
Alcohol	5.0
	100.0

Mix alcohol and the gum; add hot water, glycerin, soap, saccharine, preservative and flavor. Mix on-half hour. Mix and sieve the dry ingredients and slowly add them to the liquid. Mix untill a smooth white paste is obtained. Mill. The consistency of this paste is slightly heavy. It can be reduced by adding water.

No. 3 ACID-REACTING TOOTH PASTE

Titanium dioxide	7.0%
Talc	35.0
Glycerin	28.0
Water	16.0
Tartaric or citic acid solution (10%)	8.85
Pectin from citrus fruits	0.75
Flavor	0.75

Sugar (milk)	3.5
Sodium benzoate	0.15
	100.0

Disperse the pectin powder in the acid solution. Heat the glycerin and water; add the sugar. Mix well. Add the preservative and flavor and mix again. Sift in the dry material, mix thoroughly and mill.

No. 4 ALKALINE TOOTH PASTE

Precipitated chalk, light	25.0%
Magnesium carbonate	14.0
Borax	5.0
Glycerin	25.0
Water	28.4
Powdered neutral white soap	2.0
Saccharine	0.1
Flavor	0.5
	100.0

Make same as No. 1

No.5 MILK OF MAGNESIA TOOTH PASTE

Milk of magnesia	24.0%
Magnesium carbonate	10.0
Precipitated chalk	18.0
Soap, powdered neutral white	1.75
Glycerite of starch	12.0
Glycerin	12.0
Water	20.0
Flavor	0.5
Methyl parahydroxybenzoate	0.1
Mineral oil, heavy	1.5
Saccharine	0.15
	100.0

To boiling water add glycerin, saccharine, preservative, milk of magnesia, and the glycerite. Mix for a half hour and then add the dry

materials very slowly. Finally add flavor and mineral oil. Mix for another hour and mill. The glycerite of starch is made as follows:

GLYCERITE OF STARCH

Corn starch	40.5%
Water	24.0
Glycerin	35.5
	100.0

Mix the foregoing into a smooth paste. Then to twelve parts of this paste, add eighty-eight parts of glycerin, heated to 180 F. Mix continually, to avoid discoloring the glycerite, with constant heat for about an hour or untill a smooth translucent paste is formed. Great care must be exercised in making this preparation. This product can be purchased ready made from chemical supply houses.

No. 6 SOAPY TOOTH PASTE

Pulverized neutral white soap	20.0%
Precipitated chalk	35.0
Colloidal clay	3.0
Saccharine	0.3
Water	10.7
Glycerin	25.0
Alcohol	5.0
Flavor	1.0
	100.0

Make a hot excipient of the glycerin and water. Slowly stir in the soap. Add the flavors mixed with alcohol. Finally stir in the sifted dry ingredients. Adjust consistency to suit with chalk. Mill. This makes a very foamy paste. A small amount of gumtragacanth powder may be added.

The following formula will give a dental cream of fair consistency and is simple to manufacture:

No. 7

Precipitated chalk (light)	0.0%
Tricalcium phosphate	6.0
White soap powder	2.0
Gum tragacanth mucilage (2%)	5.0
Saccharine (soluble)	0.1
Preservative	0.1
Mineral oil	1.0
Glycerin	15.0
Water, distilled	30.3
Flavor	0.5
	100.0

Soak gum tragacanth in one-third of the water, then place in mixer with the remainder of the water and glycerin. Heat, stir thoroughly and add the sifted powders containing the saccharine; then add the flavor, preservative and mineral oil. Mix untill the paste is smooth. The larger the batch, the longer the mixing should be continued. Mill through an ointment mill. Allow to stand and then tube in the regular way.

No. 8

Precipitated chalk	42.0%
Neutral soap powder	10.0
Benzoic acid	1.0
Saccharine	1.0
Glycerin	25.0
Alcohol	20.0
Flavor	1.0
	100.0

Dissolve the saccharine and flavor in 50% of the alcohol in one container and the benzoic acid in the remaining 50% of alcohol in another container. In the mixing machine place all of the glycerin into which the alcohol containing the benzoic acid is added through a strainer. Now add the alcohol containing the saccharine and flavor in the same manner. These liquids should be well agitated. Add about one-half of the precipitated chalk and mixs well. Carefully add the soap powder, mix, and then add the remainder of the chalk. Continue the mixing for two or three hours. Mill in the usual way.

This dental cream when used will give a large quantity of suds. In pastes of this type the benzoic acid sets free a portion of the fatty acid used in manufacturing the soap while the remainder of the soap acts ad the binder and produces a satisfactory cream.

There is slight demand for an acid dental cream, the idea being that acid will remove stains from the teeth.

No. 9

Tricalcium phosphate	23.0%
Calcium sulfate	35.0
Glycerin	25.0
Water (distilled)	10.0
Glycerite of tragacanth	4.0
Mineral oil	1.0
Acid	0.1
Sodium lauryl sulfate	0.4
Methyl p-hydroxy benzoate	0.1
Flavor	1.4
	100.0

The glycerite of tragacanth should be made beforehand, using the hot method, and it is important that the glycerite be well prepared. The glycerin and glycerite of tragacanth are placed in the mixer and mixed untill a smooth, even consistency is obtained. Add the water, tricalcium phosphate and calcium sulfate, mix well and add the sodium lauryl sulfate. Then add the flavor in which the saccharine has been dissolved. The mineral oil should be added last. All the powders should be free from carbonates as the addition of the acid will liberate CO2 which will cause the tube to swell and sometimes burst.

Milk of magnesia tooth pastes are quite popular and one manufactured along the lines of the following formula will be found to give results.

No. 10

Milk of magnesia	24.0%
Precipitated chalk	32.0
White powdered soap	2.0
Glycerite of tragacanth	10.0
Glycerin	10.0
Mineral oil	1.0
Water (distilled)	20.0
Saccharine	0.1
Methyl p-hydroxy benzoate	0.1
Flavor	0.8
	100.0

Mix glycerite of tragacanth (tragacanth 10%, glycerin 78%, water 12%. Mix with heat.). Glycerin and water together, add one half of the chalk, mix; add the milk of magnesia, mix; then the soap and the rest of the chalk. Finally add the saccharine and preservative dissolved in the flavor. Mix well for two hours and mill. In making the milk of magnesia, time can be saved by buying pulverized magnesium oxide and hydrating it with hot water, then passing it through a colloid mill. The finished product should contain the required 7% of magnesium hydroxide.

No. 11 MAGNESIA TOOTH PASTE

Part 1

Magnesia-glycerin mixture:
130.0 parts milk of magnesia
110.0 parts glycerin
Mix and evaporate to 130.0 parts:

Part II

Glycerite of starch
158.0 partd glycerin
74.0 parts milk of starch
(milk of starch consists of 34.0 parts corn starch,20 parts water and 30 parts glycerin mixed.)

Heat the glycerin to 140 C. and add the milk of starch with constant agitation. Maintain the temperature for one hour.

Part III

Tooth paste:
130.0 parts magnesia-glycerin mixture (Part I)
70.0 parts glycerite of starch (special) (Part II)
30.0 parts glycerin
20.0 parts corn sugar

Part IV

Mix for 15 minutes and add:
65.0 parts precipitated chalk, light
90.0 parts dicalcium phosphate
5.8 parts powdered neutral white soap
17.0 parts magnesium carbonate, light

These powdered materials should be mixed dry and then added gradually, a process which will require approximately one hour after which the paste should be mixed at least one hour and then the following added:

Part v

3.2 parts flavor
8.0 parts heavy mineral oil

NOTE: The above tooth paste has an MgO content equivalent to approximately 53% milk of magnesia.

U.S. GOVERMENT TOOTH PASTE SPECIFICATIONS

W. Sounder and I.C. Schoonover, of the National Bureau of Standards have worked out a set of specifications for tooth paste to be purchased by the United States Goverment, and these specifications were published in the "Journal of the American Dental Association."

"Concerning material and workmanship, the tooth paste shall be free from material other than those specified and shall be uniform in composition.

"The tooth paste shall, when used in the normal manner, assist in the removal of the usual daily accumulations of debris and deposits from the exposed surfaces of the teeth without injury to the teeth, mucous membrane of the mouth or body in general. When applied undiluted to the mucous membrane of the cheeks and gums for a period of two minutes, the tooth paste must not produce irritation or unpleasant symptoms. The flavor shall be distinct and pleasant and the colour white, cream or pink. The tooth paste shall extrude from the tube in a continues mass at a temperature of 10 C. (50 F.) without the application of excessive force, and paste extrude from the tube (orifice down) to a length of 10mm. at a temperature of 20 C. (68F.), shall remain attached to the tube for at least fifteen seconds. The tooth paste shall not segregate, farment or deteriorate when cooled to a temperature of 15 C (59 F.) for one hour or when heated to a temperature of 50 C (122 F.) for seventy-two hours.

"Forty per cent or more (by weight) of the tooth paste shall consist of the following detergents: calcium carbonate, dicalcium phosphate, magnesium carbonate, magnesium hydroxide. Hard or soft soap, U.S.P. XI shall not exceed 20 per cent, sodium benzoate 2.5 per cent, and thymol 0.1 per cent. Sugars and saccharine are permitted without limit except as limited by flavor or other test. The following ingredients, as required, are permitted:

Sodium bicarbonate	Gum karaya
Sodium borate	Gum tragacanth
Sodium carbonate	Irish moss
Sodium chloride	Petroleum jelly
Boric acid	Mineral oil
Citric acid	Alcohol
Acetic acid	Ethylene glycol
Cream of tartar	Glycerin
Gelatine	Water

"Flavors and colors permitted by the U.S. Food and Drug Adminstration shall be permitted in proper amounts. One hundred per cent shall pass through a U.S. Standard No. 100 sieve and 98 per cent through U.S. Standard No. 200 sieve. Tooth paste shall not contain appreciable amounts of the commonly recognized poisonous elements such as arsenic and heavy metals. The pH value of the tooth paste (by weight) shall be greater than 4.9 and less than 10.1. The tooth paste shall not scratch glass.

"The containers shall be of the usual collapsible tube type having screw caps. The containers, including cap, shall not be attacked, chemically, by the tooth paste. Tubes shall be of tin or aluminum properly treated so that the flow of paste will cease when pressure on the tube is released. The area of the orifice through which the paste is to be extruded shall be greater than 13 square millimeters and less than 36 square millimeters. Orifices shall not have minor dimensions less than one-half the major dimension."

Before we leave our discussion of tooth pastes it should be pointed out that due to variations of raw materials, a uniform and proper consistency is not obtained under all conditions by the above formulas. For that reason it is necessary to make adjustments in liquid or solid ingredient proportions in order to obtain the desired consistency.

Liquid dentifrices do not occsasion as much detail in manufacture as pastes. The equipment required for their manufacture is more simple, consisting usually of a liquid mixing tank, storage tanks, and filling and closing equipment. The tanks should either be built from stainless steel or be glass lined. It is also advantageous to provide a suitable filter for the finished liquid before it is filled into the bottle.

For the purpose of focusing our attention on the methods used for making these three formulas, one of the older type and two of the newer type of liquid dentifrices are presented.

The formula for the older type which was used extensively in past years and still has popularity has this composition:

Olive oil castile soap	70 lbs.
Alcohol specially denatured 38-B	43 gals.
Borax	3 lbs.
Saccharine soluble	1/2lb.
Glycerin	40 lbs.
Water distilled	43 gals.
Flavor	12 lbs.
F.D.A. cert.red colour (amarnath red)	Q.S.

To put this formula together, thoroughly dissolve the soap in 40 gallons of distilled water, heated to almost the boiling point, cool down to about 90 degrees F., dissolve the borax and colour in the remaining or three gallons of hot water and add to the soap solution. Dissolve together the flavor, glycerin and alcohol and pour into the soap solution. Mix well

with the liquid stirrer in the mixing tank. Transfer to a storage tank and let the product stand for ten days to clarify. Then filter and fill.
This older type of liquid dentifrice has been largely superseded, in recent years, by those made with the aid of wetting agents. This has simplified the making procedure. Two formulas for this type of prodct follow:

1

Glycerin	180 lbs.
Crystal sugar	160 lbs.
Saccharine	1 lb.
Wetting agent (lauryl sulfate)	50 lbs.
Salt	40 lbs.
1% amarnath red colour in water	40 lbs.
Water distilled	466 lbs.
5% quince seed infusion in water	500 lbs.
Alcohol S.D. 38-B	540 lbs.
Flavor	Q.S.

2

Irish moss extract (carajel or agagel)	1 /12 lbs.
Alkyl aryl sulfate (nacconol LAL)	8 lbs.
Alcohol S.D. 38-B	75 lbs.
Water distilled	300 lbs.
Salt	1/2 lbs.
1% amarnath red colour in water	5 lbs.
Flavor	2 lbs.

To make either of these the Irish moss or quince seed are first dispersed in hot water and filtered into the mixing tank, then the wetting agent is dissolved in this dispersion followed by the sugar, salt and colour: Lastly the alcohol, in which the flavor has been dissolved, and the glycerin are mixed in. This solution is permitted to stand for from five to ten days for through clarification, after which it is filtered and filled.

In conclusion, it may again be emphasized that the public are "good-tooth" conscious. They desire teeth like gleaming white pearls, pink, firm, healthy gums and a non-offensive breath. Dentifrices alone cannot maintain these conditions. They do go far in preventing deterioration of the teeth if used faithfully in conjunction with proper diet, which consists of ample intake of milk, citrus fruits, vegetables, and green salads. It is also necessary that regular visits be made to the dentist at least twice a year for the removal of tartar which will form in spite of dentifrices, together with necessay dental attention in other directions like filling of caries. The word of the dentist himself in most cases goes further than the claims made in the advertising propaganda for these preparations. It is not easy or even possible to get most dentists to endorse any particular brand of dentifrice, but it is not difficult to arose his ill will through false and misleading claims for a dentifrice. For that reason the more successful merchandisers of these preparations emphasize the advantages of good diet and regular visits to the dentist as a wise course in presenting their product to the public. While the market is well supplied in this field, quality honest, and well presented dentifrices will continue to obtain their share of the business.

20

MOUTH WASHES

The raw materials used in various mouth washes are numerous. Among the more common antiseptic substances that find their use in these products are thymol, benzoic acid, chlorthymol, sodium perborate,. boric acid, formaldehyde, the phenol sulfonates especially zinc, menthol, salol eucalyptol and certain essential oils or their isolates, phenol resorcinol, beta napthol and potassium chlorate. Alcohol in sufficient concentration increases the antiseptic property. More recently the quaternary ammonium compounds are being used in certain directions. Certain of these ingredients like the chlorates and borates are now considered dangerous to use especially by children. Others like chlorthymol cause an unpleasant bite if used even in small quantities and the peroxides are not very stable. It must also be remembered that if bactericidal properties are assigned to combinations containing these substances their antiseptic action can be confined under conditions of use, If these products are diluted, as is the case at times, before use, the diluted product must be efficacious. Such preparations may come under two Federal laws, the Insecticide Act of 1910 and the Food, Drug and cosmetic Act of 1938, depending upon how the claims are expressed.

Other raw materials used in mouth washes consist of the flavors, astringents, colours and solvent. The flavoring oils most generally used are peppermint, methyl salicylate, cassia, anise, thyme, caraway, cloves, myrrh, spearmint, geranium, otto of rose and many others. Sugar, saccharine and salt also add to the flavor. The most commonly used astringent is zinc chloride though alum and tannin have also been used in limited amounts. In colouring mouth washes only F. D. & C. Colours should be used. These should be stable toward the rest of the ingredients. As solvents water, alcohol, glycerin and propylene glycol are used. It is permissible in U.S. to use tax-free specially denatured alcohol. This usually contains some of the flavoring ingredients of the preparation as denaturing agents.

The equipment required to make these liquids is quite simple. Suitable tanks, mixers, chilling coils if used and filters are required. The solutions are not usually difficult to make though it should be remembered it is good practice to dissolve the water insoluble ingredients in the alcohol or glycerin rather than in the water - alcohol medium. Clarification of these solutions at times is a difficult operation. The procedure outlined under the chapter "Clarification of Liquids" should be followed closely in such cases.

The following formulas are typical of the numerous types used. At the very outset as Number I we present that well-known National Formulary preparation "Liquor Antisepticus."

No. 1

Boric acid	1.5%
Thymol	0.1
Eucalyptol	0.5
Methyl salicylate	0.1
Oil of thyme	0.03
Menthol	0.1
Alcohol	30.0
Water	67.67
	100.0

Dissolve boric acid in 60% of the water and other ingredients in 60% of the alcohol. Pour water solution into alcoholic solution, add 2% of purified talc and allow mixture to stand with occasional stirring for forty-eight hours. Filter. Add rest of alcohol and water, and add caramel colouring if darker colour is desired. An interesting variation of this follows:

No. 2

Benzoic acid	1.0%
Boric acid	2.0
Alcohol	8.5
Eucalyptol	0.05
Oil of thyme	0.1
Oil of wintergreen	0.3

Water	88.0
Caramel colouring	0.05
	100.0

The boric acid is added to part of water and boiled untill completely dissolved; add this solution to the rest of the water and allow to cool. Dissolve benzoic acid in part of the alcohol. The oils are added to rest of the alcohol. Add these solutions to the water; mix rapidly and add caramel colour. Mix again for four hours. Chill in a cooling tank and filter. Or mix with 2% of purified talc, and allow to stand for 48 hours and filter.

No. 3 ALKALINE MOUTH WASH

Potassium bicarbonate	2.1%
Borax	2.0
Oil of sassafras	0.1
Thymol	0.05
Eucalyptol	0.1
Methyl salicylate	0.05
Cudbear, tr.of	0.2
Alcohol	5.0
Glycerin	9.0
Water distilled	81.4
	100.0

Dissolve the potassium bicarbonate and sodium borax in 50% of the water. Dissolve the oils in alcohol, add the alkaline solution, the tincture of cudbear, and the rest of the water. Mix thoroughly for two hours. Allow to stand for 48 hours. Chill and filter. Two per cent of purified talc may be used to aid clarification.

No. 4 CHLORO-PHENOL MOUTH WASH

Benzoic acid	1.0%
Cinnamon oil	2.0
Phenol	1.5
Chloroform	1.5
Alcohol	37.5
Oil of peppermint	0.5

Glycerin	56.0
	100.0

Dissolve the benzoic acid in the chloroform, add the glycerin and mix. Dissolve the cinnamon, peppermint and phenol in alcohol and mix two solutions together. Mix for two hours, chill and filter.

No.5 RESORCIN MOUTH WASH

Resorcinol	5.0
Zinc chloride	0.03
Menthol	0.5
Thymol	0.2
Eucalyptol	0.03
Camphor	0.03
Oil of peppermint	0.05
Alcohol	25.0
Glycerin	10.0
Water	59.16
	100.0

Dissolve resorcinol and zinc chloride in water, and the thymol, eucalyptol, wintergreen, menthol and camphor in the alcohol. Mix the two solutions together and add glycerin. Mix one hour, chill and filter.

21

FACIAL MASKS

Masks are often called "astringents." In a chemical sense astringents refer to that class of materials, such as tannic acid and alum, which precipitate protein from solution. Temporarily masks act like astringents but not in a chemical sense.

Albumen, in itself, has most of the properties for a good liquid mask, but some people are sensitive to albumen and it decomposes readily. Dextrin, casein, starch, althea and the various gums, such as acacia, tragacanth, quince seed, Tra-gum and karaya are good substitutes for albumen. Acacia gum appears to be best. It is soluble enough to make a flowing solution, and it forms a uniform layer as it dries on the face. Tragacanth base makes the mask too pasty, and desides it does not flow readily. Karaya and quince seed mucilages alone are much too stringy. Accordingly, acacia gum seems the best base for liquid mask. The gum is soluble in water and is not injured by a fairly high concentration of alcohol, which enables the mask to dry rapidly. Acacia mucilge is easy to preserve and in addition has no disagreeable odor.

If, however, acacia gum mucilage is employed solely as the base of the mask, it is apt to shrink and break up too rapidly in drying. This condition may be overcome by the addition of a small amount of glycerin. It must not be forgotten, however, that a certain contraction of the gum is necessary, for this property gives the masks its drawing power. But the directions should emphasize that the face must be covered at all times by a uniform layer of the preparation. Only then can it exert maximum contracting action.

Dextrine and starch, added to the acacia gum mucilage are said to enhance the drawing qualities of the gum. Some masks also utilize gelatine, either by itself of dissolved with other gums.

The consistency of a good mask should be about that of molasses at room temperature. It must flow easily when brushed on the skin. No mask should take longer than five minutes to dry completely. Varying the concentration of the alcohol will provide the desired drying time.

Acacia masks do not have the absorptive properties of the clay types because clay masks absorb and absorb many impurities. Acacia does this also to a limited extent, but not as effectively as the clay types. However, a small amount of colloidal clay suspended in the acacia gum solution, will make a gum mask more "absorptive."

A few masks contain irritants for the purpose of imparting a tingling sensation. This effect is supposed to stimulate the sebaceous glands and sluggish pores, but the real value of local irritants is to bring the blood to the surface of the skin.

A good mask does not require irritants to stimulate the glands. A product containing acacia gum, a small amount of dextrin, alcohol, glycerin, a non-irritating preservat. ve like the methyl ester of para-hydroxy-benzoic acid, a trace of cetyl alcohol, boric acid, and perfumed with camphor, menthol, and lavender, makes a refreshing and cooling mask. If a tingle is desired, increase the menthol a trifle untill the proper effect is obtained.

No. 1 ACACIA MASK

Part I

Acacia gum (best grade)	37.0%
Dextrin (best grade)	2.0
Boric acid	0.5
Distilled water	47.7

Part II

Alcohol	9.0
Glycerin	1.0
Cetyl alcohol	2.0
p-hydroxy-methyl-benzoate	0.15
Camphor	0.2
Oil of lavender	0.3
Menthol	0.15
	100.0

A small amount of tincture of benzoin may be added if a more opaque product is wished. In manufacturing this product the ingredients comprising Part I and Part II are mixed separately and then Part II is poured slowly, and with constant stirring, into the liquid portion. The use of a colloid mill, if possible, ensures a better product.

Using this formula and varying the different ingredients, a commercial product of any desired consistency may be made. The above preparation is removed after use on the face by water.

A formula for a facial mask in dry form which the user makes up herself by mixing with water is viz.:

No. 2

Althea (marshmallow root) (ground)	50%
Corn starch	25
Orris root powdered	24
Calcium perborate	1
Perfume	Q.S.
	100.0

This type of mask was referred to as a rejuvenator in the past but such a name is no longer permitted under existing U.S. statutes. Due to the presence of a perborate it is presumed to have some skin whitening properties.

Facial clays enjoy a fluctuating popularity. A few years ago their popularity was national in scope, but there is as yet no evidence that demand will again become nation wide.

Facial clays are pastes consisting of inert materials, water and glycerin, Sometimes rubber latex and casein are included. The following formulas are representative.

No.3

Purified kaolin	32.0%
Kieselguhr	10.0
Glycerin	15.0

Alcohol	20.0
2% acacia mucilage	10.0
Water	12.0
Perfume	1.0
	100.0

Heat the water and glycerin to 170 F. Run it into a mass mixer; add the dry materials and mix for about two hours. Then add the mucilage and the perfume dissolved in alcohol. Greater fluidity can be obtained by increasing the water content.

No. 4

Purified zinc peroxide	10.0%
Purified kaolin (colloidal clay)	24.0
Kieselguhr	5.0
Glycerin	15.0
2% acacia mucilage	10.0
Water	25.0
Alcohol	10.0
Perfume	1.0
	100.0

Use same process as for No. 1.

No. 5

Bentonite	10.0%
Alcohol	10.0
Purified kaolin	35.0
Glycerin	13.0
Tragacanth mucilage 2%	20.0
Water	10.9
Perfume	1.0
Methyl p-hydroxy-benzoate	0.1
	100.0

Same process as for No. 1.

22

COSMETIC FOR THE EYES

IN PROMOTING cosmetics for the eyes it is of tantamount importance that they do not contain any ingredients that may cause eye injury. Absolute cleanliness is necessary in making and packaging. Some plants claim that sterilized air is present during manufacturing operations by using ultra violet lamps such as used in hospital operating rooms and bacteriological laboratories. It is furthermore necessary that if any medicinal claims are made the preparation be labelled as a drug and not a cosmetic. As a matter a fact, a safe policy to pursue is to market eye lotions as medicines and then only if they contain ingredients which are not harmful. Creams, shadows and eyebrow pencils must not contain any dyestuffs that irritate the eye if any of the prepartion enters it.

Eye lotions, also termed eye washes and eye drops, are the most frequently met eye preparations. They usually consist of aqueous solutions, in some cases isotonic solutions, of such raw materials as salt, boric acid, sodium bicabonate, glycerin, potassium borate, camphor, sodium ethyl mercuric thiosalicylate, zinc sulfate, alum, witch hazel and ammonium chloride. There is no particular difficulty in making up these solutions though it is important that they be properly clarified. The purpose of eye lotions, it is claimed, is to refresh, stimulate, cleanse and soothe. In some cases claims have been made that they add to the attractiveness when used, though this is questionable.

Formulaes that have been used as eye lotions follow.

No. 1

Borax	2.0%
Salt	3.0
Bicarbonate of soda	2.0
Water	92.9
Oil of peppermint	0.1
	100.0

Dissolve each of the dry ingredients in a little water; put the remainder of the water into a mixing tank; add the borax solution, then the salt solution and finally the bicarbonate solution, mixing between each addition. Then mix the oil of peppermint with a little precipitated chalk and add this last. Mix thoroughly, age for 24 hours, and filter, preferably at low temperature.

No. 2

Boric acid	3.5%
Sodium chloride	5.0
Glycerin	3.0
Camphor water	13.0
Distilled water	75.5
	100.0

Dissolve the boric acid and borax separately in a little warm wate Mix the camphor water and the glycerin with the remainder of the water; then add the two solutions mixing between each addition.

No. 3

Boric acid	1.0%
Sodium chloride	1.0
Camphor water	53.0
Distilled water	45.0
	100.0

No. 4

Zinc chloride	0.15%
Distilled water	99.85
	100.0

No. 5

Zinc salicylate	1.0%
Camphor water	50.0
Distilled water	49.0
	100.0

No. 6

Zinc sulfate	0.2%
Boric acid	2.2
Camphor water	25.0
Distilled water	72.6
	100.0

No. 7

Zinc sulfate	0.05%
Boric acid	1.6
Glycerin	5.0
Camphor water	25.0
Distilled water	68.35
	100.0

No. 8

Zinc sulfate	0.5%
Ammonium chloride	0.2
Camphor	0.2
Alcohol	7.0
Distilled water	92.1
	100.0

Special creams for use in the areas surrounding the eyes find limited sales. These have been parcelled out in small jars. Previous to the passage of the cosmetic statute they were offered under descriptive names like wrinkle creams, crowsfoot creams and nourishing creams

These creams differ very little from the creams already described though it has been the more common custom to recommend lanolin containing or lanolin derivative containing creams for use around the eyes where wrinkles appear.

Two formulas which have been used are presented.

No. 9 EYE CREAM

Almond oil	20.0%
Olive oil	20.0
Castor oil	10.0
Lanolin	50.0
	100.0

No. 10 EYE CREAM

Lecithin	5.0%
Cholesterol	1.0
Lanolin	10.0
Yellow Wax	25.0
Expressed oil of almond	58.3
Methyl p-hydroxy-benzoate	0.2
Perfume	0.5
	100.0

23

INSECT REPELLING PREPARATIONS

Since the newer insect repellents are comparable to mineral oil in consistency anyone formulating these liquid creams should follow the processes already outlined under liquid creams replacing part of the mineral oil with the insect repellent.

It should be pointed out that these newer repellents were used without any additions. For that reason the addition of water, oil etc. reduces their repellency. Any cosmetic in which they are incorporated should contain as high a percentage of these substancesf as possible. Under no circumstances should they go below 25% for even at that figure they repel only temporarily. In diluted form they are efficacius for several hours depending upon certain conditions like temperature, air currents, perspiration and others.

The non-toxic bites of insects are annoying and at times painful. It is presumed that the irritation set up by the bite is acid in character. To temporarily allay the discomfort, concoctions that are alkaline and cooling are used. Since there is a tendency upon the part of the victim especially children to scratch in order to stop the itching occasioned by many insect bites, antiseptic substances are often incorporated.

In presenting the following formulas we point out that these are medicines and non cosmetics and must be labelled as such.

No.1 BITE LOTIONS

Ether	10.0%
Ammonia	10.0
Menthol	0.2
Thymol	0.1
Alcohol	79.7
	100.0

Dissolve the thymol and menthol in the alcohol; add the ether and the ammonia.

No. 2 BITE LOTION

Chlorthymol	0.1%
Menthol	0.1
Spirit of camphor	80.0
Ammonia	19.8
	100.0

Dissolve the chlorthymol and the menthol in the spirit of camphor and add the ammonia. Ammonia may precipitate the camphor.

No. 3 INSECT BITE LOTIONS

Menthol	0.1%
Naphthalene	2.0
Ammonia water 28%	10.0
Tincture of wormwood	20.0
Glycerin	5.0
Alcohol	62.9
	100.0

Dissolve the napthalene in the alcohol; add the tincture of wormwood and menthol. Add the glycerin and the ammonia.

No. 4 INSECT BITE CREAM

Vanishing cream	90.0%
Benzene	6.0
Naphtalene	3.0
Oil of pennyroyal	1.0
	100.0

Dissolve the naptahalene in bezéne. Add the oil of pennyroyal and slowly stir this mixture into the vanishing cream.

No. 5 INSECT BITE CREAM

Glyceryl monostearate	10.0%
Linalyl acetate	3.0
Oil of cedar leaf	0.1
Menthol	0.1
Kerosene	30.0
Water	53.8
Glycerin	3.0
	100.0

24

COSMETICS FOR BABIES

IN THE care of children, especially infants, preparations closely akin to toiltetries are of value. Besides a mild soap in bathing small children, baby oils and creams as well as powders are used.

As powders a slightly perfumed, good grade of talcum or dusting powder is satisfactory. Boric acid which has been used very generally in borating baby powders is no longer considered a good addition because of its toxic properties. The main purpose of a baby powder is to soothe and lubricate the skin. Talc with a 2% addition of zinc stearate is quite suitable for this purpose. The talc as already indicated should be as pure as obtainable and be free from lime or grit.

No. 1 BABY POWDER

Talc	70 lbs.
Kaolin	20 lbs.
Zinc stearate	5 lbs.
Precipitate chalk	5 lbs.
Hydroxyquinoline sulfate	1/4lb.
Perfume	1/4lb.

As an oily lubricant for the skin of a child pure olive oil slightly perfumed is offered. Another formula that has been used is:

No. 2 BABY OIL

White mineral oil (65-75)	45.0%
Refined peanut oil	54.7
Oxyquinolin benzoate	0.2
Maleic anhydride	0.1
	100.0

The maleic anhydride and the oxyquinolin benzoate are dissolved in the peanut oil and the mineral oil is added. Preparation is then filtered. While there is still some discussion as to the effectiveness of the test for oil-soluble antiseptics, those who have worked with oxyquinolin benzoate have testified to its effectiveness.

A cream is preferred in certain directions. Such a cream may be made by this formula:

No. 3 BABY CREAM

Anhydrous lanolin .... 3 lbs.
Paraffin (130-132 M.P.) ....1 1/8lbs.
Beeswax ....191/2lbs.
Mineral oil ....421/2lbs.
Water dist .... 35 lbs.
Absorption base .... 3/4lb.
Zinc stearate .... 1 lb.
Benzoic acid ester .... 1/8lb.
Perfume .... Q.S.

(1) Melt the waxes at 140 with the mineral oil.

(2) Mix absorption base with 20 lbs. hot water.

(3) Mix benzoic acid ester, zinc stearate and rest of water together.

Pour (2) into (1), stir well, then add (3). Mix untill homogenous and

fill at 100 OF.

No. 4 BABY CREAM

Mineral oil .... 60 lbs.
Cetyl alcohol .... 3 lbs.
Petrolatum (white) .... 24 lbs.
Paraffin .... 8 lbs.
Lanolin .... 5 lbs.
Perfume .... 1/4lbs.

Melt all together, stir well.

25

HERBAL COSMETICS FOR THE SKIN

Introduction

Making herbal cosmetics is as simple as basic cooking. Creams and emulsions are all basically mixtures of water, oils waxes and fragrances perfumery products in varuing proportions. A slight change in the quantities in the preparations changes the character of the preparation and one should be careful when measuring the ingerdients. Generally most of the creams are basically made in the same way and hence when measuring the quality the following rough equivalents should be kept in mind while formulating the the product.

1. Teaspoon + 60 drops= 5ml.
3. Teaspoon + 1 Tablespoon = 15ml.
2. Tablespoons = 1/8 cup =10ml.
4. Tablespoons = 1/4 cup =20ml.
8. Tablespoons = 1/2 cup. =40ml.
16.Tablespoons = 1 cup =80ml.
15.4 grains = = gm.
28.3 grains =1 oz.
16.oz = 1 lb. =454gms.
1kg. =2.202 lbs.

Equipment used for Herbal Preparations

1) Enamel or pyrex bowls
2) One large frying pan.
3) Measuring spoons

4) Measuring cups
5) Electric heater or manual heater
6) A good strong sieve
7) A pipette or eye dropper
8) A wool of tissue paper for wiping jars, spoons, hands etc.
9) Jars & Bottles
10) Printed/plain labels.

Cleansing Creams

Cleansing creams are used not only to lift the dust, but also to remove stale make up. Since make up has a waxy base which cannot be penetrated and cleansed simply by using soap and water thus a cleansing cream or lotion is used. The cleanser is generally applied with an upqard movement and kept on the skin for about half a minute so as to dissolve the make up and then it is removed with a tissue or damp cotton wool The dirt and grime not only dogs the pores of the skin causing block heads but also coarsens the skin.

Formulation

Bees Wax	1/2 Table spoon
Emulsifying Wax (Petrolatum)	1 Table spoon
Baby Oil	4 Table spoons
Coconut Oil	2 Table spoon
Water	2 Table spoon
Borax	1/4 Tea spoon
Witch hazel	1 Table spoon
Perfume	3-5 drops

Note:- Witch hazel is made from twigs of hamamelis or alderbush.

Process of Manufacture

The waxes and oils are mixed in an enamel bowl amd melted slowly in a pan of boiling water. In a separate bowl the water and borax are heated till the borax is completely dissolved The witch hazel is then added but the heating is not continued for long otherwise it will evaporate. When the waxes have melted both the bowls are removed from heat and mixed in water along with continuous stirring When the cooling of the cream begins the perfume is added The mixture is beaten until it begins to thicken as it cools.

Rose Water Cleansing Cream

Formulation

Beeawax or white Paraffin wax	11/2 Table spoons
Emulsifying wax (Petrolatum)	1 Table spoon
Mineral oil	4 Table spoons
Rose water	6 Table spoons
Borax	1/2 Tea spoon
Perfume	3-5 drops

Procedure

The waxes and oil are melted together and at the same time the borax and water is heated separately till it completely dissolves The heating is stopped in both bowls the borax-water contents until a white cream starts to form. A few drops of rose oil are added when the mixture begins to cool. The heating of the mixture is carried out till it thickens.

Cucumber Cleansing Cream

Formulation

Beeswax	3 Tea spoons
Coconut Oil	4 Tea spoons
Cucumber Juice	4 Table spoons
Glycerine	1 Tea spoon
Green Colourting	1 Drop

Procedure

The oils and waxes are melted the usual way over a pan of boiling water. The cucumber juice glycerine colouring and borax is heated separately in a borol ensuring that the borax dissolves thoroughly when the contents of both bowls are in molten form and warm water is added drop by drop to the oil with continuous stirring The heating is stopped and the contents of both bowls are mixed till the mixture thickens and cools. The cream is kept in a refrigeration as cucumber juice decays outside The cream is made in small letches every time.

Violet Cleansing Cream

Formulation

Lanolin	1/2 Table spoon
Petroleum Jelly	1 Table spoon
Mineral Oil	4 Table spoons
Water	10 Table spoons
Violet extract	5 drops

Procedure

The oils are heated the usual way and the water is heated separately and then mixed with constant stirring The heating is discontinued and heating of the mixture is done till it thickens and cools. It can also be used as a body lotion.

Masks

Masks have been used for beauty teatment of the face since time immemorial. They are applied on the face left on the same for ten to twenty minutes and then washed off. They provide a nourishing healing cleansing and an astringent effect These masks whip up the circulation and temporarily iron out wrinkles They freshen the skin and leave it glowing A few formulations of simple home made face masks are given as under:

Milk Mask

This is one of the cheapest and simplest masks. Cotton wool is soaked in milk and rubbed on the face and face and left to dry for 10-15 minutes and then the face is washed.

Cleansing Mask
Formulation

Powdered Brewers Yeast	1 Table spoon
Yogurt	1/2 Table spoon
Lemon Juice	1 Tea spoon
Orange Juice	1 Tea spoon
Carrot Juice	1 Tea spoon
Olive Oil	1 Tea spoon

Procedure

The above ingredients are mixed to form a paste The same is applied on the face and left for 15 minutes The mask is suitable for all types of skin. If the skin is very dry more oil is added and discarded if the skin is oily. The berwer's yeast stimulates the flow of blood to the skin and gives the complexion a healthy glow. The yogurt cleanses the skin and the fruit juices provide vitamins and minerals.

Butter Milk Mask

A cup of butter milk is heated and three table spoons of elderflower blossoms are put into it. The mixture is simered on a very low heat for about 30 minutes and then the heat is removed and allowed to cool and then used as a face mask, It helps in cleansing large pores. Both the ingredients of this mask are known for their bleaching and cleansing properties.

Meal Mask

A paste of barley meal, pea flower and rose water is applied and left on the skin for several hours to make the skin soft and supple. Another mask formulation incorporates mixing into a paste form one tablespoon each of finely ground oatmeal and milk along with a few drops of almond oil. The paste is applied on the skin and left on it for 15 minutes and then rinsed off.

Carrot and Turnip Mask

The carrot and turnip is boiled and made into a paste. This is applied for 10-15 minutes and then rinsed off with milk. This mask leaves the skin feeling fresh and clean. Carrots are rich in Vitamin. A and turnips are marvellous cleansers.

Oatmeal Mask

Dried orange peel	2 Table spoons
Oatmeal	2 Tea spoons
Cold cream	2 Table spoons

Procedure

The above ingredients are mixed into a paste and then applied generously all over face and neck. After 10 to 15 minuters when it is dry the same is rubed off using an upward circular motion. This leaves the skin smooth and shining.

Potato Mask

Potato juice	1Table spoon
Fuller's earth	1Table spoon

Procedure

The above ingerdients are mixed to form a paste and applied on the face. Potatoes contain Vit-C and clear the skin of blemishes. Fuller's rarth absorbs all the dirt and grease from the skin.

Paw Paw Mask

This is also known as Papaya Mask. Two tablespoons of ripe papaya flesh is masked and applide over a clean face and left for 10-15 minutes. Then it is rinsed with warm water. After a few days there will be a remarkable inprovement and the skin will glow with health.

Luxurious Cleansing Mask

Three straw berries are mashed into a paste and applied as a mask and then left on for 10 minutes and then washed off with rose water. Straw berries have slightly acidic properties and contain vitamin C, which cleanses the skin leaving it sparkingly clean. Another luxurious formulation consists of mashing and sieving the flesh of half a peach and then mixing it with a table spoon of brandy.

Bath Salts

Two cups of ordinary washing soda are taken and two tablespoons of potassium carbonate is added to the bath water. Baby Oil or mineral oil is not suitable as it cannot be absorbed by the skin and only remains on the skin surface. These basic oils can also be mixed with some of the herb oils or aromatic essential oil such as lavender or pine are added to the mixture and the mixture homogenised

Bath Oils

Bath oil can be prepared by adding any vegetable oil such as almond, olive or sunflower to the bath water. Baby oil or mineral oil is not suitable as it cannot be absorbed by the skin and only remains on the skin surface. These basic oils be mixed with some of the herb oils aromatic oil.

Bath Oil

Eggs	2 Nos.
Almond Oil	1/4 Cup
Sunflower Oil Corn Oil	1/4 Cup
Safflower Oil or Olive Oil	1/2 Cup
Honey	1 Tea spoon
Washing Detergent	2 Tea spoons
Vodka	1/4 Cup
Milk	1/4 Cup
Perfume	3-5 drops

Procedure

The eggs, honey the oils are blended and then the detergent is added for emulsification making the mixture thick. Beating is continued and vodka is added slowly for dispersing the bath oil. Milk is also added during the beating operation to make the oil slightly thinner and luxurious. Finally the perfume is added. This bath oil will leave the skin feeling, satiny and throughly pampered.

Holly wood Style Bubble Bath

Egg	1 No.
Shampoo	1/2 Cup
Gelatine	1 Tea spoon

Procedure

Mix the egg, shampoo and gelatine in a mixer blener and add to the bath water when the tap is running.

Bath Powder

Oatmeal Flower	3 Table spoons
Oatmeal Bran	1 Table spoons
Ground Almonds	1 Table spoons
Wheat Flour	1 Table spoon
Perfume	3-5 drops

Procedure

The abve ingredients are mixed in a jar and a small quantity is used in the bath water.

Massage Preparations

The is a special recipe for brides to be used daily at the time of bath for ten days before marriage. The following ingredients are mixed to a paste and rubbed vigorously. They cleanse and stimulate the skin leaving it soft, supple and shiny.

Dries, ground and shiny orange peel	
Dried, ground and shiny.	1 Table spoon
Dried, ground and sieved lemon peel	1 Table spoon
Ground Almond	2 Table spoons
Salt	1 Pinch
Ground Thyme	1 Table spoon
Ground all spice	1 Pinch
Almond Oil	Sufficient to make a paste.
Jasmine Oil (Perfume)	3-5 drops

Massage Paste

This consists of wheat flour or oatmeal mixed into a paste with double cream. The paste has a deep cleansing effect on the skin and removes dead cells and dirt.

Massage Cream

Lamolin	4 Table spoons
Sunflower or Safflower Oil	4 Table spoon
Rose Water	9 Table spoon

Proceduer

The oils heated and then the heated water is slowly added along with a table spoon of winter green or camphour oil to make a really invigorating massage cream.

Massage Oil

Almond oil	1/2 Cup
Castor Oil	1/2 Cup
Camphour Oil	1 Tea spoon

Body Lotions

Mix three table spoons of rose water, one table spoon of glycerine and two spoons lime juice. This mixture is used after the bath if you suffer from dry skin. The proportion of this lotion is to suit the type of skin. The lotion no longer feels sticky and mixed into the skin easily. It has to be stored in a refrigerator.

Blue Ratin Body Lotion

Soap Flakes	3 Table spoons
Glycerine	1 Tea spoon
Witch Hazel	1 Tea spoon

Olive Oil	4 Tea spoon
Water	4 Tea spoons
Blue Colouring	3-5 drops
Perfume	3-5 drops

Procedure

The soap flakes and water are heated in a saucepan till they dissolve. Then glycerine is added along with olive oil and witch hazel. Stirring is continued until the same gets cooled amd then the blue colour and perfume is added. A lovely thin creamy blue mixture thus made is an ideal non-greasy, after-bath body lotion which leaves the skin glowing like satin.

Lavender Body Lotion

Dissolve 1 teaspoon of borax in 1 cup of rose water and then add 2 tablespoon warmed oilve oil with continuous beating. When all the oil has been added to the water and an emulsion has been formed the lavender water is added. The lavender water is made by infusing a handful of lavender flowers in 2 cups of boiling water. The above mixture is allowed to stand for an hour and then strained for use.

Almond Body Lotion

Lanolin	3 Tea spoons
Almond Oil	1 Tea spoon
Petroleum Jelly	1 Tea spoon
Vegetable Lard	1 Tea spoon
Glycerine	2 Tea spoons
Water	10 Table spoons
Soap Flakes	1Tea spoon
Cornflower	1 Tea spoon
Perfume or Almond Essence	q.s.

Procedure

The water and the oils are heated separately and then mixed till the mixture becomes cool. It is then poured into a bottle and shook vigorously. Now the perfume is added.

Moisturising Creams

Almond Oil Moisturising Cream

Beeswax	2 Tea spoons
Emulsifying Wax (Petrolatum)	1 Tea spoon
Almond Oil	5 Tea spoons

Procedure

The emulsifying wax and beeswax are taken in a bowl and heated in a water bath until they melt. Then the almond oil is added. In a separate bowl the water is heated in the same water bath so that the two bowls are at the same temperature. Then the water is slowly added to the melted waxes and oils, stirring all the time. After a few minutes the heating is stopped and the stirring continued till the contents cool down. When cool a few drops of lavender oil is added.

Herb Cream (Comfrey Cream)

Lanoiln	1 Table spoon
White Emulsifying Wax	2 Table spoons
Beeswax	6 Table spoons
Almond Oil Herb Lotion	6 Table spoons
or Infusion	6 Table spoons

Procedure

The oils and waxes are melted over a water bath, cooled and stored in refrigerator. A few teaspoons of this cream is taken, melted and a teaspoon of any herb lotion or infusion of your choice is added. Comfrey is a healing herb which is ideal for the sensitive skin or for skin having irritations or spots. A handful of comfrey is taken, liquidised and then strained. The comfrey residue need not be thrown away. A tea spoon honey may be added to tablespoon of this residue to form a paste and this can be used as a face mask.

Avocado Almond Cream

Beeswax	3 Tea spoons
Emulsifying Wax (Petroleum Wax)	3Tea spoons
Almond Oil	1/2 Cup
Avocado Oil	1/4 Cup
Rose Water	3 Table spoons

Procedure

The waxes are melted in an enamel pan over a water bath. The avocado and the almond oils are then added. Now the heated rose water is added drop by drop with constant stirring. The heat is then stopped and the stirring is continued till it is cool. After cooling a few drops of the perfume is added. The avocado and almond oils are both rich for the skin.

Sun Flower Cream

Lanolin	4 Tea spoons
Emulsifyng wax petrolatum	2 Tea spoons
Beeswax	2 Tea spoons
Sunflower Oil	5 Table spoons
Water	6 Table spoons
Glycerine	2 Tea spoons
Borax	1/2 Tea spoon

Procedure

The waxes, oil and lanolin are heated over a water bath till they melt. The water, glycerine and borax are heated separately in a similar manner, till the borax gets completely dissolved. While the melted oils and waxes are still on the heat, the water is added drop by drop with continuous heating with a wooden spoon til a whitish thick and creamy textured rich cream is formed. This is a good moisturising cream leaving the skin looking soft and moist.

Jasmine Moisturising Cream

Emulsifuing Wax (Petrolatum)	2 Table spoons
Almond or Sunflower Oil	2 Table spoons
Lanolin	Tea spoon
Borax	1/2 Tea spoon
Witch Hazel	1 Tea spoon
Glycerine	1/2 Tea spoon
Water	8 Table spoon
Jasmine Oil	3-5 drops

Procedure

The wax, oil and lanolin are heated over a water batch till they melt. In a separate bowl the water, glycerine and borax are heated till the borax gets completely dissolved and then the witch hazel is added. Water is added drop by drop to the oils and stirring continued until cool. A few drops of Jasmine oil are added. This non-greasy cream is suitable for normal and greasy skins.

Mourishing Creams

Preparations of this type include all skin nutrients whether they are oil based or of the moisturizing type. They may be light and immediately absorbed or heavy and sticky reqiring to be managed into the skin. The nourishing creams comprise of Hormone creams and lotions, vitamin products, screen ampoules, antiwrinkle creams and lotions, and biologically active preparations. A few formulations of nourishing creams are given as under:-

Cocoa Butter	2 Table spoons
Emulsifying Wax (Petroleum Wax)	2 Table spoons
Beeswax	1 Table spoons
Sesame Oil	4 Table spoons
Almond Oil	1 Table spoons

Procedure

All the above ingredients are taken in a bowl and heated in a water bath till they melt. Stirring is continued for homogenisation. The heating is then stopped and the mixture stirred. This cream leaves the skin smooth without being greasy. If waxes are not easily available two tablespoons of almond oil (or safflower or sesame oil) are melted in a water bath. This cream is really good for dry skin and neglected areas such as elbows, feet and neck. In case the cream has to be applied on as oily skin 2 tablespoon of rosewater (or ordinary soft water) is added

Elder Flower Cream

Almond Oil	3 Table spoons
Elder Flower Blossoms	4 Table spoons
Lanolin	1 Table spoon

Procedure

The above ingredients are mixedd togetther in a bowl over a water bath and allowed to simmer together for an hour. It is then strained and then warm water is added slowly with constantt stirring.

Wheatt Germ Cream

Beeswax	1 Tea spoon
Emulsifying Wax (Petrolatum)	1 Tea spoon
Lanolin	5 Table spoons
Sesame Oil	3 Table spoons
Wheat Germ Oil	2 Table spoons
Water	5 Table spoons
Witch Hazel	1 Table spoons
Borax	1/2 Tea spoons
Perfume	3-5 drops

Procedure

The waxes an oils are melted over a water bath The water and borax are heated separately in the water bath till the borax gets completely dissolved. Now the borax-water mixture is added slowly to the melted oils and waxes. Stirring is continued until a glossy nourishing cream is ready. Lanolin and wheat germ oil both conain vitamin-E.

Honey Cream

Honey is a very useful ingredient creams used for dry. coarse and senistive skin. For a nourishing honey cream for shallow skin 3 tables spoons of lanolin alongwith 1/2 table spoon honey and 1 tea spoon of lecithin are taken in a bowl and melted in a water bath Warm water is added of the above very sloely with continuous heating to the extent of 4 table spoons. Beating is done until the mixture cools.

Vitamin Cream

Beeswax	1 Table spoon
Emulsifying Wax	1 Table spoon
Lanolin	1 Table spoon

Wheat Germ Oil (vitamin-E Capsules 2 No)	3 Table spoons
Carrot Oil (or Vit-A Capsules -2 Nos)	3 Table spoons
Borax	1/2 Tea spoons
Distilled Water	6 Table spoon
Tincture of Benzoin	6 Table spoons
Orange-Flower Oil	3-5 drops

Procedure

The waxes and oils are heated in a bowl over a water bath and at the same time in a separate bowl the borax is dissolved in warm water. Both the bowls are maintained at the same temperature of the water bath for some time and then the water is quickly added to the oils and heating continued until the mixture cools down Then the tinure of benzoin is added and the beating is continued until a thick nourishing cream is formed When the mixing of vitamin capsules is done the capsules are pricked open and contents poured in.

Mixed Vegetable Cream

Beeswax	2 Table spoons
Emulsifying Wax (Petrolatum)	4 Table spoons
Lanolin	3 Table spoons
Almond Oil	4 Table spoons
Sesame Oil	Table spoons
Avocado Oil	2 Table spoons
Safflower Oil	2 Table spoons
Sun Flower Oil	2 Table spoons
Water	5 Table spoons
Borax	1/2 Tea spoons
Amber Oil	3-5 drops

Procedure

The waxes and the oils are mixed in a bowl and heated in a water bath. The borax is disaolved separately is warm water.

26

HAIR SHAMPOOS

Introduction

A shampoo may be defined as the preparation of surfaceactive materials which when used will remove surface grease, dirt and skin debris from the hair and scalp without affecting adversely the hair, scalp or health of the user. Apart from the cleansing action it must leave the hair fragrant lustrous, soft and manageable. Hence unlike the detergent cakes, a shampoo is not only a detergent but a cosmetic as well.

Generally shampoos are cleansing water solutions or suspensions of cleansing agents mixed with such ingredients which may improve the performance. Synthetic detergents are more effective and soaps have no place in good quality shampoos.

Functions of a Shampoo

A good shampoo, therefore, required to have the following properties:-

(1) It should remove dirt grease and skin debris from the hair and scalp.

(2) It should give adequate foam in both hard and soft water.

(3) It should be pleasantly perfumed.

(4) It should be easily washable, and

(5) It should leave the hair in soft, lustrous and easily manageable condition.

(6) It must be non iretating and should not permanently damage the sensitive eye tissue in case of accidental occurrence in eye.

Types of Shampoos

The shampoos may be made in any suitable form viz liquid solid or powder. Some of the common type or shampoos are liquid clear shampoos, liquid cream or cream lotion shampoos cream paste shampoos big shampoos herbal shampoos dry shampoos liquid dry shampoos, colour shampoos and aerosol shampoos.

Modern shampoos are based on sulphated fatty alcohols and sulphonated fatty alcohol ethers. Triethanolamine lauryl sulphate is a brown transparent viscous lipuid and is the most widely accepted cleansing agent used in shampoos. Sodium lauryl sulphate is a powder highly solufle in water and is a good emulsifier, it may also be obtained as a paste Monoethamolamine lauryl sulphate is similar to triethanolamine lauryl sulphate and its viscosity can be increased by adding sodium chloride. Turkey red oil or sulphated castor oil is a viscous water miscible liquid having good detergent and emulsifying properties.

A Clear Liquid Shampoos:- These are relatively straight forward water solutions of one or more shampoo detergents or soap together with other ingredients. In a clear liquid shampoo it is important that the base detergents or soap have good water solubility and a relativey low cloud point. Solubilizing agents are sometimes used to improve and maintain clarity and to aid the solubility of various additives. Thickners, such as alkytolmides, are usually employed to increase viscosity.

B Baby Shampoos:- These are based upon detergents which provide the so called no eye sting feature. The imidazoline-type (cycloimidium type) amphoteric detergent has been recommended for this purpose. Unique sulphosuccinic acid esters have also been suggested.

C Medicated Dandruff Shampoos:- These are recommended for the control of and correction of dandruff. Today a large number of medicated dandruff shampoos enjoy a reputation for appreciable effectiveness. One such product obtainable only by prescription is a shampoo in the form of 2.5% suspension of selenium disulphide in a detergent base. Another contains Zinc Puridinethine (Zinc-2-pyridinethiol 1-oxide.) as the base detergent. A wide range and assortment of other antidandruff ingredients are used in shampoo. These include lacteristatic compounds such as hexachlorophene, heavy metals such as cadmium sulphide and tellurium oxide, hydroxy quinolines, liphanamine hydrochloride (2-diethylamino) ethyl 2-hydroxy-3-bi-phenyl carvoxylate hydrochloride), a poly vinyl pyrrolidone-iodene compoex quatrrused polytyionatis allantoin and many others.

D Soap shampoos :- Soap offers an appreciable advanvtage over synthetic detergents in respect to the manageability and conition of the hair following shampooing. Modern soap shampoos are generally based upon alkano amine soaps rather than the soda or potash soaps that were once used. The alkanolamine soaps are prepared by reacting the amine with the appropriate fatty acid. In the perparation of soap based shampoos generally mono or triethanolamine is reacted with a mixture of coconut fatty acid and oleic acid Solubilizing-coupling agents are included to achieve and maintain clarity.

E Solid Shampoos:- These shampoos consist of either detergent or soap pressed into a bar form or tablet shape. In another type the detergent is dried or pressed as a thin sheet or leaf.

F) Liquid Cream or Lotion Shampoos:- These are opaque viscous liquid shampoos which have the appearance of cosmetic skin lotions. These are not truly emulsions but contain generous concentrations of suspended opacifiers such as glycol stearates. Less soluble detergents procesing a high point are generally used in this type of product and relatively heavy viscosities are usually required to maintain a long-term suspension of the opacifiers.

G Powder Shampoos:- These are of two types. The first is the powdered detergent which is dissolved in water before use. The second is the so called dry shampoos consisting of mixtures of oil absorbing powders such as fullers earth, starch, kaolin, talc and the like. This product is simply spread through the hair and then brushed out after it has absorbed the surface oil from the hair.

H Jelly Type (Gel) Shampoos:- These are very similar to clear liquids but tend to be more concentrated. Heavy visciosity is generally achieved by using relatively high concentrations of alkylamide, soap or synthetic gum.

I Cream or Paste Shampoos:- These are similar to liquid cream products except that they have a firm pastelike consistency which is achieved by incorporating relatively insoluble faty ingredients such as sodium stearate and using certain liquids which serve to salt out some of the basic ingredients. In such products less soluble detergents are employed.

Additives used in Shampoos

To get a good shampoo it is necessary to add certain additives to basic detergents to impart certain good properties. Alkyl amides are used to increase stability of lather and control of viscosity. Additives such as lanolin or egg powder are claimed to give lustre and make the hair manageable. Opacifiers like spermaceti common salt magnesium stearate and magnesium silicate etc. are used. To get clear shampoo, some additives are used such as butyl alcohol, isopropyl alcohol, ethyl alcohol yerpineol, pine oil, diethulene glycol STPP and TSP Protecine shampoos contain hygroscopic materials mainly amino acids. Glycerol, propylene glycol sorbitol and urea help to retain moisture thus keeping the hair soft; this conditions the hair. All such additives are categorised and discussed as under.

1 Opacifiers:- These are used to make shampoos opaque. They are usually waxy materials which are relatively insoluble but readily dispersible in the shampoo. It is important that they should not have any detrimental effect on shampoo properties such as lather formation. Some opacifiers solidify or crystallize in such a manner that they give the product a shimmering pearlescent effect. Generally, esters such as glycol and glyceryl stearates, are used. Higher alcohols such as stearyl and cetyl alcohol, stearate soaps, and waxy alkylomides, such as stearic amides also find application.

2 Solufilizers:- These are ingerdients used to clear shampoos. They are used to solubilize poorly soluble ingredients such as perfume oils, preservatives, and bacteriostatic alcohol, have been used for this purpose as ether. Surfactants with hydrotropic properties are also used as solubilizers.

3 Thickners:- These are used to increase the viscosity of the shan poo preparations and provide the desired consistency in gel and cream form. The alkyloamides are generally used. In case of shampoos based on sodium lauryl sulphate the addition of inorganic saits increases the viscosity of the liquid product and hardens the consistency of cream

shampoos. It has been noted however that too much of the electrolyte causes softening. Sodium stearte and stearic amides are excellent thickners for cream type shampoos through poly vinyl alcohol, methylcellulose and sodium alginate have also been used in formulations.

4 Conditioning Agents:- These are substances used to improve the manageafility and the texture of the hair. Various oils, fatty alcohols, glycol esters humectants and protein derivatives are used. TO improve lanolin is used extensively as hair conditioner and is important ingredient of cream and liquid cream shampoos. Lanolin oil and derivatives of lanolin have also been recommended and been the subject of considerable investigation. The selection of the base ingredient is an important factor in hair conditioning. There are several types of surfactants including alkyloamides, fatty amine oxides, fatty acid peptide condensates and cationic anionic complexes are considered to contribute to hair conditioning.

Preservatives

These are mecessary ingredients of shampoos based on surfactants since these producers are capable of inhibiting mould and bacteria growth. The preservatives generally used are methyl and propyl parabens such as para-hydroxy benzoates and parachlorametacresol. Formaldehyde and dehydracetic acid salts have also been recommended. Phenyl mercuric salts are used in very dilute concentrations wherever regulations permit the use of such components.

Surfaceactive Agents (Detergents)

The most important synthetic detergents used in shampoo are the anionic - fatty alkyl sulphates. The primary alkyl sulphates the detergent work horses of the shampoo industry. They are generally esters fatty alcohols made by sulphation with chlorosulfuric acid or sulphuric acid. The alcohols are usually prepared by the catalytic hydrogenation or by sodium reduction of the corresponding fatty acids. The primary alkyl sulphate which is generally used in shampoos is the so called lauryl sulphate which contains a mixture of C10 to C18 compounds with C12 compound predominating. Various salts of lauryl sulphate are available including sodium, potassium, calcium, zinc, ammonium, maganesium as well as mono, di, and triethanolamine. The lauryl sulphates are generally sold as paste or as water solution. Those with metallic cations are generally offered as 30% active water solutions or in the form pastes containing upto 2.5% free alcohol and 1-1.5% of the inorganic salt. The alkanolamine salts will contain more active ingerdient on a total solid basis because of the much larger cation but actually no more on a fat autent basis. The various salts vary drastically in their properties particularly in respect to colour, coludpoint and viscosity. The viscosity of the sodium salt is especially affected by the inorganic salt content. Since there is some danter of hydrolysis, the fatty alkyl sulphate is generally buffered on the alkaline side by the manufacturer. The concentrations lauryl sulphate in the shampoos generally ranges from about 7 to 15% on an anhydrous basis. Osco process alcohols produced by the oxidation of paraffins are also sulphated and find some applications in shampoo. Tridecyl alcohol sulphated is also used in shampoos as its properties are similar to lauryl sulphates.

Liquid silicones also contribute to foam stability, gloss and setting properties. To finish the bacteria of the scalp, certain antibacterials like chlorosaicylamilide, thymol, bacitracin and hexachlorophene are added.

Various Formulations

(Sulphonated Oil-Soap Less Shampoos)

		Percent
1)	Sulphonated olive oil	16.0
	Sulphonated castor oil	16.0
	Water	68.0
	Colour	q.s.
	Perfume	q.s.
2)	Sulphonated castor oil	77
	Mineral oil light grade	3
	Olecyl alcohol	3
	Water (Distilled) 14	

Formulations(Coconut Oil Shampoo)

		Percent
1)	Coconut oil	16
	Potassium Hydroxide 85%	4
	Water	80

2)	Coconut oil	37
	Potassium hydroxide	29
	Water	5.0
	Glycerol	29
	Perfume	q.s.

		Percent
3)	Coconut oil	21
	Potassium hydroxide	4.1
	Water	54
	Perfume	0.5
	Olive oil	3
	Sodium hydroxide	1.9
	Ethyl alcohol	15
	Ethylene diamine tetra acetic acid	0.5

		Percent
4)	Coconut oil	7.0
	Potassium hydroxide	1.1
	Water	68.7
	Perfume	1.0
	Olive oil	9.9
	Sodium hydroxide	95% 4.4
	Ethylacohol	2.8
	Palm oil	5.1

		Percent
5)	Coconut oil	20
	Potassium hydroxide	4.1
	Water	1.0
	Perfume	4.0
	Olive oil	1.9
	Sodium hydroxide	1.9
	Ethyl alcohol	15

		Percent
6)	Coconut oil	14.0
	Potassium hydroxide	6.0
	Water	57.0
	Glycerol	11.5
	Perfume	0.5
	Sodium hydroxide	95% 0.5

Formulation (Vegetable Oil Shampoos)

1)	Coconut	15
	Palm oil	5
	Potassium hydroxide	90% 3
	Sodium hydroxide	1.0
	Ethyl alcohol	7
	Water	69

		Percent
2)	Coconut oil	7.0
	Potassium hydroxide 90% (to make pH 9.0)	q.s.
	Stearic acid	14
	Glycerol	2
	Perfume	0.5
	Sodium lauryl sulphate	3
	Water (to make 10 parts)	q.s.

		Percent
3)	Potassium hydroxide	14.5
	Ethyl alcohol	37.0
	Perfume	6.0
	Corn oil	34
	Sodium lauryl sulphate	8.5

Formulations for Powder Shampoos

Powder shampoos are not very common. These are made by mixing diluent or extrueder with soap powder. Diluents commonly used are sodium cardonate sodium sesquicarbonate disodium phosphate or borax.

Formulation No.1

Sodium bicarbonate	500 parts
Disoium phosphate	200 parts

Perfume 0.5% of the formulate batch may be added.

Formulations No.2

Henno powder	5
Borax	15
Sodium carbonate	25
Potassium carbonate	5
Soap powder	50

In addition perfume may be added upto 0.5% of the mass of the formulation.

Formulation for Shampoo Pastes and Creams

These shampoos are based on sodium and alkyl sulphates and are more viscous than liquid.

Formulation No.1

Sodium lauryl sulphate	400 parts
Cetyl alcohol	75 parts
Distilled water	525 parts

An alkylomide such as coconut diethanolamide in 1 to 2% is added as stabilizer.

Formulation No.2

Sodium lauryl sulphate	450 parts
Cetyl alcohol	50 parts
Distilled water	500 parts

Process of Manufacture

The detergent is heated together with water at about 80 ^{0}C in steam-jacketed pan fitted with a stirrer. The cetyl alcohol (wax) is added and stirring continued for 15 minutes. The mix is allowed to cool to 40-45 ^{0}C. Any perfume and colour is then added and stirring is continued until the mix is uniform.

Formulation No.3

	% by weight
Sodium lauryl sulphate (Paste)	25
Stearic acid	6.5
Lanolin	0.25
Caustic soda	1.0
Cetyl alcohol	0.5
Water	67.25

Process of Manufacture

Stearic acid sodium lauryl sulphate and lanolin are heated with 80% water to 80 ^{0}C and stirred until homogenous. Caustic soda and remainder of the water are also heated and this solution is added to the previous one with stirring colour and perfume are added after cooling the mass to 40 ^{0}C

Formulation 4

	% by weight
Sodium lauryl sulphate paste	25
Diethylene glycol monostearate	2
Sodium hydroxide	0.75
Stearic acid	5
Water	67.25

Process of Manufacture

Sodium hydroxide is dissolved in water and heated to 70 C. The other ingredients are heated to 70 C and added to the caustic solution. After cooling colour perfume and preservative are added. In addition coconut diethanolamide or lauric propanolamide in concentration of about 1 to 2% is added as foam stabilizer.

Formulation No.5

	% by weight
Sodium alginate	16
Sodium lauryl sulphate paste	30
Sodium chloride	4
Water	50

Process of Manufacture

The sodium alginate is dissolved in water and heated to 70 ^{0}C Sodium chloride is mixed with sulphonated lauryl sulphate paste and mix it with water solution while stirring. The mass is cooled to 40 ^{0}C and perfume and colour are added.

Formulation for Liquid Creams or Lotion Shampoos

Liquid creams or lotion shampoos are made from fatty alcohol sulphate pastes or from clear liquid detergents by mixing with suitable stabilizing and opacifying agent. Liquid creams are based for a large number of shampoos. Egg lanolin lemon protein brandy strawberry etc. are sometimes added and the resulting product is known with the name of the additive used such as egg shampoo lemon shampoo etc. These have less cleansing powder and thus the shampoo becomes wider in action. A few formulatiions on these bases are given below.

Formulation No.1 (Thick Pearly Cream)

	% by weight
Fatty alcohol sulphate paste	50
Sodium chloride	0.3
Water	49.7

Process of Manufacture

Sodium chloride is first dissolved in water and added slowly to the paste with continuous washing.

Formulation No.2 (Pearly Cream)

	Percent
Triethanolamine lauryl sulphate	45
Coconut monoethanolamide	2
Water	53

Process of Manufacture

First two items are heated to about 65 ^{0}C water and preservative are also added to 65 C. Both the solutions are mixed together and cooled. Perfume is then added.

Formulation No.3 (Rich Foam Cream)

	Percent
Monoethanolamine lauryl sulphate	40
Lauric isopropanolamide	1.5
Ethylene glycol monostearate	5
Water	53.5

Formulation for Specific Shampoos

(1)Egg Shampoo	% by weight
Fatty Alcohol sulphate Paste	27.5
Lauric isopropanolamide	1
Ethylene glycol monostearate	3
Egg powder	0.25
Water	68.25

Process of Manufacture

A paste is made by adding water or glycerine into egg powder and then it is dilute with detergent. The other ingredients are then mixed separately and then with the paste.

(2) Anti Dandruff Shampoos

To prevent and cure dandruff from the hair medicated shampoo are used. A typical formulation of such an anti dandruff shampoo is given below :-

Thymol	0.5 parte
Menthol	0.2 parte
Camphor	0.2 parte
Triethanolamine lauryl sulphate	100 parte
Water	89.5 parte

Process of Manufacture

Thymol camphor and menthol are mixed together. Perfume oils are added and mixed with a small quantity of the detergent. Detergent is added with continuous and gentle stirring. Water is finally added to adjust the thickness of the shampoo.

Formulation for Anti Bactreia Shampoo

Antibacterial Shampoo

	%
Cetrimide	17.5
Alcohol	10
Diethyl phthalate	2
Water	70.5

Process of Manufacture

Cetrimide is dissolved in water using gentle heating. It is cooled to 35 ^{0}C. A mixture of diethyl phthalate and alcohol is then made separately. This mixture is then added slowly to the previous solution. Perfume is finally added and the mass is stirred gently until a homogenous mass is obtained.

Antiseptic Shampoo

Precipitated sulphur is used as a mild antiseptic and parasiticide. Salicylic acid is also used as a bacterostatic and fungicide. Both are used in the concentration of 2%. A typical formulation is :-

	% by weight
Sodium lauryl sulphate	25
Stearic acid	7
Sodium hydroxide	1
Very fine sulphur powder	2
Distilled water	65

Process of Manufacture

Sodium hydroxide is dissolved in water and heated to 75 ^{0}C. Sulphur powder is then made in a pulverizer and added to sodium hydroxide solution. Stearic acid and sodium lauryl sulphate paste are then mixed together and heated to 60 ^{0}C. This mixture is then added to the aqueous solution with stirring. Perfume and preservatives are finally added.

Clinium Type Shampoo

Selenium sulphide a bright orange powder is a modern material used in shampoos for anti dandruff purpose. It also destroys bacterias. It is insoluble in water and hence should be mixed with a suitable inert diluent before mixing with the surface active agent.

The Formulation is	% by Weight
Selenium disulphide	2.5
Bentonite	5
Sodium lauryl sulphate (paste)	40
Water	52.5

Process of Manufacture

Selenium disulphide and bentonite are mixed properly. Sodium lauryl sulphate and water are heated to 90 ^{0}C with stirring. Small amount of this solution is added carefully to the previous mixture and mixed with stirring until homogeneous. This is added to the main solution with stirring. It is cooled to 40-45 ^{0}C and prefume etc. are added in it. If a firmer cream is desired 0.5 to 1.5% cetyl alcohol is also incorporated in the formulation.

Formulation for Hair Rinses

Cream form	
Triton X-400 Concentrate (Stearyldimethyl	%
Benzyle-ammonium chloride)	2.3
Cetyl alcohol	0.3
Potassium chloride	0.8
Water	96.6

Note:- Triton X-400 is available as stearalkonium chloride.

The pH. of the formulation is 4.4 These rinses should be diluted for use at the rate of 11b Sp. to 802 of water. Heat approximately 1/2 of the water to 180 ^{0}F. Add the cetyl alchol and stir slowly until molten. Use slow speed agitation during the entire manufacturing process. Care should be taken to prevent the incorporation of air into the product.

Heat the triton x-400 to 170 ^{0}F and add to the water slowly. Then reduce the temperature of the mixture to 170 ^{0}F and add to the water slowly for at least 1/2 hour to ensure uniformity and maximum emulsion stability. reduce the temperature further 120 ^{0}F. Dissolive the potassium chloride in the balance of the water and heat to 120F. Then slowly add this solution to the triton X-400 cetyl alcohol emulsion. Remove the heat source and agitate the baten slowly for an additional hour, or until the mixture gels. Colouring agents and perfumes solubilized in triton X-100 may then be added.

27

ANTI DANDRUFF PREPARATIONS

Introduction

Dandruff or scaly disease of the scalp exists when the continuous but normally imperceptible sloughing of the outer epidermal layers of the skin becomes grossly visible. The dandruff consists of desquamated epidermal cells plus accumulated sechetion and acquired soil. Any disturbance in the balance established between the constant production of new cells and the rate of sloughing of the old may lead to the visilbe masses of epidermal cellular debris called dandruff. Another factor which greatly influences the production of dandruff of visible scale is the amount and quality of emolliency or ebum secretion.

A product which clears tne scalp press it of adherent debris and regulates the amount of residual scalp and hair oils to retain healthful scalp conditions is an antidandruff preparation.

All properly formulated shampoos as well as most of the non medicated hair lotions or grooming agents fall into this group. The ideal shampoo should clean both the scalp and hair without irritating the epithelium or causing excessive reduction of the natural oils. The modern shampoo preparation may be an antidandruff product not only because it removes scale and oil debris but also because it destroys bacteria.

Formulations

1. Selsum type Suspension Antidandruff Preparation

	%
Selenium disulfide	2.5
Surfactant	17
Inert stabilizer	5.2
Water	75.3

2. Cosmetic Scalp Lotion	%
Liquid paraffin	99
Perfume	1
Colour	q.s

3. Emulsified preparation	%
Mineral oil	38
Fatty acid compound	4-5
Gluceryl monostearate (Tegacid)	3-4
Fatty acid derivatives	4-5
Fatty alcohol	4-5
Water to make	100
Perfume and colour	q.s

4. Alcoholic Preparation	%
Castor oil	18
Ethyl alcohol 90%	82
Perfume	q.s
Colour	q.s

5. Alcoholic Complex Preparation	%
Castor oil	15
Tincture of Benzoin	2
Ethyl alcohol SD 40	83
Perfume & Colour	q.s

6. Emulsified Preparation

Part A:-	%
Petrolatum	6.0
Mineral oil	37.5
Lanolin	3.0
Beeswax	12
Arlacel 83	3.0
Arlacel 20	1.0
Tween 20	2.0

Part B:-

Borax	0.5
Water	35
Preservative	q.s
Perfume	q.s

Process of Manufacture

Heat A to 70 ^{0}C and B to 75 ^{0}C. Add B to A slowly, with agitation. Add perfume at 45 ^{0}C. Stir untill cool.

Quality Control Aspects

The product should be preserved from oxidation (resulting in rancidity) from potency deterioration and from mold and fungus growth. It is still difficult to use the many desirable unsaturated natural fats and oils because of their tendency to decompose. Due to this, formulations are limited to the more stable vegetable oils, the fully saturated hydrocarbons, and the animal lipid substance, lanolin. The formualtions in future will undoubtedly contain natural unsaturates stabilised with antioxidants of the food presevative type. The potency of the product is to be maintained inspite of addition of germistatic antidandruff agent. Except where attepts are made to use them in conjunction with emulsifier and stabilizers with which they are chemically incompatible. The quaternaries do not retain their full potency in the presence of soaps and anionic detergents.

Another manufacturing problem is that of avoiding the use of agents which are or will become toxic to the skin. Formerly the perfume used in the preparation was the greatest offender, followed by therapeutic agents but today we not only have these reactions to contend with but also a host of new ones due to the addition of emulsifiers, stabilizers, preservatives, antioxidants, and synthetic germicidal agents to the formulation. It is therefore customary to retain maximum simplicity consistent with cosmetic elegance and practical usefulness.

HAIR - GROOMING PREPARATIONS - 3

Introduction

Hair-grooming preparations are used to give in hair a natural and healthy appearance. Hair dressings of one type or another have had a popular appeal for men and women throughout the ages. Most of the products formerly used were home-made, being derived from special recipes. These were commonly wines, herbs, animal and plant by products. Improvements were constantly being made and newer products are being introduced frequently. The need for hair dressings appears to be constantly increasing. Hair not only acts as a protective covering for the head but is also an attractive feature of both men and women. Both of these factors- protection and attraction-are best-accomplished by healthy hair is a measure of its health and of the efficiency with which it accomplishes its taste.

Characteristics of a Good Hair Dressing:-

Hair - dressing preparations are used for protection and attraction of hair. A good hair dressing preparation should have the following characteristics-

(1) Good grooming

(2) Luster wihout greasiness

(3) Protection from the elements

(4) Some degree of hair conditioning

(5) Good wetting action

(6) Should leave a uniformaly thin film

(7) Dandruff control.

Classification of Hair-Dressings

The hair dressings preparations can be divided into 7 groups viz.

1. Alcholic lotions

2. Brilliatines

3. Gum-base hair dressings

4. Hair Tonics

5. Oil-in-water emulsion

6. Two, layer systems

7. Water-in-oil emulsions

Alcoholic Lotions

Alcoholic lotions have been quite popular as hair dressings. These are made by diluting viscous oils with alcohol. This lotion when applied leaves a uniform thin layer of oil after the evaporation of the alcohol. It gives good wetting action.

Formulations for Alcoholic lotions

Formula No.1

	% by weight
Ethyl Alcohol	50
Castor oil	50
Colour & Perfume	q.s.

Formula No.2

	% by weight
Ethyl alcohol	80
Castor oil	20
Colour & Perfume	q.s.

Formula No.3

	% by weight
Ethyl alcohol	60
Castor oil	10
Glycerol	30
Colour & Perfume	q.s.

Formula No. 4

	% by weight
Ethyl alcohol	83
Castor oil	15
Tincture of benzoin	2
Colour & Perfume	q.s.

Process of Manufacture (For Formula No. 1 to 4)

The ingredients are mixed well at room temperature and filtered bright. The raw materials used should be of purest grade. The perfume is added dissolving it in a solvent.

Formula No. 5

	% by weight
Isopropyl myristate	5
Glycerol	5
Ethyl alcohol	90
Colour & Perfume	q.s.

Formula No. 6

	% by weight
Glycerol	40
Ethyl alcohol	40
Water	20
Colour & Perfume	q.s.

Formula No.7

	% by weight
Ethyl alcohol	96
Oleic acid	4
Colour & Perfume	q.s.

Attempts have been made to solubilize other oils in alcohol. Such a preparation is described in a patent in which solubilizing of deodorized kerosene is done. The formulation is given as under:-

Formula No. 8

	Percent
Ethyl alcohol	54
Olive oil	19
Kerosene	27
Colour & Perfume	q.s.

Brilliantines

The main pupose of a brilliantine is to add a measure of grooming and to afford a sheen to the hair. Mineral oil and deodorized kerosene are usuall formulated in the brilliantines preparation. There are two types of brilliantines viz.

(1) Liquid brilliantine viz.
(2) Solid brilliantines

Liquid Brilliantines

Liquid brilliantines result in easier spreading and penetration, and after evaporation of the volatile deodorized kerosene, the deposition of a thin, uniform layer of a various oil which does a good grooming job and imparts a high gloss to the hair.

Formulations for Liquid Brilliantines of Manufacture

Formula No. 1

Mineral oil, light	100%
Colour & Perfume	q.s.

Formula No. 2

	% by weight
Mineral oil, light	75
Deodorized kerosene	25
Colour & Perfume	q.s.

Process of Manufacture (For Formula No. 1 & 2)

Mix the ingredients thoroughly and filter the solution.

Formula No. 3

	% by weight
Castor oil	80
Almond oil	20
Colour & Perfume	q.s.

Formula No.4

	% by weight
Castor oil	6
Almond oil	49
Olive oil	45
Colour & Perfume	q.s.

Formula No. 5

	% by weight
Castor oil	15
Deodorized kerosene	85
Colour & Perfume	q.s.

Process of Manufacture (For Formula No. 3 to 5)

All ingredients are mixed thoroughly to dissolve the colour and perfume. It is then filtered bright.

Formula No. 6

	% by weight
Mineral oil	80
Peanut oil	34
Colour & Perfume	q.s.

Formula No. 7

	% by weight
Mineral oil	80
Almond oil	10
Castor oil	10
Colour & Perfume	q.s.

Process of Manufacture (For Formula No. 6 and 7)

The ingredients are mixed thoroughly and then filtered bright.

Formulations for Solid Brilliantines

Solid brilliantines are best suited for unruly or pinky hair which has to be forcibly held in place and are very popular for use on closely cropped hair. These are usually vegetable or mineral oil, which have been stiffened to the desired consistency with the aid of certain waxes.

Formula No. 1	% by weight
Stearic acid	23
Mineral oil	77
Colour & Perfume	q.s.

Process of Manufacture

First of all melt the two ingredients together at 60 to 70 ^{0}C and add colour and perfume. Fill the hot melt a marbled product which crumbles at the touch.

Formula No. 2

	% by weight
Paraffin wax	15
Mineral oil	25
Petolatum	60
Colour & Perfume	q.s.

Formula No. 3

	% by weight
Paraffin wax	20
Mineral oil	50
Petrolatum	30
Colour & Perfume	q.s.

Formula No. 4

	% by weight
Mineral oil	86
Spermaceti	10

Beeswax	4
Colour & Perfume	q.s.

Formula No. 5

	% by weight
Mineral oil	70
Spermaceti	5
Paraffin wax	15
Stearic acid	10
Colour & Perfume	q.s.

Process of Manufacture

Melt all the ingredients at the lowest temperature. As the cooling occurs, perfume is added into it and the material is run into warmed jars. Allow to cool slowly, until completely solidify.

Gum Base Hair Dressings

A hair dressings which almost approaches a wave set in its action can be based on any of the available gums. These preparations do not impart much sheen to the hair but they hold unruly strands in place for long periods and are excellent for fixing the hair of children. A variety of natural and synthetic gums are used in such preparations. Gum tragacanth and karaya are used most often although quince seed mucilage is preferred by some. Pectins such as Irish moss, gum arabic, gelatin, flax seed, mucilage, and water soluble shellac.

Hair dressings based on gums vary from 0.5 to 2 percent in gum content depending upon the type of gum and on the viscosity desired. When applied to the hair, the products based on the gums will gradually dry out leaving a continuous and more or less flexible film which holds the hair in place. Polyvinyl alcohols, polyethylene glycols (such as the carbowaxes, soluble starches and abietic. Esters are other basic ingredients which can be and have been used to prepare mucilaginous hair dressings. Perfumes for gum base hair dressings should be chosen with care since of them will cause the product to discolour with age.

Formulation for Gum Base Hair Dressing

	1	2	3
Gum Karya	-	-	2
Gum Tragacanth	1.2	1.0	-
Ethyl Alcohol	15	6.0	5
Glycerol	2.0	1.0	-
Castor Oil	-	2.0	-
Water	81.8	90.0	93.0
Preservative	q.s.	q.s.	q.s.
Perfume & Colour	q.s.	q.s.	q.s.

Procedure

The gum is first welled with the alcohol and stirred slowly to expel the air. The glycerol preservative, castor oil and perfume is added and then the water is added all at once. Stirring is continued until all the gum is dispersed uniformly and then it is filtered or strained and allowed to reach its maximum viscosity upon standing for a few hours The addition of castor oil aids in plasticizing the gum film and prevents dulness.

Formulation for Gum Based Cream Hair Dressing

	Percent
Gum tragacanth Powdered	1.0
Isopropyl alcohol	2.0
Glycerol	4.0
Mineral oil, heavy	1.8
Water	91.0
Formalin	0.2
Perfume & Colour	q.s.

Procedure

The powdered tragacanth is mixed with alcohol and then the glycerol, perfume and the mineral oil is added along with all the water. The mixture is stirred well untill the dispersion is complete and then allowed to stand for several hours to thicken up before straining. The appearance of the product can be improved by parsing it through a homogeniser

Formulations for Gum-Base Hair-Dressings

	Percent 4	Percent 5
Sodium Alginate	1.25	1.5
Glycerol	2.5	3.0
Calcium Citrate	0.10	0.3
Distilled water	96.15	86.2
Tincture of Benzoin	-	40
Balsam Peru	-	5.0
Preservative	q.s.	q.s.
Colour & Perfume	q.s.	q.s.

Procedure

The sodium alginate is added to half of the water and then glycerol and perfume is added. The mixture is then stirred well to dissolve. The calcium citrate is dissolved separately in the remainder of the water. When the alginate solution is smooth the calcium solution is poured in. The mixture is stirred well and allowed to 'body up' by standing for few hours. The glycerol can be increased by adding more calcium citrate or citric acid.

Hair Tonics

Hair tonics have generally been used for specific pupose of curing baldness, releiving oily or dry scalp and preventing or curing dandruff. These contain a combination of atleast two of the three igredients of a hair tonic such as a sebaceous-gland stimulant, a rubefacient and an antiseptic. The rubefacients commonly used include chloral hydrate (2-4%), formic acid spirits (10-20%), quinine and its salts (0.1 to 1.0%), tincture of cantharides (1 to 50%), tincture of cinchona (1 to 10%), and such tars as cade, pine, and birch 0.1 to 1.0%. Most of the antiseptics used are of phenolic character, although quinine, salicylic, formaldehyde, and ethyl or isopropyl alcohol will also contribute an antiseptic. Antiseptics are added in the formulation to the extent of less than 1% except for resorcinol which can be used to the extent of 5%. Among the various materials used to stimulate the sebaceous glands are the following: Quinine and its salts, tincture of Jaborandi leaves or Pilocarpine, resorcinal and resorcinol monoacetate cholesterol, salicylic acid, ethyl alcohol, methyl linoleate, sulphur and lecithin. Quinine and pilocarpine when adminstered internally are believed to be able to stimulate hair growth.

Formulations

The formulation presented are roughly divided into those intended to retard loss of hair, those to control dandruff and allivate oily scalp and those designated for dry scalp. Bay rum is very popular item and still is often used as the vehicle for some of the drugs and antiseptics.

Bay Rum Hair Tonics

	Percent
1. Jamaica rum	12
Ethyl alcohol	45
Oil of bay	2
Glycerol	5
Water	36
2. Jamaica rum	10
Ethyl alcohol	50
Oil of bay	2
Water	37.5
Oil of Piemento	0.5

Procedure for 1 and 2: Dissolve the oils in the alcohol, add the remainder of the ingredients and mix well.

	Percent
	0.15
3. Oil of bay	0.15
Ethyl alcohol	60
Tincture of quillaia	10
Water	29.55
Ethyl acetate	0.15
4. Oil of bay	0.25
Water	65
Oil of Cinnamon leaf	34.59
Quassia extract, solid	0.10
Heptaldehyde	0.01

Procedure for 3 and 4

The essential oils are dissolved in the alcohol and ethyl acetate or heptaldehyde is added, the quassia extract is dissolved in the water with heat and then mixed with the rest of the materials. The preparation is stirred well and filtered bright.

Formulation for Resorcinol Hair Tonics

	Percent
1. Resorcinol	5
Tincture of capsicum	5
Ethyl alcohol	85
Castor oil	5
Perfume and Colour	q.s.

	Percent
2. Resorcinol	0.8
Chloral hydrate	1.5
Ethyl alcohol	80
B Napthol	0.8
Sulphonated castor oil	16.9
Perfume and Colour	q.s.

	Percent
3. Resorcinol	0.3
Pine Tar oil	2.7
Soft soap	0.5
Potassium sulphate	3.0
Water	93.5
Perfume and Colour	q.s.

	Percent
4. Resorcinol monoacetate	3
Spirits of formic acid	20
Ethyl alcohol	70
Castor oil	7
Perfume and Colour	q.s.

	Percent
5. Resorcinol monoacetate	2.5
Ethyl alcohol	93
Methyl linoleate	2-5
Cinnamn	2.0
Perfume and Colour	q.s.

Procedure

The tinctures and oils are added to the alcohol in which the resorcinol or resorcinol based monoacetate has been dissolved. The perfume and colour is then added. The mixture is stirred well and then filtered.

Formulation for Jaborandi Hair Tonics

Percent

1. Tincture of Jaborandi	5.0
Tartaric acid	0.5
Ethyl alcohol	5.0
Triple rose water	82.5
Glycerol	7
Perfume	q.s.

	Percent
2. Ethyl alcohol	9.0
Pelocarpine nitrate	0.05
Tincture of cantharidine	0.95
Water	85.0
Glyceryl borate	5.0
Perfume	q.s.

Procedure

The tinctures and the oils are added to the alcohol in which the resorcinol or the resorcinol based monoacetate has been dissolved. The perfume and colour is then added. Care has to be taken to ensure a brilliantly clear product on filtration.

Formulations for Dry Scalp Tonics

	Percent
Ammonia water	1.5
Sulphonated castor oil	9.5
Tincture of capsicum	0.8
Ethyl alcohol	88.2
Perfume	q.s.

	Percent
3. Ethyl alcohol	2.5
Potassium sulphate	5.5
Water	91.7
Hydrochloric acid	0.004
Glacial acetic acid	0.006
Pine tar oil	0.300
Perfume	q.s.

Procedure

The ingredients are thoroughly mixed and filtered to obtain a brilliant product.

Formulations for Oily Scalp Tonics

	Percent
Tannin	5
Formaldehyde	0.75
Water	83.75
Ethyl alcohol	10.5
Perfume	q.s.

	Percent
Water	32.5
Bary rum	30.0
Rose water	24.5
Ammonia 26^0	5.0
Glyceryl borate	7.0
Tincture of capsicum	1.0

Perfume	q.s.

	Percent
Ethyl alcohol	70
Rose water	6
Eau de colgne	10
Glyceroil	4
Tincture of cinchona	4
Tincture quillaia	6
Perfume	q.s.

	Percent
Water	56.5
Ethyl alcohol	40.0
Tincture of capsicum	3.0
Chlorothyniol	0.1
Quinine sulphate	0.1
Benzoic acid	0.30
Perfume	q.s.

Procedure

The water soluble materials are dissolved in the water and the oils, tinctures, and perfume in the alcohol. The mixture is stirred well and filtered bright.

Oil-in-Water Emulsions

Emulsions provide a smooth attractive cream like product for a hair dressing. A good pouring and spreading consistency can be obtained resulting in a thin uniform film of oil on the hair. The greasy feel is greatly reduced and the residue on the hands can be easily removed. From the manufacturers point of view such emulsions offer an advantage of being economical since a portion of the raw materials is replaced with water. Moreover these emulsions have to be well balanced and stable. Due to evaporation of water and absoption of it by the hair, the emulsion is soon broken leaving continuous film of residual oils and fats to protect the hair shaft, seal in the absorbed moisture and to afford grooming and lustre. Efficient preservatives and antioxidants are necessary in the formulation of emulsion to prevent the risk of bacterial and mold attack. Uniform welling of the hair usually is obtained with oil in water emulsions since the emulsifiers lower the surface tension of the aqueous phase.

The main factors to be considered in evolving a formulation for an emulsified hair dressing are:-

a) Selection of appropriate emulsifying agent
b) Proper balance between the oil and water phases
c) Correct viscosity of both phases.

Formulations

Ingredients	Percent 1	2	3	4
Mineral oil	44	25	43	40
Stearic acid	6	-	2.4	3.5
Water	48.5	65	48.7	49
Triethanolamine	1.5	-	1.2	1.5
Perfume and Colour	q.s.	-	-	-
Triethanolamine stearate	-	7	-	-
Beeswax white	-	-	3	1.5
Bees wax	-	3	-	-
Colour and Perfume	-	q.s.	-	-
Stearic acid	-	-	2.4	-
Glyceryl monostearate	-	-	0.2	-
Carnauba wax	-	-	-	1.0
Stearamide carbitol solution	-	-	1.5	2.5
Colour and preservative	-	-	q.s.	q.s.

Procedure (for No. 1)

Mineral oil and stearic acid is heated to about 70 °C until the solution is complete. The water and triethanolamine is heated to about 2 °C higher and then slowly run into the heated oil under moderate agitation. The agitation is continued till the emulsion gets cooled and then the perfume is added, at around 45 to 50C. The emulsion should be stable at this temperature and hence it should not be necessary to cool below 40 °C.

Procedure (for No. 2)

The triethanolamine stearate is dissolved in the water and heated to 70 °C, The mineral oil and beeswax is heated to 72 °C and slowly run into the aqueous phase. The agitation is continued until cool with the addition of perfume at 45 °C to 50 °C. The mixture is then passed through a colloid mill or a homogeniser to ensure stability.

Procedure (for No.3)

The heated aqueous triethanolamine solution is added to the melted oils and fats at 75 °C to 80 °C and stirred until cool, and then perfumed below 45C. The perfume is dissolved in carbitol solution as a means of solubilizing and for better dispersion throughout the emulsion.

Procedure (for No.4)

The melted oils are poured into the aqueous triethanolamine at 75 °C to 80 °C with vigorous agitation. The agitation is done more slowly upon cooling.

Formulation No. 5

	Percent
Stearic acid	2
Cetyl and Stearyl alcohol (10% sulphated)	2
Soft white paraffin	8
Cocoa butter	4
Mineral	50
Water	33
Borax	1
Colour and Perfume	q.s.

Procedure

The borax is heated and water is added to the hot fats at 75° to 80 °C with moderate stirring. The stirring is continued until the emulsion is cool and then the perfume is added at 45 °C.

Formulations (Hair Creams) Percent

Ingredients	6	7	8
Diglycol laurate	-	-	14
Diglycol stearate	7	8	-
Mineral stearate	20	-	36
Water	73	60	50
Castor oil	-	16	-
Almond oil	-	1	-
Perfume and Preservative			

Water-in-Oil Emulsions

Water-in-oil emulsions have been used on and off as hair grooming preparations and seen to be more popular with men than with women due to the greater grooming action and the slightly oil feel. Several types of emulsifiers have been used to prepare the water-in-oil hair dressings of which the polyvalent soaps are probably the oldest although beeswax and borax have long been used. The other enmusifiers for the water in oil enulsion on which are used are calcium oleate, calcium stearate, zinc stearate, aluminium stearate.

Formulations (Emulsified Hair Grooming Preparation)

No. 1	Percent
Mineral oil	62.55
Beeswax white	2.5
Water	34.8
Borax	0.15
Perfume	q.s.

Procedure

The wax is melted in half of the mineral oil and hot borax water is added. The remainder of the oil is then added and the whole mixture is then homogenised.

Formulations (Emulsified Hair Grooming Prepartion)
Percent

Ingredients	2	3	4	5
Oleic acid	12	20	1.0	-
Beeswax	2	1	1.5	2.5
Mineral oil	45	-	41.7	48
Lanolin	2	0.5	-	-
Lime water	19	33.5	53.8	-
Saccharated lime water	20	5	-	-
Olive oil	-	40	-	-
Magnesium sulphate (25%)	-	-	2.0	-
Stearic acid	-	-	-	1.5
Absorption base	-	-	-	5.0
Petrolatum	-	-	-	12.5
Magnesium oleate	-	-	-	2.5
Water	-	-	-	28
Perfume and Preservative	q.s.	q.s.	q.s.	q.s.

Procedure

The aqueous phase is added to the heated oils at 70 to 75 ^{0}C with moderate agitation and stirring is continued until cool. In formulation No. 3 the magnesium sulphate solution is added after the lime emulsion has been prepared and then stirring is continued till the emulsion gets cooled.

Formulation No. 6 (Emulsified Hair Cream)

	Percent
Mineral oil	40
Petolatum	19.4
Beeswax, white	17.6
Oleic acid	0.40
Lanolin absorption base	0.8
Borax	0.4
Magnesium sulphate	1.0
Sodium hydroxide	0.4
Water	20.0
Perfume and Preservative	q.s.

Procedure

The magnesium sulphate and the sodium hydroxide is dissolved in half of the water and the borax in the other half. The two aqueous phases are mixed and added to the heated oils, both at 65 ^{0}C. The mixture is stirred until it gets cooled to 45 ^{0}C and then perfume is added. The preparation is then passed, through a homogeniser.

HERBAL COSMETICS FOR THE HAIR

Introduction

Herbal Cosmetics generally imply those cosmetics which are made with an ayurvedic base with the addition of some ayurvedic or medicinal compounds which contribute the desired additional specific properties to the prepartion. Among the herbal cosmetics for the hair, preparations such as herbal hair oil, herbal shampoos can be included. Hair Care products and cures comprising of herbal Hair Rinses, Hair tonics, Shampoos, Heena powders, are designed to restore beauty and health to the hair. They contain extracts known for their qualities of stimulating hair growth, improving hair texture and colour.

Range of Market Products

Herbal Hair Conditioners:- This is a powerful combination of invaluable herbal ingredients like Amla, Sandalwood, Brahmi, Lichens and other precious herbs. It makes the hair strong, healthy and lustrous. Prevents hair loss and acts as a scalp deep cleanser while maintaining the natural moisture balance. It provides body to dull lifeless hair.

Herbal Hair Oil:- This is an effective combination of arnica, Henna, Thikkakai and other herbal extracts, especially created to prevent hair loss and promote luxurious hair growth.

Herbal Henna:- This is an effective combination of pure Henna Leaves with a number of herbal ingredients used in this preparation make the hair lustrous, manageable and silky. It also works as a powerful treatment for scalp disorders and gives a mild natural colour and sheen to the hair.

Herbal Hair Tonic:- This preparation is a formulation for controlling hair loss/dandruff/greying hair. It stimulates hair growth and thickness. It is a specialised tonic treatment for revitalising the hair and generating a natural lustroics glow. It serves well for texturising rough brittle hair and split ends.

Herbal Henna Shampoo (for normal to oily hair):- This preparation is a unique blend of Henna and other herbal extracts to cleanse the scalp and controls excessive secretion of scalp oils and imparts sheen to dull hair making it tangle free.

Herbal Amla Shampoo (for normal to dry hair):- This preparation is made from extracts of Amla, Dater and Arnica and other rare herbs. This shampoo makes the hair lustrous, healthier and manageable and cleanses the scalp while retaining and stimulating its natural oil.

Hair Treatment Cream:- This preparation is an effective, medicated antiseptic ointment for the treatment of dandruff scalp disorders, seborrhoea and sealy skin conditions and is used for the treatment of dandruff and falling hair.

Herbal Mint/Hair Gloss Conditioner:- It is used as a hair sheen and can be used just before shampoo for providing texture and conditioning to the hair.

Herbal Hair Rinse:- This is a combination of mint, brahmi and other herbal extracts and is an effective control for dandruff and scalp disorders and promotes hair growth.

Formulations

Herbal Hair Oils (Medicated):- Medicated herbal oils are also used as scenting material for the hair. The base oil may be a mineral oil such as coconut oil, groundnut oil, castor oil, neem etc. To make an oil ayurvedic or a herbal product certain essential oils are added which provide certain specific characteristics of the individual used in the formualation.

Formulations

Herbal Hair Oil:- There is no unique formulation for herbal hair oil. The formulations of the manufacturers are trade secrets. However the following formulation can be taken as a standard base and it can be changed according to requirements.

Til Oil	91	ml.
Mollha Kankola	0.3	ml.
Whees Charrila	0.3	ml.
Sailag Nagar	0.03	ml.
Chander	0.04	ml.
Long Dalchini	0.03	ml.
Ratanjot	0.02	ml.
Kapur Kachuri	0.05	ml.
Satabar	.02	ml.
Tejpat	.03	gms.
Howber	.03	gms.
Balhere	.06	gms.
Amla	.08	gms.
Harrar	0.06	gms.
Chanpa	0.03	gms.
Keora (keya)	0.06	gms.
Gulabphul	0.03	gms.
Alaichi (Big)	0.02	gms.
Pudhina	0.4	gms.
Perfume	0.3 - 15	gms.
Quath water	1.5	kg.
Menthol	0.2	

Herbal Shampoos

These products have a good demand in hard-water areas. Quillaja Saponania is one of a whole class of Saponias widely distributed in nature. Commercially sponin is extracted with water and alcohol from the Quillaja bark or from the soap root. Preparations of saponin are genrally intended to cleanse the scalp and to reduce scaliness. These are generally compounded with rosemary or celandine and in addition to its use in shampoos saponin has found some use in bubble baths. Some formulaions for Herbal Shampoos are given as under:-

Percent

i)	Quillaja bark, powdered	5
	Ammonium carbonate	1

	Borax	1
	Bay leaf oil	0.1
	Water	92.9
ii)	Sodium carbonate anhydrous	19.4
	Powdered soap	79.0
	Saponin	1.6
	Perfume	q.s.
iii)	Borax	20
	Sodium, sesquicarbonate	40
	Powdered soap	35
	Saponin	5
	Perfume	q.s.

Henna Hair Dye

Of the vegetable dyes only henna is of any real importance today. It consists of the dried powdered leaves of Lawsonia alba, Lawsonia spinosa and Lawsonia inemis, which are removed from the plants prior to flowing. Henna owes it hair dyeing properties to the presence of 2-hydroxy-1, 4-napthaquinone, after termed lawsonia, which is soluble in hot water and is, in acid solution, a substantive dye for Keratine. In dyeing hair with henna a paste of the powdered henna and hot water, slightly acidified with citric acid, adipic or other suitable acids to an optimum pH of about 5-5, is applied to the washed hair. The "henna Pack" is kept in place by means of a towel and is allowed to remain on the head for the required time varying from five to sixty minutes after which the hair is thoroughly shampooed, rinsed and dried.

Natural Organic Dyes

The earliest known dyes were natural organic substances from plants and used as infusions, decorations or packs. Many of these are still utilized for the dyeing and blending of postiche but only henna and camomile persist in this trade.

(A) Henna

The henna plant is shrub. "Lawsonia alba lans" of bears small, fragrant, greenish-white flowers, but as the only plant utilized for dye are the leaves and stems, the plants are frequently at back. For infusions, used as rasies the leaves are usually left whole, but is the more common commercial form of henna, the leaves and stems are ground to a powder, about the colour of dark unstand and with characteristic earthy odour.

The principal advantage offered by henna as a modern hair dye is that it is harmless to the system and causes no irritations on the skin. A few applications impart a slight amount of colour to the entire hair shift and depending on the original colour of the hair, a whole range of reddish pure vegetable shades - tomato, beet, egg plant - can be produced. If it is plied often enough, therefore, hair of any and all original shades can be brought to the same characteristics orangered.

Applications of Heena

Despite the intense dark red shade of solutions of henna, the active dyeing principle, is only about 1% of it. This dye is used mostly in beauty shops, as a rinse or as a pack.

(a) Henna Rinse

For slight change of colour, bring out high lights on dark hair, henna levels are steeped in boiling water until all the dye is extracted. This solution is then poured several times over freshly shampooed hair. Commercial preparations of a henna rinse should be acidified with 1 to 2% of some mild organic acid viz-adific acid, citric acid, tartaric.

(b) Henna Pack

For a more decided, or more lasting, change in shade, powdered henna leaves are made into a paste with boiling water. This is applied to all the hair, which is allowed to remain and undisturbed until test on a single strand shows that the desired shade has been attained. The subsequent treatment, the colour can be kept uniform by applying the paste to only the new growth of hair.

To prepare henna powder, the fresh leaves are ground extremely fine. Fresh powder is dark browinsh-green, as it ages bearing yellowish red. It is usually packed in waxed paper in cans or boxes that can be tightly sealed.

(c) Henna Shampoos

Because hena dye works best in acid media may attempt to utilize it as a coloured shampoo were ineffective. Five percent of henna mixed with sodium or tri-ethnolamine sulphate and 5% of boric or adipic acid, makes a satisfactory shampoo of the type, when freshly prepared. It is usually recommended for dark hair on which it may be desirable to bring out warm highlights.

(d) Henna Mixtures

To modify the often unpleasing reddish shades that are the only ones possible with henna alone, this plant was long ago mixed with indigo. The dried and powdered leaves of indigo origin are either mixed with ground henna or applied alternatively with henna, to produce a good shades from light brings to black can be produced by varying the proportions of henna and indigo.

(e) Camomile

Another of the few plants that are still used for colouring the hair is camomile. Several varieties of related plants are found in U.K., Western Europe, and the U.S.A., of which only two - camomile and German or Hungarian camomile - are used to any extent. The essential oil distilled from camomile flowers in pale blue, due to the presence of some hydrocarbon azuline.

Applications of Camomile

Like henna, camomile can be used as a rinse, a pack, or a shampoo.

(a) Rinse

For the rinse, a strong infusion of either German or Roman camomile should be made with boiling water. While it is still warm, this liquid should be poured repeatedly over freshly shampooed hair. A commercial product would best be made by preparing first a concentrated infusion, by percolating the materials according to the following formulation:-

Roman camomile, powdered - 40%
Oil of camomile - 0.2%
Alcohol (20%) q.s. to make 100

(b) Camomile Pack

As camomile flowers alone do not form a cohesive pack, they should be powdered, mixed (2 parts) with kaolin or fullers earth (1 part), and made into a thin paste with boiling water. The shade produced depends on the original shade of the hair and the time of contact, and the change in colour lasts considerably longer than the glints produced by a rinse. As with the henna pack the paste must be kept hot during the entire application, and the marketed as powders and as liquids.

Formulation of Powder Shampoo

Camomile German Powdered	- 10%
Mild organic acid	- 5%
Sodium sulphate	- 85%
Oil of camomile	q.s. (for perfume)

A liquid shampoo is most effective when freshly prepared. Hence it may be made in concentrated form, accompanied by information on the amount of water to be added or the moment by use.

Formulation of Liquid Shampoo

Camomile infusion	- 10%
Sodium laurge sulfate	- 30 to 40%
Water	- 60 to 50%

d) Camomile-Henna Mixtures.

To modify the harsh colours produced by either substance above henna and camomile are mixed in varying proportions. Pack of this type may be prepared to very good effect to produce a fair range of colour on hair of different basic shades as shown below.

Formualtions for Camomile - Henna Mixture Formulation

	1	2	3
Camomile	75	50	25
Henna	25	50	75

Original Colour	Shade Produced
Blond	Golden-blond
	Red - Gold
	Golden - Red
Light Brown	Light auburn
	Auburn
	Bright auburn
	Chest Nut
Dark Brown	Reddish - Brown
	Dark auburn

Henna Reng Dye

By the addition of other substance to henna shades other than auburn may be obtained, such as mixture of powdered indigo leaves and henna produces blue shades and such mixtures are known as henna rengs.

Camomile Herbal Dye

Of the various species of camomile, only 'Anthemis nobilis' (Roma Camomile) and Matricaria camomile (German camomile) have been used in cosmetics and are useful in tinting the hair. The active ingredient of these flowers in 1, 3, 4 - tri hydronyflavore, known as apigenin. Either an aqueous extract or a paste of the ground flower heads are generally used. To lighten the hair a paste consisting of 2 parts camomile and 1-2 parts kaolin mixed to a thin cream with hot water is applied to the head for a period varying from 15 minutes to 60 minutes depending upon the shade required. While making a formulation it is essential that at least 5% camomile or its equivalent in extract, must be present to produce any effect at all and the azulene also present in camomile contributes to the brightening effect.

Fresh Soap-wort Shampoo

Soap-wort contains saponina, chemicals that produce foam when added to water. All parts of the plant produce a gentle cleansing lather that does not sting the eyes or make the hair brittle. It can be combined with other herbs that suit particular types of hair and colour.

Formulation No. 1

Leafy Soapwort stems 6-8 long	10 Nos.
Water	500 ml.
Strong Herb or flower infusion	3 Tablespoon

For making an infusion use the following amounts. To each 1/2 litre of boiling bottled spring water add

Dried Herbs:-	14 gms for weak infusion
	28 gms for normal strength
	56 gms for strong infusion
Fresh Herbs	1 1/2 handfuls for weak infusion
	3 handfuls for normal strength
	3 handfuls for strong infusion

Dried herbs of any of the flowers given below can be used.

- Chamomile, Lime flower, yarrow.
- Rosemary, sage, comfrey, henna (powder)
- Marigold flowers.
- Lavender, peppermint, white, dead nettle.
- Marsh mallow, comfrey
- Southerriwood, stinging nettle.
- Elder flower, Uiyme, rosemary.

Procedure

The stems are cut into short lengths and put into an enamel sauce pan. The same are then bruised lightly with a wooden spoon and water is added. The mixture is boiled and then covered and allowed to simmer for 15 minutes with continuous stirring, till cool. Then the contents are strained and bottled for future use. A flower infusion is prepared and 3 tablespoon of strong herb or flower is added. The shampoo is covered and then allowed to cool and then strained. The whole of the above liquid is used for one hair wash.

Dried Soapwort Root Shampoo
Formulation No. 2

Dried soapwort root	30 gms.
Boiling water	500 ml.
Dried Herbs & flowers	30 gms.

Dried herbs are the same as used in formulation - 1.

Procedure

Boiling water is poured on the broken up roots and then covered and left for soaking for 12 hours or overnight. The contents are transferred to an enamel pan and heated to boil and then simmered for 15 minutes. The dried herbs or flowers are then added, stirred, covered and left to cool. The mixture is then stirred into a fug and used for one hair wash.

Nettle Rinse and Conditioner

Nettle is an excellent hair conditioner. It is an acidic plant and promotes a healthy gloss.

Formulation No. 3

- A big handful size bunch of nettles.
- Water.

Procedure

Wear rubber gloves to cut the nettles. Wash thoroughly and put the bunch into an enamel sauce pan with enough cold water to cover. Heat it to boil and then cover and allow to simmer for 15 minutes. Strain the mixture into a jug and allow it to cool.

Lotion for Unruly Hair
Formulation No. 4

-Herb or flower infusion of normal strength	- 8 Tablespoons.
- Eau de cologne	- 1 Tablespoon
- Glycerine	- 1 Tablespoon

The first two ingredients are poured into a bottle. Add the glycerine one drop at a lime and then shake well. The herbs used for formulations can be used.

Horsetail Hair Rinse and Tonic.

Herbal hair tonics and conditioners help restore the scalps natural acidity and strengthen the circulation giving a healthy shine to the hair. Horsetail contains saponins which create lather, flavore-glycosides which act on the scalps tiny blood vessels to stimulate the circulation and silica which provides body to the hair. The conditioning herbs that you can use instead of horsetail are rosemary southern wood and stringing nettle..

Formulation No.5

Horsetail stems "6-8" long (or other conditioning herbs)	8 Nos.
Water	500 ml.

The horestail stems are bruised with a spoon before adding the boiling water to make an infusion. They are then coverd and left until lukewarm and then strained. After shampooing and rinsing, the infusion is poure on the hair and massaged on the scalp. The excess moisture is blotted with a towel and the hair is combed. The head is then coverd with a warm towel and then waited for ten minutes before drying the hair the usual way.

Tonic Shampoo

Put 135 gms each of dried reetha, shikakai and amla into one litre water. Keep it for 24 hours. Boil and then allow to cool. Filter the mixture and use as a shampoo.

Herb Shampoo

Wash 210 gms each of dried olives and shikakai leanns in cold water and then soak overnight in an iron pot. Next morning boil them for 10 - 15 minutes and strain liquidige the flesh that remains and use the paste to wash your hair. This shampoo leaves your hair soft and shing.

DEPILATORIES

Introduction

Present - day fashions in women created a large demand for depilatories. Good grooming requires that one want to keep the legs, arms and armpits free from unsightly hair the year around if bathing and casual attire, sheer hosiery and 'off-the-shoulder' dress are to be worn without embrrassment.

The desire for removal of hair for social and other purposes or for improving personal appearance has led men and women since ancient times to try the most varied of measures. It is recorded that the primitives used singeing, as well as mineral, vegetable or animal matter in ointment and paste form, for the removal of unwanted hair or to prevent its growth.

Now-a-days shaving by women is usually a biweekly procedure, and the process is made more convenient by specially designed razors and elegantly formulated shaving creams. But this too is not an easy method as it is not possible to shave all the parts of the body which require this process along with the added disadvantage of incurring cuts and scratures. Therefore the use of depilatories has increased tremendously the demand for such preparations. These can be available in various forms such as semisolid or cream form or as a waxy preparations. The process of removal of the unwanted hair is termed as epilation when the relatively intact hair is removed by plucking, electrolysis, X' Ray etc., and the term depilation is reserved only in cases where the removal is the result of chemical degradation of the human hair fibre by inorganic and organic chemicals.

Epilatory Compositions

Such compositions are essentially adhesive mixture of two genral types.

a) Wax rosin compositions designed to be applied in the molten state to the hairy area and allowed to solidify, so that the hair becomes enmeshed in the plastic mass. The subsequent removal of the waxy film from the site uproots and removes the hair.

d) Adhesive semisolid compositions which are permanently sticky at room temperatures and applied usually on a flexible backing material such as cloth. On removal of the adhesive composition by stripping the hair gets removed without injury to the skin.

Formulations for Hair-Full Type Dpilatory

	%by weight
Rosin	69.00
Beeswax	20
Burgundy pitch	4
Gum camphor	3
Oil of bergamot	2
Oil of eucalyptus	1
Oil of skurik	1

Note:- Epilatories of the hair-full type generally give satisfactory results when the epilatory is applied and removed by a beautician. When a woman applies the material to her skin, she winces from the pain attendant to the epilation and frequently removes the composition slowly and carefully instead of sharply and firmly. By doing so, epilation is often incomplete. Consequently, epilatories of this type are opt to be ineffective when applied at house.

Formulation for Rosin-Based Epilatories

Formulation No- 1

	% by weight
Rosin	42
Beeswax	37
Carnauba wax	6
Mineral oil	15

Formula No. 2

Rosin	50
Beeswax	24
Paraffins	20
Petrolatum	4
Benzocaine	2

Formula No. 3

Rosin	64
Beeswax	8
Carnauba wax	24
Linseed oil	4

Formula No. 4

Rosin	68
Beeswax	22
Ceresin	10

Chemical Depilatories

Great advances have been made in the art of removal of superfluous hair through the use of chemical agents in paste and cream form with the result that a number of cosmetic depilatory creams have become popular. An ideal chemical depilatory formualtion should possess the following attributes:-

(a) It should convert human hair completely in 2-5 minutes to a soft, plastic mass easily removed from the skin by wiping or rinsing.

(b) It should be nontoseic systematiclly and non irritating to the skin even on long contact.

(c) It should be easily applied, economical to use, and stable in the tube or far.

(d) It should be cosmetically elegant, odourless or pleasantly perfumed, white or neutral in colour, stainless to the clothing and noninjurious. to the skin.

Formulations for Powder Depilatory
Formula No. 1

	% by weight
Barium sulphide	31.00
Titanium dioxide	18.00
Corn starch	50.5
Menthol	0.25

Note:- Mix the water at time of application.

Formula No. 2

Strontium sulphide	35.0
Corn starch	35.0
Powder soap	5.0
Zinc oxide	23.0
Benzocaine	0.2
Perfume	1.8

Formula No. 3

Strontium sulphide	50.0
Starch powders	30.0
Talc	20.0

Procedures

The powders are mixed together in a tharough manner and kept in a dry bottle which is well stoppered

Application

A small quantity of the powder is taken and mixed with water to form a paste. This should be mixed immediately before use.

Note:- Mix with water at the time of application.

Formulation for Paste Depilatories

Formulation No. 1

	% by weight
Sodium sulphide	4
Calcium hydroxide	4
Glycerol	1
Kaolin	32
Water	59

Formulation No. 2

Barium sulphide	8.0
Calcium carbonate	32
Powdered soap	4
Glycerol	2
Water	54

Formulation No. 3

Strontium sulphide	30.0
Zinc oxide	8
Glycerol	2
Methyl cellulose	2.5
Menthol	1.0
Water	50.5

Formulation No. 4

Strontium sulphide	35.0
Titanium dioxide	4.0
Glycerol	5.0
Menthol	2.5
Perfume	1.0
Water	52.5

Formulation No. 5

Strontium sulphide extra	35
Titanium dioxide	5
Glycerine	5
Petroleum	3
Triethanolamine	1
Tylose-5 in 4% solution	
(or carboxy methyl cellulose) Menthol	1

Formulation No. 6

Strontium sulphide	30.0
Corn starch	15
Precipitated chalk	15.

Glycerine.	10
Water	29
Lavender oil	1

Procedure:- Add the glycerine to the water. Mix in the strontium sulphate. When the solution has ben effected, mix and sift in the precipitated chalk and the starch, then add the perfume. Mix thoroughly until smooth paste is obtained.

Formulation No. 7 (Thioglycolate Depilatories)

	% by weight
Calcium thioglycolate, trihydrate	6.0
Calcium carbonate, light U.S.R.	21.0
Calcium hydroxide, USP	1.5
Cetyl alcohol flakes N F	4.5
Sodium lauryl sulphate USP	0.5
Sodium silicate solution,42.5 BC'	3.5
Perfume	0.5
Distilled or deionized water to inches	100.0

Process of Manufacture

Dissolve 4.5 gm of sodium lauryl sulphate in 155 ml. of hot water (65 °C). Add sodium silicate solution and mix. Add method cetyl alcohol to this mixture while hot, then agitate while cooling, to form an emulsion. In a separate vessel, mix clacium carbonate with 360 ml. of hot distilled water. Add previously prepared emulsion to this slung and agitate for 30 minutes at 40 °C. In another vessel, make a suspension by mixing the calcium hydroxide and calcium thiglycolate in 110 ml. of distilled water containing 0.5 gm. of sodium lauryl sulphate. Add perfume and continue agitation for 30 minutes. Add water, if necessary, to make proper weight. Product is roller-milled and it should be free from entrapped air. Fill cream into wax-lined lead tubes when cooled to room temperature.

Formulation No. 8

Calcium thioglycolate	15 gms.
Calcium hydroxide	5 gms.
Calcium carbonate	60 gms.
Sodium lauryl sulphate	0.5 gms.

Formulation No. 9

Mercapto - Acetic acid	12 ml.
Strontium hydrate	50 gms.
Calcium oxide	12 gms.
Colloidal clay	102 gms.
Methyl cellulose	11 gms.
Perfume	0.8 gms.
Water	300 ml.

Formulation 10 (Depilatory Cream)	Parts
Starch powdered	8.0
Glycerine	8.0
Strontium sulphide	20.0
Zinc oxide	16.0
Wool fat	8.0
Sodium sulphide	2.0
Distilled water	37.0
Tragacanth	1.0

Procedure

The starch and glycerine is mixed alongwith 4 ml. of the distilled water until a thin paste is formed. The mixture is stirred continuously and heated gently until the mass stiffens. The strontium sulphide and zinc oxide is mixed together and then sifted. The wool fat is melted and the mixed powders are incorporated. The sodium sulphide is dissolved in the remaining water and worked into the wool fat and powders. Now the starch paste is incorporated and finally the tragacanth.

Formulation No. 11 (Depilatory Wax)

Paste Colophony (Fusible natural resin-80, Beeswax-20)

Procedure

The above ingredients are melted and stirred continuously, when the mixture becomes thick but still pourable it is given a final sting and allowed to stand for a few seconds that small bits of solid impurities may fall to the bottom. The above is now poured into moulds or saucepans.

Formulation No. 12 (Wax Mask)

These are usually moulded into a small tablets, each sufficient for one application.

Olive oil	5.0 parts
Soft paraffin	25.0 parts
Hard paraffin	70.0 parts

Procedure

Melt the two paraffins on a water bath with the oil when almost cool, pour into suitable moulds. These tablets are usually delicately tined. Any oil soluble dye can be used to obtain this effect.

28

HAIR STRAIGHTENERS

Introduction

Throughout the ages, in mans' eternal quest for beautification, it has been observed that the individual with straight hair wants curly hair and the individual with curly hair believes straight hair to be esthetically desirable. The most accepted theory relative to the inherent difference between straight and curly hair is related to the configuration of the hair shaft. When cross sectioned examinations of the hair shaft are made, the straight hair appears circular and the curly or pinky hair gives the appearance of a very oblate spheroid.

The method of hair straightening of greatest antiquity was that of plastering down the hair by the use of gums or resinous-fatty vehicles, as given in the following formulations:-

Formulations

Formulation No. 1

	Percent
Quince seed	3
Ethyl alcohol	25
Water	72
Perfume and colour	q.s.

Procedure

Soak the quince seed overnight in 50 parts of water. Strain the resulting mucilage through a cloth and add the balance of the water, alcohol, odour and perfume.

Formulaion No. 2

	Percent
Gum karaya	1.5
Ethyl alcohol	5.0
Glycol bori-borate	1.5
Water	82.0
Preservative, colour and perfume	q.s.

Procedure

Make a mucilage of karaya, alcohol and water. Add teh glycol boriborate, colour and perfume prior to passing through a colloid milt.

Formulation No. 3

	Percent
Petrolatum	90
Paraffin	10
Perfume and colour	q.s.

Procedure

Melt, mix and add perfume and colour, as desired. waxes other than paraffin, such as beeswax or ozokerite may be used in formulation No. 3. Whenever heavier products are required, cersin can be incorporated to achieve the desired hardness. Certain resins can also be incorporated in product of this type. The degree of tackiness wax, more than 20% is seldom used, as the product becomes too hard for easy application.

The disadvantages of the products made from formulation 1 to 3 are many. Formost they do not affect the hair chemically. They function as a result soley of the adhesive qualities of the product.

When the curly or pinky hair is not changed chemically into a different pattern, the hair returns to its natural state. Moisture accelerates this action. Attempts have been made to imcoporate water repellents, such as aluminium stearate into the poundes. A formulation of this kind is given below.

Formulation No. 4

	Percent
Petrolatum	95
Aluminium distearate	5
Perfume and colour	5.5

Procedure

Melt the petrolatum and add the aluminium distearate, perfume and colour.

Physical Method of Hair Straightening

The physical rather than the chemical method of hair straightening is more useful. In this method, the hair is washed and dried thoroughly. Then the petrolatum product is applied to the hair. The comb, which is heated is placed on the hair, and the hair is then stretched while the heated comb is applied.

A simple preparation that represents a product for use with hot combs is given in Formulation 5 and a more complex preparation along the same lines is shown in Formulation 6, while still another type of hair straightener in current use is the caustic alkali product, represented by

Formulations 7 and 8.

The consistency of these creams can be varied by changing the amount of stearate or the ratio of stearic and oleic acids. The proportion of sodium hydroxide, incorporated in formulas of this type varies with the base used. Of stearic acid, oleic acid or mixtures thereof are used, a greater amount of alkali is required, due to the saponification of the fats. Many products on the market utilize between 5 and 7%. Naturally as the amount of alkali is increased, the quicker is the action on the hair and the greater is the need for caution in applictation.

The alkali type of straigtener is used primarily by the men, where straightness is desired and no styling required.

Formulation No. 6

	Percent
Petrolatum	100%
Perfume and colour	q.s.

Process of Manufacture

Melt the petrolatum and add the perfume and colour.

Formulation No. 6

	Percent
Beeswax	7
Ceresin	3
Petrolatum	30
Mineral oil	30
Water	29.25
Borax	0.75
Perfume	5.5

Process of Manufacture

Melt the oils and waxes on a water-bath and bring to 70 °C. Dissolve borax in water and bring 72 °C. Add latter solution to oil-wax mixture with rapid agitation slowly, cooling to 55 °C, at which time the perfume is added. Continue to cool with agitation to 40 °C and fill into jars.

Formulation No. 7

	Percent
Sodium hydroxide	5
Glyceryl monostearate	15
Glycerol	5
Water	75
Perfume	9.5

Process of Manufacture

Heat the glyceryl monostearарte, glycerol and water to 95 ^{0}C. Cool to 60 ^{0}C, then add the sodium hydroxide which has been dissolved in a small amount of water. Cool with agitations to 40C, add perfume and fill. It is important that the sodium hydroxide not be added of too high a temperature, otherwise the glyceryl monostearate will be saponified.

Formulation No.8

	Percent
Stearic acid	15
Oleic acid	5
Glycerol	5
Sodium hydroxide	10
Water	65
Perfume	9.5

Process of Manufacture

Dissolve the sodium hydroxide and glycerol in the water and heat to 90 ^{0}C. Heat the stearic acid and oleic acid to 95 ^{0}C. And add to the water solution with agitation. Cool with agitations to 40 ^{0}C, add perfume and fill.

Other Formulations

The larger number by thioglycolate straighteners on the market are of the emulsified oil in water type, although viscous liquids have also been introduced. An example of this type of product is given below:-

Formualtion No.9

	Percent
Glyceryl monostearate	15
Stearic acid	3
Ceresin	1.5
Paraffin	1.0
Sodium lauryl sulphate	7.0
Distilled water	51.9

Thioglycolic acid	6.6
Ammonium hydroxide (26 °C)	20.0
Perfume	9.5

Process of Manufacture

Mix the glyceryl monostearate, stearic acid, paraffin and sodium lauryl sulphate in a kettle, with 40 parts of the water and heat with constant agitation to 95 °C. Then cool to 50C, still under agitation. While this is being done, add the thioglycolic acid to the remaining water and to this solution slowly add the ammonium hydroxide. As considerable heat is generated, it is necessary to provide some method of cooling to keep the temperature below 50 °C. For this reason, it is preferable to use ammonium thioglycolate, as obtainable commercially and reduce the amount of ammonium hydroxide by 16 parts. Slowly add the thioglycolate solution to the stearate mixture both being of 50 °C. It is important that the thioglycolate solution not to be allowed to go above 50 °C, otherwise there will be a decomposition of the ammonium thioglycolate. Care should be taken that the thioglycolate solution is mixed in thoroughly as it is added. Cool the resulting mixture rapidly to 40 °C, to avoid saponification of the glyceryl monostearate, add perfume and package.

Formulation No. 10

	Percent
Sodium bromate	14
Propylene glycol	2
Lanolin, anhydrous	2
Sorbitan monopalmitate	1
Sorbitan trioleate	2
Sodium cetyl alcohol sulphate	3
Water	76
Perfume	9.5

Process of Manufacture

Dissolve the sodium bromate in the water and propylene glycol and heat to 60 °C. Add the mixture of the remaining ingredients, which have been heated to 60 °C. Cool to 35 °C with agitation, add perfume, and package. Because of the high concentration of salt, this product may have a tendency to separate over a period of time, especially in hot weather. It is therefore advisable to use a 'Shake Well' label.

Formulation No. 11

	Percent
Cresol sulphonic acid	7.5
Isopropyl Naphthaline sulphonic acid	7.5
Formaldehyde	10.0
Water	75.0

Precautions

Before recommending the use of a thioglycolate product, following precautions must be specified to the customer.

1. Do not use the hair straightener if you have abrasions or cuts on your scalp. Wait until they have heated before straightening the hair.

2. Do not straighten your hair if you are sick, since hair is affected by one's physical condition.

3. Do not substitute hot water when directions call for warm water.

4. Do not use the treatment unless you are all of the neutralizer in the kit.

5. For those whose hair are in a very damaged condition the following is recommended.

6. If you have used hot combs, mancel vions, harst dye straighteners, dyes or bleaches, you may have abused your hair. Do not use hair straightener it your hair has been abused. For this condition, it is recommended to use hair conditioner for about two weeks or longer before straightening.

29

HAIR DYES, BLEACHES, COLOURINGS AND DYE REMOVERS

Introduction

Hair dyeing is one of the most important acts of adornment for men as well as women since time immemorial. The usual reasons for dyeing the hair are to change the natural colour, to colour the white hair which begin to appear with middle age, or to alter the colour of the hair temporarily for a particular occasion. The development of hair colourings followed the traditional use of simple and complex substances from plants, metallic compounds, and mixtures of these two types, and there was little change in colouring products and processes until the mid-ninteenth century. The discovery of some new synthetic organic compounds suitable as dyes for animal fibre gave impetus to the development of new-type hair colourings. For long the use of hair dyes, either at house or in beauty shops was kept a secret. Promoting hair colourings of all kinds as a feature in the ensemble of fashion i.e. something to be used as freely and as openly as facial makeup. With the exception of a few antiquated recipes of freely published in formularies, all the best known hair-colouring in cement use are proprietary products and therefore the compositors given in this chapter indicate only the typical compositions for the respective product.

Classification of Colouring Agents

The hair colouring in general use fall into two groups, depending on whether they are intended to colour the hair temporarily or permanently. The various types of products may be classified as below:-

(1) Bleaching Agents
(2) Temporary colourings
(3) Permanent colourings
(4) Natural Organic dyes.

1. BLEACHING AGENTS

Like dyes, bleaching agents are among the oldest products in this family. The early days, native minerals such as rock alum, quicklime, crude soda, and wood-ash, occasionally combined with old wine and water, served as favourite 'blond washes'. These preparations were left on the hair overnight or for several days and the resulting reddish gold shades were usually considered satisfactory. If the hair happened to be completely destroyed, the ladies frequently demanded and the hair be shorn from the captives and made into wigs for them.

Chemical Bleaches

The chemical bleaching compounds are mainly oxygen releasing. For use on living human hair, a chemical bleaching agent must have the following properties:-

(1) It should be nontoxic
(2) It should be mild in action
(3) It should be free of harmful residue.

These requirements rule out many effective oxidizing agents, in fact they narrow the possibility to sodium hypochlorite and hydrogen peroxide. As the former is of it in cosmetology is limited to the removal of dye stains. The reducing action of sulphur dioxide is also utilized to a limited extent.

Hydrogen Peroxide

The most satisfactory bleaching agent for human hair has always been hydrogen peroxide, because after its available oxygen has been released nothing but water remains.

Hydrogen peroxide made electrolytically is now more commonly used. To maintain desired quality, solutions of hydrogen peroxide must be stabilized with chemicals viz. acetanilide, dilute acids, sodium stannate or stannic hydroxide. To aid in preventing deterioration through carelessness, the peroxide should be bought in the pound bottle, rather than large containers.

Process of Bleaching

In practice, the peroxide solution is activated by the additions of ammonium hydroxide (28%, 0.880 sp. gr.), usually 15 to 20 drops to the ounce of peroxide in the simplest method of bleaching, the hair should be well shampooed and dried and the peroxide solution applied to the full length of it, stand by stand. The bleaching action, which oxidizes the colour to lighter shades, can be continued as long as desired by touching the hair saturated with the peroxide, and it can usually be stopped at any stage by colious rinsing with hot water.

In addition to solutions of hydrogen peroxide, which are marketed under various proprietary names, some of the other commercial forms are:

1. Solid Hydrogen Peroxide

Tablets made of peroxide and urea, or mixtures of sodium perborate and, for example, tartaric acid. These are to be dissolved in water at the time use.

2. White Henna

This is the commercial name for magnesium carbonate, to be mixed with hydrogen peroxide and ammonia and applied in the same manner as the clear liquid. The formulation of a modified white henna is given below.

Formulation for Modified White Henna

Magnesium carbonate	70%
Sodium carbonate	30%

Proprietary products may specify mixing with either water or hydrogen peroxide. The former should be satisfactory for all practical purposes, depending on the previous treatment of the hair, use of hydrogen peroxide in such a mixture may be disastrous

3. Peroxide Shampoo

This is usually a mixture of hydrogen peroxide and soap solution. The products may be mixture of melting agents and sodium carbonate.

4. Brightening Rinse

In simplest form, as used in beauty shops to bring out highlights in the hair, this is usually a mixture of hydrogen peroxide and water as given below:-

Hydrogen peroxide (20v)	40 to 50%
Water	60 to 50%

This is poured over the hair repeatediy until the desired shade is seen.

Formulation of Brightening Rinse, Modified

Hydrogen peroxide, 3%	97%
Quaternary ammonium salt or Quaternary monopholinium alkyl sulphate	1.5%
Adific (or tartaric acid)	0.8%
Sodium stannate (or hydrophosphate)	0.6%

5. Plantinum Bleaching

Under ordinary conditions , even the lightest shade obtainable from bleaching with hydrogen peroxide is always a decidedly yellowish tinge. To produce really the white 'Platinum blond' shade which is intermittently popular, the hair must first be bleached as light as possible, and then carefully raised with a dilute solution of some dye that can neutralize the residual yellow. Methyl violet, Methyl blue and nigrosine have proved to be satisfactory for this purpose.

Bleaching of Hair

Besides the golden red and yellow shades of hair, obtainable with hydrogen peroxide, there has been an intermittent and sporadic demand for some means of turning mixed gray hair an even snowy white. For such a treatment, the reducing action of sulphur dioxide may be recommended.

2. TEMPORARY COLOURINGS

Temporary colouring are the products used at any time to effect a physical change in the shade of the hair. These may include powders, cragois, lacquers and certain rinses.

(A) Powders

The use of powder for changing the colour of the hair is now largely contained to theatrical makeup otherwise it is limited to the occasional freshening of the wigs worn by judges and certain other participants in courts of law. The first coloured powders consisted of starch with various percentage of burnt sienna, umber, or other pigments for brownish shades and hidia ink for black. Metallic powders were also used in large amounts in a wide range of shades and still available in the market.

The modivn powder as in any basic mixture of a hair powder, externally light powders e.g. magnesium carbonate, should not be included. Following is the typical composition of such a powder:-

Formulation of Powder

Talc	20%
Starch	25%
Potato meal	45%
Powdered orris root	10%

Powders of different colours can be made by adding various mineral pigments and lamp black to this basic mixture.

(B) Crayons

Sticks or blocks of colouring, similar to the mascara have been used since long times as crayons. These coloured crayons for the hair are made of mixtures of natural or synthetic waxes, with a soap, such as triethanolamine stevate into which dyes or pigments are thoroughly incorporated. They are usually offered in a good range of shades, stimulating the average colours of natural hair, so that these will blend with other dyes that may be on the hair. The consistency of the finished product must be such that the colour can be easily applied as the stick is rubbed directly over the hair, or transferred from the stick to the hair by a moist brush. Typical composition for two types of crayons for the hair are shown in the following paragraphs as a soap base product and a wax-base product.

Formulation for a Soap-based Crayons

Water	26.5%
Gum arabic	27.5%
Sodium stearate	15.0%
Glycerol	15.0%
Colour	16.0%

Process of Manufacture

Mix water and glycerol, add gum arabic to half of this solution and allow it to stand, add stearic acid to remainder and warm mixture until it is dissolved. Mix all ingredients, add colour mill thoroughly, run paste into moulds, and dry in heat.

Formulation for a Wax-based Crayons

Triethanolamine	70.0%
Glyceryl monolaurate	5.5%
Gum tragacanth	2.5%
Stearic acid	13.5%
Bees wax	50.0%
Carnauba wax	13.5%
Ozokerite	8.0%
Colour	9.5%

Process of Manufacture

Heat first three ingredients to 70 ^{0}C, add stearic acid and raise the temperature to 75 ^{0}C. Melt waxes at 75 to 80 ^{0}C, add them to other mixture and stir until well blended. Add colour and mix thoroughly, pour into moulds at 68 to 70 ^{0}C.

C) COLOURED RINSES

The coloured rinses (also called tint rinses) for the hair were originally patterned on a similar product commonly used to restore or change the shade of lingeric, contains or other articles used in the households. Tinted rinses are similar in composition to the proprietary acid rinses, used as accessories to a shampoo. The base may be tartaric acid (adipic, citric, acetic and other acids may also be used, either alone or in combination), with which various water-soluble azo dyes are carefully bleded. All dyes should be selected from the official list of colours suitable for cosmetics, as published by the Food and Drug Controller. Most lines of coloured rinses are offered in twelve to sixteen shades, from golden and silver-blond, through various reddish and brownish shades, to black. Most commonly used and certified colours for hair rinses are listed below:-

1. Naphtol yellow S
2. Taratrazine
3. Sunset yellow FCF
4. Metanil yellow
5. Quinvlime yellow YS
6. Orange G
7. Orange II, I
8. Poncean 3 R
9. Amaranth
10. Poncean SX
11. Eusion YS
12. Acid Fuchsin D
13. Fast acid fuchsin CD
14. Naphthaline Red B
15. Viulamine R
16. Rose Bengale TDK
17. Fast Red A
18. Azo Rubin Extra
19. Croceine Scarlet MOO
20. A Light Green SF
21. Fast Green FCT
22. Alizarine Cyanine Green C
23. Acid Fast Green
24. Brilliant Blue FCT
25. Indigotin
26. Alpazurine FG
27. Evioglaucine
28. Methyline Blue
29. Acid Violet 6B
30. Resorcin Brown
31. Naphtol Blue Black
32. Fast Black BB
33. Sulfo-cyanine Black B.

Formulations For Coloured Rinses

Formulation No. 1 (Gold - Blond)

Tartrazine	64%
Orange No. 1	20%
Poncean 3R	3%
Acid Violet 6B	8%
Naphtol Blue Black	5%
G. Dyes/Ib. acid	3%

Formulaion No. 2 (Auburn)

Orange No. 1	76%
Poncean 3R	11%
Acid Violet 6B	13%
G. Dyesh/Ib. acid	7%

In manufacturing these rinses, solutions of the colours-especially mixtures must be thoroughly worked into the crystal of the acid. The finished product is usually sold in envelope of cellophane or translucent moisture proof paper, cotaining about 400 gms.

Rinses for Grey Hair

To neutralize the yellowish tinge that commonly appears in natural grey and white hair, and to produce 'Platinum blond' in bleached hair, rinses based on methylene blue, acid violet 6B, and water-soluble nigrosine are sold both as dry crystals and in solution. The accompanying instructions should insure a concentration of no more than 0.001% in the solution, as prepared for the application to the hair.

For all practical purpose, it is well to prepare these dyes as 1% solutions. The methylene blue and nigrosine should be dissolved in 1 part alcohol and 3 parts water, the acid violet 6B in alcohol alone. A rinse of proper concentration can then be prepared by mixing one part of any of these solutions with 500 to 1000 parts of water. To make them more attractive, these bluing or silvering rinses are usually compounded with adific acid, citric acid or tartaric acid.

(D) MISCELLANEOUS TEMPORARY COLOURINGS

(i) Colour Shampoos

In addition to the rinses in various forms as described earlier, azo dyes have been used in combination with shampoos of different types. Earlier, these products used a natural soap but most of the colour shampoos are now based on synthetic suface-active agents with melting and detergent properties. Example of this kind is sulfonated oils. The average line offers four to ten shades, in 0.5 to 2.0% concentrations of colour, suitable for blond, reddish, light and dark-brown hair.

(ii) Wave Sets

The mucilages and gums, both natural and synthetic, which are used for setting the hair in finger waving or sculpture curls, may also serve as carriers for setting the hair in finger waving or sculpture curls; may also serve as carriers for colouring intended to impart high lights.

(iii) Lacquers

Another possibility for imparting a slight tinge of colour to the hair has been found in the fine lacquers and 'non lacquers' commonly used to hold a finished coiffuse in place. These fixatives may be of several types viz. shellac, ethyl cellulose or polyvinyl pyrrolidone.

3. Permanent Colourings

The use of temporary colourings for the hair is of relatively recent origin. However permanent colouring, once upon a time, also drew the attention of experts in this field. The permanent dyes in general use are of three genral types:

(a) Natural Organic
(b) Synthetic Organic and
(c) Metallic preparations

The following requirements are however essential for a satisfactory permanent colouring agent.

(1) It must not be injurious to the general health.
(2) It must dye the hair, but not the skin.
(3) It must have no ill effect on the structure of the hair.
(4) It must not require a long time for the production of its effect.
(5) It must have no irritating effect on the hair.
(6) It must produce shades that are natural in appearnce and reasonably lasting.
(7) It must be compatible with other treatments, such as permanent waving.

(A) Natural, Organic Dyes

The earliest known hair dyes were natural organic substances obtained from plant origin and used as infusions, decoctions, or packs. A number of these are still utilised for the dyeing and blending postiche but the most popularly used organic materials of plant origin are 'Henna' and Camomile. A discussion on the same has been taken up separatly in the section on, 'Herbal Cosmetics for the hair.'

(B) Synthetic Organic Dyes

These dyes are organic synthetic compounds and are easily applied, produce natural-looking shades, and have no adverse effect on normal hair. They have entirely superseded the hennas and other natural dyes and seems to be increasingly popular for use both at home and at beauty shops. Examples of these compounds contains pyrogallol and also the azo dyes and other dyes covered under the heading of 'Coloured rinses'. Essentially the same compounds and compositions are available under many trade names. All are applied cold and all depend for development of the shade on hydrogen peroxide or some other non-contaminating compound that readily liberates oxygen.

(i) Pyrogallol

The first synthetic organic dye to be used on human hair was pyrogallol. The effectiveness of many of the natural substance used to produce brown shades is due to the pyrogallol, which is either present or developed in one or another of the ingredients. Used alone, pyrogallol acts as a progressive dye. A freshly prepared aquarium solution gradually darkens when exposed to the air, the addition of dilute ammonia hastens the development of the colour. It has often been added to henna packs to take advantage of the strong dying property of the latter but produce brown shades.

Without still other ingredients to fix the colour, these co-called 'Vegetable packs' are usually unsatisfactory, because the brownish tung soon wars off, leaving the characteristic red shade of the henna.

(ii) Amino Dyes

The first of the amino dyes used on human hair was phenylenediamine. For the dying of living hair, the earliest method of applying phenylenediamine was in two steps.

a) Wetting the hair with a 1 to 3% soloution of the dye, made alkaline with caustic soda, sodium carbonate, or ammonia water.

b) Applying oxidizing agent to bring out the colour many familiar oxidizing agents are: Ferric cheoride, potassium dichromate and permanganate, hydrogen peroxide. The best results are however, found with ammonia as the alkalizer and hydrogen peroxide as the developer, and by mixing the two solutions immediately before use.

The compounds used as bases for the organic synthetic dyes are more properly called countermediates because their actual dying properties are developed only on oxidation.

Formulation for Amino Dyes

Following compounds are also added in the formulation of amino dyes:-

(i) Antioxidants

Because of the readiness with which the amino dyes oxidize and darken even in the air, all manufacturing processes must be carefully guarded against access of air. The most generally used preservative is now sodium sulfite.

(ii) Alkalizers

Ammonium hydroxide has for many years been considered the best alkali for dye compositions because it helps efficiently in softening the hair and leaves no foreign residence as the fixed alkalies do. The amount to be added to the dye not exceed 1 to 2% is the final mixture that is to be applied to the hair.

(iii) Other Adjuvants

For various reasons, it has beocome common manufacturing practice to improve a good dye solution by adding one or more substances with special properties viz. sequestearing, foaming or the cleaning agents etc.

Formulation for Black Oxidation Dye

P -Amino diphenylamine	0.05%
1,5 - Dihydroxynaphthaline	0.06%
P - Phyenylinediamine	3.75%
4 - Nitro - O - Phenylenediamine	0.8%
2 - Nitro - P - Phenylenediamine	0.05%
Sodium Sulfite	0.2%

Formulation for Dark Brown Oxidation Dye

P - Amino diphenylamine	0.05%
4 - Amino - 2 - Nitorphenol	0.10%
P - Aminophenol	0.21%
2 - Nitro - P - Phenylenediamine	0.10%
4 - Nitro - O - Phenylenediamine	0.2%
Pyrogallol	0.2%
Resorcinol	1.4%
Sodium sulfite	0.2%

Medium Brown

P - Aminodiphenylamine	0.2%
O - Aminophenol	0.2%
P - Aminophenol	0.2%
P - Methylamino phenol sulfate	0.15%
4 - Nitro - O - Phenylenediamine	0.15%
2 - Nitro - P - Phenylenediamine	0.15%
P - Phenylenediamine	2.0%
Resorcinol	1.0%

Sodium sulfite	0.4%

Medium Red

4 - Amino - 2 - Nitrophenol	1.5%
P - Aminophenol	1.0%
4 - Nitro - O - Phenylenediamine	0.5%
2 - Nitro - P - Phenylenediamine	2.5%
P - Phenylenediamine	1.0%
2 - Nitro - P - Pheylenediamine (Fusion (Mixture)	0.15%
Pyrogallol	2.0%
Resorcinol	0.3%
Sodium sulfite	0.8%

Golden Blond

P - Aminophenylamine	0.10%
O - Aminophenol	0.13%
P - Methyl amino phenol sulfate	0.4%
P - Phenylenediamine	0.4%
Pyrocatechol	0.2%
Pyrogallol	0.5%
Resorcinol	0.2%
Sodium sulfite	0.2%

Blue Violet

P - Aminophenol	0.9%
1,5 - Dihydroxynaphtaline	0.8%
P - Phenylenediamine	0.55%
2, 4 - Diaminoanisole sulfate	0.25%
Pyrocatechol	0.8%
Sodium sulfite	0.3%

Steel Gray

1, 5 - Dihydroxynaphthalene	0.4%
P - Methylaminophenol sulfate	0.25%
P - Phenylenediamine	0.6%
2, 4 - Diaminoanisole sulfate	0.55%

Sodium sulfate	0.6%

Colour Shampoos

These products are intended to impart merely a temporary tinge of colour to hair of any shade. The colour shampoos are usually prepared in only a few shades for example, one gold, one red, one or two browns and a silvery blue. A typical base for a modified colour shampoo is given below:-

Ammonium lauryl alcohol sulfate	25 - 35%
Fatty acids alkanolamide	2 - 6%
Water 9.5 to make	100%

(C) Metallic Hair Dyes

The metallic dyes are based principally on lead, silver and copper. Nickel alone is rare, but is found with silver, iron is found in most copper preparations. Bismuth, manganese and cobalt are fairly common in foreign products.

1. Lead Dyes

Most of the 'Colour restores' based on lead consist of dilute solutions of lead acetate or nitrate. Many compositions call for the addition of finely divided powdered sulphur, glycerol and either rose water or bay rum as perfume. All lead dyes are classified as 'Progressive dyes'

Following are some typical formulations for lead dyes.

Formulation No. 1

Lead acetate	1.5%
Precipitated sulphur	0.2%
Glycerol	1.5%
Distilled water or rose water, to make	100%

Formulation No. 2

Lead acetate	0.6%
Sodium thiosulfate	7.8%

Glycerol	5.0%
Ethyl alcohol	6.0%
Water, to make	100%

Formulation No. 3

I. Lead acetate	2.5%
Water to make	100%
II. Sodium sulfite	2.5%
Water, to make	100%

Preparation

Mix equal qualities of I and II at time of use.

2. Silver Dyes

The principal underlying the so-called restorers based on silver is two fold:-

a) All silver salts darkens on exposure to the light, and
b) Silver combines readily with protein, forming a brown stain.

In the oldest preparations, silver nitrate was used alone, in a dilute solution which was combed through the hair and allowed to remain undisturbed during exposure to strong sunlight. If the shade obtained was too light, the application of solution and exposure were repeated on incessive days. Used in this way, silver dyes may be classified as 'Progressive Dyes'.

As later improvements in these compositions, varying amounts of ammonia were added to the silver solution, thereby inhibiting certain proportions of silver and producing a fair gradation in shades. Sodium thiosulfate, also known as 'type was adopted as developer.

Restorers of this type are classified as instantaneous. For best effect, the hair must be absolutely clean, so it should be freshly shampooed and dried. The developer or mordant is combed through the hair first and distributed evenly. This may be allowed to dry or is followed immediately by the silver solution which brings out the colour. In genral, silver dyes are more satisfactory than those based on lead. The user may have trouble, however, after the first application, in the retouching of new growth of hair. Repeated applications to the same portion of hair cause the hair to become progressively darken and to develop an unpleasant metallic or indescent sheen.

Formulations for Silver Dyes

1. Black

(I) Pyrogallol	5%
Distilled water, to make	100
(II) Silver nitrate	15%
Ammonia water, 10%	9.5
Distilled water, to make	100

2. Dark Brown

(I) Pyrogallol	3%
Distilled water, to make	100
(II) Silver nitrate	8%
Ammonia water, 10%	9.5%
Distilled water, to make	100

3. Light Brown

(I) Pyrogallol	2%
Distilled water, to make	100
(II) Silver nitrate	4%
Ammonia water 10%	9.5
Distilled water, to make	100

4. Blond

(I) Pyrogallol	1%
Distilledj water, to make	100
(II) Silver nitrate	0.5
Ammonia water, 10%	9.5
Distilled water, to make	100

Procedure

In making II, use sufficient ammonia water to dissolve precipitate that forms. As a precaution against deterioration, the ammoniacal silver nitrate should always be in a dark blue or amber bottle, closed securely against escape of ammonia.

3. Copper Dyes

The modern hair based on copper have been evolved from the ancient rastiks, in that the same essential ingredients are combined in liquid form instead of powders. Use of copper sulphate alone with pyrogallol produces a rather good brown, if ferric chloride is added, the resulting shade is a much darker brown or black. By varying the proportions of the metallic salts some variation can be affected in the shade produced, but copper is usually not to be considered for lighter shades of hair.

Formulation for Copper Dyes

Formula No. 1

Copper chloride	2%
Pyrogallol	2%
Nitric acid	0.5
Distilled water, to make	100

Formula No. 2

Copper sulphate	1%
Pyrogallol	2
Ammonium chloride	0.5
Distilled water, to make	100

Formula No. 3

Copper chloride	1.8%
Pyrogallol	3.8
Hydrochloric acid	0.8
Distilled water, to make	100

Miscellaneous Metallic Dyes

To produce a wider range of shades, and especially lighter shades than is possible with the metallic dyes just described, the following metals have been employed from time to time, and may still be found in present products.

Bismuth

The use of bismuth citrate as an innovation in hair dyes was first proposed in 1875 in France but discontinued due to the use of pure smelling sulphur compounds in order to obtain good shades.

As bismuth sulfide is chocolate brown, these dyes can be used to produce medium and light brown shades. Neutral bismuth nitrate first dissolved in glycerol and then carefully diluted with water can serve as a progressive dye as sodium thiosulfate is commonly offered in a second bottle as a developer. The action is very slow, and as the light shades fade relating quickly, the solutions must be applied repeatedly. Combinations with silver nitrate act more quickly and produce more lasting shades.

2. Cobalt

It is used with a developer (Hydrosulfide or pyrogallol) to produce light brown shades. The use of cobalt nitrate, either alone or in mixtures with silver and ammonium compounds permitted the introduction of a full line of 20 shades of dyes, from blonds to black. The developer was pyrogallol with or without other phenolic compounds and iron salts.

3. Iron

The least harmful to the hair, but also the least effective metal whose salts are used as hair dyes. Ferrous sulphate was commonly employed in old progressive dyes. Used alone, iron salts produce unsatisfactory blond shades because they tend to darken, and the darker shades from more concentrated solutions are drigy, grayish, and fluting. As modifiers in compositions with copper, cobalt, and other salts, ferrous sulphate and ferric chloride have been used for many years. As the developer for now salts, pyrogallol has supplanted the evil-smelling hydrosuphides formerly used.

4. Nickel

Occasionally found alone, but usually combined with silver, cobalt or copper. Nickel nitrate produces fair dark-brown shades, ammonium hydroxide or carbonate is usually included, and the developer is usually pyrogallol.

5. Other Metals

To widen the range of shades obtainable with metallic dyes, both stannic chloride and cadmium sulphate have been recommended and tried by various experimenters.

6. Manganese

A saturated solution of potassium or sodium permanganate, which is reduced to manganese dioxide in contact with organic matter produces a good brown shade when it is combed through the hair. However in the trade and industry permanganates are considered quite obsolete.

Advantages and Disadvantages of Metallic Dyes

The principal advantage that can be claimed for metallic dyes is that, unless they are accidently taken internally, by mouth or through abrasions in the skin, they are generally considered harmless to the skin and to the system.

The disadvantages of metallic dyes as now constituted are numerous viz.-

(i) The range of shades normally produced is limited to harsh dark browns and black,

(ii) Lighter shade darken unpredictably or fade,

(iii) All metallic dyes deposit a plating on the hair which frequently causes unpleasant off-shades, and eventually makes the hair stiff and brittle,

(iv) because of abnormal changes in texture, such hair frequently is adversely affected by permanent waving.

DYE REMOVERS

The removal of a hair dye, especially if there is any question of changing from one type of dye to another, is a serious and important undertaking, which is best left to an experienced hair dresser or cosmetologist.

Hot-oil Treatments

An entirely safe treatment for all dyed hair is a good soaping in oil. Various mixtures have been used successfully e.g. crude oil alone, or preferably mixed with olive oil or any readily available less expensive vegetable oil. Mineral oil may also be mixed with olive oil or any good blend. Instructions should specify that the hair be completely covered with the oil and heated by slipping strands of it through a heated iron. A marcel iron, a pressing iron, or a metal pressing comb, such as used for strengthening the hair, serves the purpose. The hair is then to be rubbed, strand by strand, with a towel, and thoroughly shampooed.

Vegetable Dyes

Of the 'Coating dye' those compounded of only natural organic substances offer relatively little trouble. Plain henna is the one most commonly encountered now. Depending on the nuber of times the colouring has been applied, the texture of the hair may be stiffer and harsher than normal, but it usually responds to relatively few of the oil treatments.

Metallic Dyes

Of the three metals commonly found in modern hair dyes, lead is most easily removed. Silver and its combinations are more assistant but usually tractable. Copper, either alone or with other metals, is often troublesome because the mordants that are now always used with it fix the dye in the hair. During the course of oil-treatment, lead dyes develop a purplish tinge, silver dye become distinctly greenish, and copper dye, reddish.

Synthetic Organic Dyes

As originally presented, that is, as clear ammoniacal solutions, to be applied to hair that was shampooed and pretreated with hydrogen peroxide, the amino dyes penetrated the hair and coloured it throughout. Hair so dyed usually does not respond to treatments with the simple oil mixtures described.

Colour rinses, presumably temporary, have been made more lasting by the addition of surface-active chemicals. If there is any appreciable deposit on the hair after the application of these rinses, it can be removed by one two heating treatments with oils.

Sulfonated Oils

At any time, sulfonated oils must be used with caution, because they can be strip even the natural colour from the hair and frequently bring out unpleasant streaks.

Sulfonated castor oil has long been used to remove all types of dyes. It offers an advantage over the simple oils because being water miscible other chemicals for special purpose can be added to it.

To remove henna and metallic dyes, sulfonated castor oil is more effective with the addition of 1 to 2% salicylic acid. For amino dyes, a portion of the oil may be mixed with half its quantity of 20 ml. hydrogen peroxide.

Formulation for Acquous Dye - Remover

Sodium thiosulfate	5%
Sulfuric acid	2
Distilled water	93

Following solutions are also recommended for this purpose:-

1. Sodium hydrosulfite.
2. Sodium formaldehydesulfoxylate.
3. Hydrogen peroxide

30

ORAL HERBAL PREPARATIONS (TOOTH PASTE AND POWDER)

Many herbs have cleansing and antiseptic properties which made them suitable for oral hygiene. The most commonly used important herbs for Oral hygiene are sage (astrigent), cloves, peppermint & thyme (antiseptics) parsley, marjoram, bramble and black current leaves & Juniper berries. Chewing Juniper berries, peppermint or parsley kills the bad odour of onion, garlic or alcohol. Rubbing the teeth with sage cleans them and sweetens the breath strawberries impart a whitening effect and clean the teeth and remove the decay. An effective mouth wash can be prepared with a normal infusion of sage, mint, thyme or marjoram. Another useful herbs for the mouth cones from the tree salvadora persica popularly known as the "Tooth brush tree' or Mustard Tree or 'Salt Bust It is a large, much branched evergreen shrub or a tree much resembling saloadora olcoides found in the dry & Ariel regions of India and on the Saline Lands and in Coastal regions just above the high water mark. Tooth pastes made from this tree are now available in the market.

TOOTH PASTES AND TOOTH POWDER

Tooth Paste (Peppermint)

This mixture cleans the teeth and freshesing the mouth. It is to be used generally with a damp tooth brush.

Arrowroot	1 Table spoon
Milled Sea Salt	1 Table spoon
Sodium Bi-carbonate	1/2 Tea spoon
Peppermint oil	15-20 Drops

Procedure

The ingredients are mixed with a spoon and then beaten into a paste with a pestle and then stored in a screw topped jar.

Arrow root	1 Table spoon
Milled sea salt	1 Table spoon
Ground of Cloves	1 Table spoon
Oil of Cloves	15 Drops.

Procedure

The ingredients are mixed with a spoon and then beaten to a dry paste with a pestle and mortar.

Tooth Powder with Sage

Fresh sage leaves	1 Small handful
Sea Salt miled	1 Tea spoon

Fresh sage is used for this powder. The sage is washed and the fresh leaves are picked off and finely chopped. To each spoonful of the chooped sage a half teaspoon of miled sea salt is added the contents are transferred to a heating dish and baked in an oven at a temperature of 150 °C for twenty minutes until the sage is dry. Then it is removed from the oven & the mixture is ground to a fine powder with a pestle and mortar. The mixture is again kept in an oven for a further 15 minutes until powdery. The product is cooled and stored in a screw topped jar. Fresh sage leaves used in this powder taste good and the volatile oil has antiseptic to be rinsed well after use.

Mouth Wash

Black currant or Bramble leaves	1 handful
Water	500 Ml.
Lemon Juice	2 Teaspoons.

Procedure

The leaves are picked when they are young and fresh and are chosen from the tops of the steins. The leaves and water are taken into an open saucepan and boiled until the liquid is reduced by half. The Lemon Juice is then added and after straining used immediately.

Mouth Wash.

Vinegar	1/4 Cup.
Wine	1/2 Cup.
Honey	1/4 Cup.
Powdered Cloves.	1 Teaspoon

Procedure

The above ingredients are taken in a bowl and boiled till the mixture is homogeneous. It is then cooled and used as a mouth wash.

31

GOVT. REGULATIONS AND ACTS ON DRUGS AND COSMETICS

There are several Acts pertaining to manufacture and sale of Drugs and Cosmetics in India. There are also rules framed under the procedure of these laws which govern the production and sale of drugs and cosmetics. The following laws operate at present in the country.

The Drugs and Cosmetics Act of 1940 as amended by the Drugs (Amendment) Act, 1950,

- The Drugs (Amendment) Act, 1960,
- The Drugs (Amendment) Act, 1962,
- The Drugs and Cosmetics (Amendment) Act, 1964,
- The Drugs and Cosmetics (Amendment) Act, 1972,
- The Drugs and Cosmetics (Amendment) Act, 1982,
- The Drugs and Cosmetics Act, 1986.

2. The Drugs and Cosmetics Rules 1945
3. The Drugs and Cosmetics (Amendment) 1964
4. The Drugs and Cosmetics (Amendment) 1972
5. The Drugs and Cosmetics (Amendment) Act of 1982
6. The Drugs and Cosmetics (Amendment) Act, of 1986
7. The Medicinal and Toilet Preparations (Excise Duties) Act of 1956.
8. The Medicinal and Toilet Preparations (Excise Duties) Rules of 1956.

THE DRUGS AND COSMETICS ACT OF 1940

OBJECTIVE

The object of the Act is to regulate the import, manufacture, distribution and sale of drug and cosmetics under the provisions of this Act. The Central Government appoints the Drug Technical Advisory Board to advise the Central Government and the State Government on technical matters arising out of the adminstration of this Act. The Central Government has also to establish a control of a Director to carry out the functions entrusted to it by this Act.

The Drug and Cosmetics Act prohibits the following:

a) Import of any drug (or cosmetic) which is not of standard quality.
b) Import of any misbranded drug or misbranded or spurious cosmetics.
c) Import of any adulterated or spurious drug.
d) Import of any drug, for the import of which licence is prescribed.
e) Import of any patent drug if it is not labelled in prescribed manner displaying its true formula.
f) Import of any drug which claims to cure and mitigate disease prescribed.
g) Import of any drug the import of which is banned under the Act.

The Drug and Cosmetics Act further prohibits the manufacture for sale or for distribution or sale or stock or exhibit or offer for sale the following:

a) Any drug which is not of standard quality or is misbranded, adulterated or spurious.
b) Any drug which is not of standard quality or is misbranded or spurious.
c) Any patent drug which does not bear on the label the true formula or list of active ingredients together with quantities.
d) Any drug which claims to cure and mitigate prescribed diseases.
e) Any cosmetic containing any ingredient making it unsafe for use.
f) Any drug the manufacture of which is prohibited under the Act.
g) Any drug or cosmetic manufactured in contravention of any of the provisions of the Act or rules made thereunder.

THE DRUG AND COSMETIC ACT - 1940 (As modified upto the Ist June 1984)

SYNOPSIS OF CHAPTER I

Section

1. Short title, extent and commencement
2. Application of other laws not barred.
3. Definition.
3a. Construction of reference to any law not in force or any functionary not in existence in the State of Jammu and Kashmir.
4. Presumption as to poisonous substances.

1Ins. by Act 13 of 1964, s. 2 (w.e.f. 1964).
2Subs. by 'Act 68 of 1982, s. 2 for certain words (w.e.f. 1-2-1983).
3 Subs. by s. 3, ibid., for certain words (w.e.f. 1-2-1983).
4 Original clasue (a) was relettered as cl. (aa) and subs. by Act 13 of

1964, s. 2 (w.e.f. 15-9-1964).
5. Ins. by Act 21 of 1962, s. 4 (w.e.f. 27-7-1964).
6. Relettered by Act 13 of 1964, s. 2(w.e.f. 15-9-1964).
7. Certain words omitted by Act 68 of 1982, s. 3 (w.e.f. 1-2-1983).
8. Subs. by Act 11 of 1955, s. 2 for cl. (b).
9. Subs. by Act 68 of 1982, s. 3, for sub-clause (i) (w.e.f. 1-2-1983).
10. Subs. by Act 13 of 1964, s. 2, for "vermins" (w.e.f.15-9-1964).
11. Ins. by Act 68 of 1982, s.3 (w.e.f. 1-2-1983).

SECTION 3. (Definitions)

In this Act, unless there is anything repugnant in the subject or context,-

1[(a) "2[Ayurvedic, Siddha or Unani] drug" includes all medicines intended for internal or external use for or in the diagnosis, treatment, mitigation or prevention of 3[Ayurvedic, Siddha and Unani tib system of medicine, specified in the First Schedule;]

4[(aa) "the Board" means-

(i) in relation to 2[Ayurvedic, Siddha or Unani] drug the 3[Ayurvedic, Siddha and Unani Drugs Technical Advisory Board] constituted under section 33C; and

(ii) in relation to any other drug or cosmetic, the Drugs Technical Advisory Board constituted under section 5;]

5[6[aaa)] "cosmetic" means any article intended to be rubbed, poured, sprinkled or sprayed on, or introduced into, or otherwise applied to, the human body or any part thereof for cleansing, beautifying, promoting attractiveness, or altering the appearance, and includes any article intended for use as a component of cosmetic7 * * *;]

8[(b) "drug" includes-

9[(i) all medicines for internal or external use of human beings or animals and all substances intended to be used for or in the diagnosis, treatment, mitigation or prevention of any disease or disorder in human beings or animals, including preparations applied on human body for the purpose of repelling insects like mosquitoes:]

(ii) such substances (other than food) intended to affect the structure or any function of the human body or intended to be used for the destruction of 10[vermin] or insects which cause disease in human beings or animals, as may be specified from time to time by the Central Government by notification in the Official Gazette;]

11[(iii) all substances intended for use as components of a drug including empty gelatin capsules; and

---

1 Subs. by Act 13 of 1964, s.2, for cl. (r) w.e.f. 15-9-1964).
2 Subs. by Act 68 of 1982, s.2. for certain words of w.e.f. 1-2-1983).
3 Cl. (d) omitted by Act 19 of 1972, s.3.
4 Subs. by Act 13 of 1964, s.2, for cl. (e) (w.e.f. 15-9-1964).
5 Cl. (bbb) ins. by Act 11 of 1955,s.2.
6 Cl. (bbb) relettered as cl. (f) by Act 35 of 1960, s.2 (w.e.f. 16-3-1983).
7 Ins.by Act 21 of 1962,s.4 (w.e.f.27-7-1964).
8 Subs.by Act68 of 1982, s.3 for "sale and distribution"(w.e.f. 1-2-1983).
9 Subs. by Act 21 of 1962,s.4 for "or packing of any drug".
10 Cls. (c), (d) and (e) relettered as cls.(g),(h) and(i) respectively by Act 35 of 1960,s.2 (w.e.f. 16-3-1961).
11 Subs. by Act 3 of 1951,s.3 and Sch., for "the States".
12Ins.by Act21 of 1962,s.5,(w.e.f. 27-7-1964).

(iv) such devices intended for internal or external use in the diagnosis, treatment, mitigation or prevention of disease or disorder in human beings or animals, as may be specified from time to time by the Central Government by notification in the Official Gazette, after consultation with the Board:]

1[(c) "Government Analyst" means-

(i) in relation to 2[Ayurvedic, Siddha or Unani] drug, a Government Analyst appointed by the Central Government or a State Government under section 33F: and

(ii) in relation to any other drug or cosmetic, a Government Analyst appointed by the Central Government or a State Government under section 20:]

* * * * * * *

4[(e) "Inspector" means-

(i) in relation to 2[Ayurvedic, Siddha or Unani] drug, an Inspector appointed by the Central Government or a State Government under section 33G; and

(ii) in relation to any other drug or cosmetic, an Inspector appointed by the Central Government or a State Government under section 21:]

5[6[(f) "manufacture" in relation to any drug 7[for cosmetic] includes any process or part of a process for making, altering, or ornamenting, finishing, packing, labelling, breaking up or otherwise treating or adopting any drug 7[or cosmetic] with a view to its8[sale or distribution] but does not include the compounding or dispensing 9[of any drug, or the packing of any drug or cosmetic.] in the ordinary course of retail business; and "to manufacture" shall be construed accordingly;]

10[(g)] "to import" with its grammatical variations and cognate expressions means to bring into 11[India];

12[(h) "patent or proprietary medicine" means.-

(i) in relation to Aurvedic, Siddha or Unani Tibi systems of medicine all formulations containing only such ingredients mentioned in the formulae described in the authoritative books of Ayurveda. Siddha or Unani Tibi systems of medicine specified in the First Schedule, but does not include a medicine which is administered by parenteral route and also a formulation included in the authoritative books as specified in clause (a):

(ii) in relation to any other systems of medicine, a drug which is a remedy or prescription presented in a form ready for internal or external administration of human beings or animals and which is not included in the edition at the Indian pharmacopoeia for the time being or any other pharmacopoeia authorised in this behalf by the Central Government after consultation with the Drugs Technical Advisory Board constituted under section 5;]

1[2[(i) " prescribed" means prescribed by rules made under this Act.]

*   *   *   *   *   *

4[3A. Any reference in this Act to any law which is not in force, or any functionary not in existence, in the State of Jammu and Kashmir, shall, in relation to that State, be constructed as a reference to the corresponding law in force, or to the corresponding functionary in existence, in that State.]

SYNOPSIS OF CHAPTER

5. The Drug Technical Advisory Board
6. The Central Drug laboratory
7. The Drug consultation committee.
7 a. Section 5 and 7 not to apply to Ayurvedic Sidha or Unani

SYNOPSIS OF CHAPTER
IMPORTS OF DRUGS AND COSMETICS

SECTIONS
8. Standards of quality
9. Misbranded Drug
9. A. Adulterated Drug
9. B. Spurious Drug
9. C. Misbranded Cosmetics
9. D. Spurious Cosmetics
10. Prohibition of import of certain drug and cosmetics
10 A. Power of Central Govt. to prohibit import of drug and cosmetics in public interest
11. Application of law relating to sea custom and powers of Customs officers.
12. Power of the Central Govt. to make rules.
13. Offences
14. Confisaction
15. Jurisdiction

SECTION 9C (Misbranded Cosmetics)
For the purposes of this chapter a cosmetic shall be deemed to be misbranded.
a) If it contains a colour which is not prescribed or
b) If it is not labled in the prescribed manner, or
c) If the label or container or anything accompanying the cosmetic bears any statement which is false or misleading in any particular.

SECTION 9D (Spurious Cosmetics)

For the purposes of this chapter a cosmetic shall be deemed to be spurious:-

a) If it is imported under a name which belongs to another cosmetic; or

b) If it is an imitation of or is a substiute for, another cosmetic or resembles another cosmetic in a manner likely to deceivre or bears upon its label or container the name of another cosmetic unless it is plainly and conspicuously marked so as to reveal its true characters and its lack of identity with such other cosmetic; or

c) If the name of an industry or a company purporting to be the manufacturer of the cosmetic which industry or company is fictitions or does not exist; or

d) If it is an imitation of or is a substitute for another drug, or is not truly a product.

SECTION 10 (Prohibition of import or certain drug or cosmetics).
From such date as may be fixed by the Central Government by notification in the official gazette in this behalf no person shall import.

a) any drug (or cosmetic) which is not of standard quality,

b) any misbranded drug (or misbranded or spurious cosmetic) or any adulterated or spurious drug),

c) any drug (or cosmetic) for the import of which a licence is prescribed, otherwise than under and in accordance with such licence,

d) any patent or proprietary medicine, unless there is displayed in the prescribed manner on the label or container therof (the true formula or list of active ingredients contained in it together with the quantities thereof;,

e) any drug which by no means of any statement, design or device accompanying it or by any other means, purports to claim to cure or mitigate any such disease or ailiment or to have any such other effect as may be prescribed,

f) any cosmetic containing any ingredient which may render it unsafe or harmful for use under the directions, indicated or recommended,

f) any drug (or cosmetic) the import of which is prohibited by rule made under this chapter:

Provided that nothing in this section shall apply to the import subject to prescribed condition of small quantities of any drug for the purpose of examination, test or analysis or for personal use.

Provided further that the central government may, after consultation with Board by notification in the official Gazette, permit, subject to any condition specified of any drug or class of drug not being standard quality.

SYNOPSIS OF CHAPTER

MANUFACTURE, SALE AND DISTRIBUTION OF DRUG AND COSMETICS

SECTIONS

16. Standards of quality
17. Misbranded drug
17a. Adulterated drug
17b. Spurious drugs
17c. Misbranded cosmetics
17d. Spurious cosmetics
18. Prohibition of, manufacture and sale of certain drugs and cosmetics
18a. Disclosure of the name of the manufacturer etc.
18b. Manufacture of records and furnishing of information
19. Pleas
20. Government analysis
21. Inspectors
22. Power of inspectors
23. Procedure of Inspectors
24. Persons bond to disclose place where drugs or cosmetics are manufactured.
25. Reports of Government Analyst.
26. Purchaser of drug or cosmetic enabled to obtain test or analysis.

26a. Powers of central government to probihit, manufacture etc. of drug and cosmetic in public interest.
27. Penalty for manufacture, sale, etc. of drug in contravention of this chapter.
27a. Penalty for manufacture, sale, etc. of cosmetics in contravention of this chapter.
28. Penalty for non-disclosure of the name of the manufacturer etc.
28a. Penalty for not keeping documents etc. and for non-disclosure of information.
28b. Penalty for manufacture etc. of drugs or cosmetics in contravention of section 26a.
29. Penalty for use fo government analyst's report for advertising
30. Penalty for subsequant offences.
31. Confiscation
31.a Application of provisions to government department.
32. Cognizance of offences
32a. Power of court to implead the manufacture, etc.
33. Power of Central Government to make rules.
33a. Chapter not to apply to Ayurvedic, Siddha or Unani Drugs.

SYNOPSIS OF CHAPTER

Provisions relating to Ayurvedic siddha Unani Drugs

SECTIONS
33B. Application of chapter.
33C. Ayurvedic and Unani Drugs Technical Adivsory Board.
33D. The Ayurvedic, Sidha and Unani Drug consultative committee.
33E. Misbranded drugs
33EE. Adulterated Drugs
33EEA. Spurious Drugs
33EEB. Regulation of manufacture and sale of Ayurvedic, Siddha and Unani Drugs.
33EEC. Prohibition of manufacture and sale of certain Ayurvedic, Siddha and Unani Drugs.
33EED. Power of the Central Government to prohibit manufacture etc. of Ayurvedic, Siddha or Unani Drugs in public interest.
33F. Government Analysts.
33G. Inspectors.
33H. Application of provisions of section 22, 23, 24, 25

33I. Penalty for manufacture, sale, etc. of Ayurvedic, Siddha or Unani Drug in contravention of this chapter.
33J. Penalty for subsequent offences.
33K. Confiscation.
33L. Application of visions to government departments.
33M. Cognizance of offences.
33N. Power of Central Government to make rules.
33O. Power to amend first schedule.

SYNOPSIS OF CHAPTER
MISCELLANEOUS

33P. Power to give direction
34. Offences by companies
34A. Offence by government department.
34AA. Penalty for vexatious search or seizure.
35. Publication of sentences passed under this Act.
36. Magistrates power to impose enhanced penalties.
36A. Certain offences to be tried summarily.
37. Protection of action taken in good faith.
38. Rules to be laid befor Parliament

32

BATH PREPARATIONS

Introduction

Modern bath preparations are usually formulated for several or all of the following purposes:-

1. To make the user full refreshed.
2. To help soften hard water.
3. To add a pleasing effect to the bath, by means of perfume and colour.
4. To clean the body by removing list and odour, and to add a pleasing fragrance to the body.
5. To prevent a ring from forming around the bath tube.

Bath prepartions may be classified as below:-
1) Bath salts
2) Bath oils
3) Bubble bath
4) Bath powders.

Bath Salts

Bath salts are of two types viz.

a) Those that are primarily intended to impart perfume and colour to the bath, and
b) Those that, in addition to the above two qualities also help soften hard water and make cleansing easier.

The first type is formulating usually with rock salt crystals (or glauber's salts) coloured and perfumed. This type of bath salt is neutral in character and not soften the water or help in the cleansing action of the bath soap. The salt crystals of the desired size are placed in a ribbon powder mixer, and a solution of the perfume oil, alcohol and the desired colour is added to the crystals, with mixing. From 0.5 to 1.0% of the perfume oil is the usual quantity used. After the crystals are uniformly coloured, they are placed on trays to allow the alcohol to evaporate, and are then ready to be packaged.

In second type of bath salts is usually based on one of the sodium phosphates or on sodium sesquicarbonate. Trisodium phosphate is the most common for this purpose. However, the latter is seldom used alone for bath salts, because of its high alkalinity. Usually sodium sesquicarbonate or borax, or both, are mixed with the trisodium phosphate to buffer its high alkalinity. The advantages of this type of bath salts are that it does have some water-softening properties and that it aids the cleansing action of the soap. Moreover, the surface tension of the water is lowered which allows easier metting of the skin. The disadvantage of this is that due to high alkalinity, some people respond to skin irritation. The other disadvantages is that only certain perfumes and colours can be used in such preparations due to high alkalinity.

Formulations for Bath Salts

Formula No. 1

	Parts
Trisodium Phosphate	50 to 49
Sodium Sesquicarbonate	49.5 to 49
Perfume	0.5 to 2
Colour	q.s.

Formula No. 2

Trisodiumk Phosphate	50 to 49
Rock Salt or Sodium Chloride	49.5 to 49
Perfume	0.5 to 2
Colour	q.s.

Formula No. 3

Sodium Sesquicarbonate	80 to 90
Borax, powdered	18 to 8
Perfume	0.5 to 2
Colour	q.s.

Formula No. 4

	%
Sodium Bicarbonate	45
Tartaric Acid	37.5
Sodium Hexametaphosphate	10.0
Carboxymethylcellulose	2.0
Sodium Lauryl Sulphate	5.0
Perfume	0.5

Process of Manufacture

Combine the dry ingredients in powdered form and mix until uniform. Dissolve the perfume in enough isopropyl alcohol to moisture the batch (about 2 pints to 100 pounds) and add to the material. Stir the mixture until perfumed uniformly, then granulate through a 1/8 inch screen, and dry. The finished product is packaged in air-tight containers or pressed into screen, and dry. The finished product is packaged in air-tight containers or pressed into tablets, preferably about 11/4 inch in diameter and 1/4 inch thick, which are placed in the airtight containers.

Formula No. 5

	Parts
Sodium Sesquicarbonate	100
Rose artificial	0.001
Phenyl Ethyl Alcohol	0.001
Rhodamine B.S.	0.001

Use water in a sufficient quantity to dissolve the rhodamine.

Bath Oils

Bath oils are of two main type viz.-

1) One is an oily type that is not miscible or emulsifable with water, and

2) Second is either soluble or emulsifiable in water.

The first type is perhaps less popular. It can be made in several ways. One formula calls for castor oil, for instance, with the viscosity adjusted by means of alcohol, and with about 3% of perfume and an oil-soluble colour, if desired. A little or then it is put into the tube, and water pressure is allowed to distriubute it in the bath. The water then takes up much of the perfume oil and the latter floats as a thin film on the surface, which, of course, is transferred to the body while bathing. Other oils can be used but castor oil is the only common oil that can be diluted with alcohol to give the desired viscosity. Some of the synthetic oil esters may be used for such purpoe. Isopropyl myristate or palmitate, butyl stearate, and others are easily perfumed and coloured. Following are some of thė typical formualtions:-

Formula No. 1

	%
Castor Oil	30 to 80
Ethyl Alcohol	0 to 10
Perfume	10
Colour	q.s.

Formula No. 2

	%
Isopropyl Myristate	90 to 95
Perfume	5 to 10
Colour	q.s.

Formula No. 3

Castor Oil, sulfated 50%	97
Perfume	3
Colour	q.s.

Formula No. 4

	%
Castor Oil, sulfated 50%	50
Ethyl Alcohol	10 to 0
Solubilizer	7

Perfume	3
Colour	q.s.
Water	30 to 40

Formula No. 5

A bath oil based on a sulphated detergent, non-foaming type, is shown in following formula.

	Parts
Sulfated Detergent	30 to 40
Water	60 to 50
Solubilizer	7
Perfume oil	3
Colour	q.s.

Formula No. 6

Pinc Oil Bath Foam	Parts
Flourescein	0.1
Bromyl Acetate	10.1
Oil of Pinc	5.0
Alcohol	20.0
Sulphonated Castror Oil	100.0

Formula No. 7

Bath Cubes	Parts by wt.
Crex	84.5
Talc	5
Starch	8
Borax	2
Perfume	0.2

Bubble Bath

Bubble bathes are by far the most popular of the bath accessory preparations. They take on many physical forms: Powder, liquid, tablets, capsules, crystals, and soap cakes.

Characteristics of Bubble Bath

1) The product should bubble easily without the need of excessive water pressure.

2) The foam product should be stable in both hard and soft water, and also in the presence of soap.
3) The product should prevent the formation of a ring around the bath tube.
4) At the dilution used in the tube, it should be nonirritating to the skin and mucous membrane.
5) The cost of ingredients should be low enough to allow it to be sold at a reasonable price in the proper package.

Formulations for Bubble-Bath

Formula No. 1

	%
Sodium Lauryl Sulphate	30
Sodium Hexametaphosphate	5
Sodium Carboxymethyl Cellulose, low viscosity	2
Sodium Chloride, fine, granular	60
Perfume	3

Formula No. 2

	%
Sodium Lauryl Sulfoacetate	20
Sodium Chloride, fine, granular	47
Alkyl Benzene Sodium Sulphonate	30
Perfume	3

Formula No. 3

	%
Sodium Lauryl Sulfoacetate	60
Sodium Tripolyphosphate	38
Perfume	2

Procedure

Mix the dry ingredients until uniform, then add thc perfume, and mix again until uniformly distributed. If difficulty is experienced with non-uniformity of odour, the perfume should first be dissolved in a little alcohol.

The liquid bubble bath is a most popular product. Earlier such formulas were based on liquid soap with phosphate and with other sequestering agents added to keep insoluble soaps from forming in the bath.

More modern liquid bubble baths are based on the synthetic surface active agent especially the good foamers, whether they are good detergents or not. However, it is easy to add a good detergent to a good foamer and thus have bath qualities present.

The ingredients of a liquid bubble bath must be selected so that a clear solution is obtained over a wide range of temperatures. If the product is to be coloured other than brown, a light-coloured solution must result. Some excellent preparations can be made from the following formualtions. In all these formulas, the perfume content is arbitraily set at 3%, it should, however, be adjusted, according to the type of fragrance used, and the remainder of the formula changed accordingly. Colour may also be added to any of these preparations, if desired.

Formula No. 1

	%
Fatty Acid Amine Condesate	40
Water	57
Perfume	3

Formula No. 2

	%
Fatty Acid Amine Condensate	30
Alkyl Sulfonate	15
Water	52
Perfume	3

Formula No. 3

	%
Fatty Acid Amine Condensate	20
Sodium Lauryl Sulphate	20
Water	57
Perfume	3

Formula No. 4

	%
Sodium Lauryl Sulphate	30
Water	67
Perfume	3

Formula No. 5

	%
Triethanolamine Lauryl Sulphate	30
Water	67
Perfume	3

Formula No. 6

	%
Alkyl Aryl Polyethyl Ether	7
Dioctyl Ester of Sodium Succinic Acid	6
Ethyl Alcohol	10
Water	100
Perfume	3

Bath Powders

Bath powders have in the last been based on corn and rice starch and boric acid, but modern bath powders are generally made with from 60 to 90% of talc. Many other ingredients in smaller amounts are used to give desired properties to the finished product. These are chalk, zinc oxide, magnesium carbonate, kaolin, titanium dioxide, and zinc stearate.

Special perfumes are needed for bath powder to cover up the earthy odour of the ingredients. Small amounts of the synthetic musk like fixatives generally do a good job. About 5% of magnesium carbonate is used to absorb this perfume and hold it in the finished product. The perfume oil is mixed with magnesium carbonate before being added to the rest of the ingredients. A small amount of titanium dioxide, 1 to 2% will give some opacity to the talc, if this properly is desired.

Zinc oxide and chalk can be added to impart greater bulking tensity and to assist in packaging by giving a good fill in the container. Kaolin will help the powder cling to the body, and zinc stearate will give a desired slip to the product.

If colour is desired in the bath powder, the earth oxide colours should be used. Cosmetic grade from oxide will give a light pink colour, and odor a light tan one. A mixture of these two will produce a flesh tint. This type of colour should be added as an extender to the other ingredients, after they are uniformly blended. The extender should consist of about 25% of dry colour and 75% talc, mixed until uniform, and then micropulverized.

Formulations for Bath Powders

Formula No. 1

	%
Talc	80
Magnesium Carbonate	5
Kaolin	5
Titanium Dioxide	2
Zinc Stearate	7
Perfume	1
Colour & Extender	q.s.

Formula No. 2

	%
Talc	70
Magnesium Carbonate	5
Kaolin	7
Zinc Stearate	4
Zinc Oxide	3
Chalk, Heavy	10
Perfume	1
Colour & Extender	q.s.

Formula No. 3

	%
Talc	90
Magnesium Carbonate	4
Zinc Stearate	5
Perfume	1
Colour & Extender	q.s.

Formula No. 4

	%
Talc	60
Magnesium Carbonate	5
Titanium Dioxide	2
Zinc Stearate	10
Zinc Oxide	12
Chalk, Heavy	10
Perfume	1
Colour & Extender	q.s.

Procedure

Place the dry ingredients, except the magnesium carbonate, in a powder mixer and mix until uniform. If a perfume fixative is to be added to counteract the earthy odour, it is incorporated at this point in the form of a 1% alcoholic solution, at the rate of one point to 100 pounds of the finished batch. Mix the alcoholic solution into the dry ingredients, until uniformly distributed. Mix the magnesium carbonate and the perfume in a separate container and sift into the batch while mixing. If colour desired, add the extender at this time and mix the batch until the colur is uniformly distributed. Then run the batch through a micropulverizer or through a bolting screen, and it is ready to be packaged. The bath powder should be packaged in a large diameter, round or square, flat box, so that a large puff can be enclosed.

33

BABY PREPARATIONS

Introduction

The increase sale fo the baby toiletries is of equal importance to the manufacturers and consumers of such products. Years of research work have made it possible for some such preparations and the care of the new born is still a subject of the scholars and much more is expected to come forward in the years to come.

The skin of the new born and infants is quite different from that of a child and an adult. It is thinner, less cornified, less hairy, contains a higher proportion of water and extracellular fluid minerals, has a tendency towards peeling and flaking. After removed of this membranous covering of the new born formed by fatty decomposition of epidermic cells, the skin is pink, soft, and silky in touch and has a very delicate texture. Therefore, the care of baby skin requires some special preparations. These can be in the form of powder, oil, lotion, cream, soap, shampoo, cotton swals, soft wash clothes and brushes.

A dermatological approach to the formulation of products designed for use on the new born and infant skin is of considerable value. A knowledge of the epidermal physiology of the new born, infant, and adult skin, including the structural anatomy, biochemistry, penetration and absorption, is a necessary requisite. The marked difference between the infant and adult skin, seen especially in the statum corneum require the most precise evaluation of each component and of the final product for sensitization and irritational potential. Of equal importance is the clinical and consumer testing of the product for its prophylactic and therapeutic effects.

The ingredients used in the formulation of body toiletries are selected from those generally used in adult cosmetics, and hence conform to the same standard. Raw materials should be selected which have minimal odour characteristics, so that very low perfume concentrations may be used. The choice of perfume oil should be based on results of through testing on adult and infant skin to be certain that they include no ingredients which may react unfavourably on the sensitive skin of infants. The raw materials for baby toiletries may include emollient oils and waxes, emulsifiers, humectants, antiseptics, preservatives, antioxidants, talc, corn starch, zinc oxide, detergent and perfume oils.

Emollients used in Baby Preparations

Following oil-soluble emollients may be used in the formulations of baby toiletries.

1. Wax esters like spermaceti, beeswax, lanolin.
2. Steroid alcohols: cholesterol and other lanolin alcohols.
3. Fatty alcohol: lauryl, cetyl, oleyl, and stearyl alcohols.
4. Triglyceride esters: animall and vegetable fats and oils.
5. Pospholipids: lecithin and cephalin.
6. Polyhdric alcohol esters: mono-and di-fatty acid esters of ethylene glycol, diethylene glycol, polythylene glycol, glycerol, sorbitol, mannitol etc.
7. Fatty alcohol ethers: cetyl, stearyl, and uleyl ethers of ethylene oxide polymers.
8. Alkyl fatty esters: methyl isopropyl , and butyl esters of fatty acids.
9. Hydrocarbon oils and waxes: mineral oils, petrolatum, and paraffin.
10. Hydrophilic lanolin derivatives: polyoxyethylene-sorbitol lanolin and polyoxyethylen lanolin derivatives.
11. Hydrophilic beeswax derivatives: polyoxyethylene sorbitol beeswax.
12. Silicone oils: dow-corning 200 series and 555 series etc.

Formulations for Baby Oils

The principal ingredients of baby oil is light mineral oil, with addition of other emollients such as vegetables oil, and lanolin or its oil soluble derivatives. Antiseptics, antioxidants, and perfume oils are generally added when desired.

Formula No. 1

	%
Light Mineral Oil	98.9
Hexachlorophene	1
Perfume	0.1

Formula No. 2

	%
Light Mineral Oil	73.85
Vegetable Oil	25
Hexachlorophene	1
Antioxidant	0.05
Perfume	0.10

Formula No. 3

	%
Mineral Oil, light	49.4
Lanolin	5
Isopropyl Myristate	19.5
Lantrol	25
Hexachlorophene	1.0
Perfume	0.1

Formula No. 4

	%
Mineral Oil, light	39.4
Isopropyl Myristate	9.5
Lantrol	50
Hexachlorophene	1.0
Perfume	0.1

Formula No. 5

	%
Mineral Oil, light	88.9
Isopropyl Myristate	7
Lanogene	3
Hexachlorophene	1
Perfume	0.1

Formula No. 6

	%
Mineral Oil, light	79.85
Isopropylan No. 50	20

Chlorothymol	0.25
Perfume	0.1

Formula No. 7

	%
Mineral Oil, light	87.85
Lanosol	12
Chlorothymol	0.05
Perfume	0.1

Formula No. 8

	%
Mineral Oil, light	93.9
Acetulan	5
Hexachlorophene	1
Perfume	0.1

Formula No. 9

	%
Mineral Oil, light	93.9
Moldulan	5
Hexachlorophene	1.0
Perfume	0.1

Formula No. 10

	%
Mineral Oil, light	58.9
Myracet type 9-40	30
Lanolin	10
Hexachlorophene	1.0
Perfume	0.1

Formula No. 11

	%
White Mineral Oil (65-75)	45
Refined Peanut Oil	54.7

Oxyquinoline Benzoate	0.2
Maleic Anhydride	0.1

Formula No. 12

	%
Mineral Oil	90.0
Lanolin	3.0
Ethyl Stearate	7.0

Fomula No. 13

	%
Mineral Oil	97
Cetyl Alcohol	3.0

Process of Manufacture

Dissolve the hexachlorophene in the isopropyl myristate (for formula 3, 4, 5) or in the mineral oil (for formula 1, 2, 8, 9, 10), by heating to 65 ^{0}C. Add the remaining ingredients (except the perfume), and cool to room temperature under constant stirring. Add the perfume oil, filter clear and fill . Formula 6 and 7 may be prepared by mixing all ingredients at room temperatures and filtering clear before filling .

Formulation for Baby Lotion

A popular product for cleaning the diaper area and for applying on emollient material to the skin is in the form of a lotion emulsion. The oil-in-water lotions usually contain more water than the corresponding creams, while the water in oil types may have the same water content, with oily components replacing part of the wax like materials.

These lotions be formulated with anionic, nonionic or cationic emulsifiers, as well as with nonionic-anionic and nonionic-cationic combinations. The nonionic and nonionic-cationic emulsions have the advantage over ther types of permitting formulations which contain to the acidic pH of normal skin. The emollients, antiseptics, and other additives may include those in the groups described previously.

Formulas for Baby Lotions oil/Water Nonionic Types

Formula No. 1

Part A	%
Lanolin	1
Cetyl Alcohcl	1
Arlacel 80	2.1
Tween 80	4.9
Velvasil Silicone fluid 1000	5
Mineral Oil, light	35
Propyl Paraben	0.15
Part B	
Methyl Paraben	0.15
Water	50.60
Perfume	0.10

Formula No. 2

Part A	%
Arlacel 83	2
Atlas G-1425	4.5
Beeswax	2.0
Petrolatum	7.5
Mineral Oil, light	37.50
Propyl Paraben	0.15
Part B	
Methyl Paraben	0.15
Water	46.10
Perfume	0.10

Formulas for Baby Lotions oil/Water Nonionic-Anionic Types

Formula No. 1

Part A	%
Cetyl Alcohol	0.20
Tween 60	0.50
Stearic Acid	1.0
Beeswax	2.0
Arlacel 60	5.0
Lantrol	10.0
Isopropyl Palmitate	10.0
Mineral Oil, light	10.0
Propyl Paraben	0.15

Part B	%
Methyl Paraben	0.15
Glycerol	5.0
Triethanolamine	0.40
Borax	0.10
Water	55.25
Perfume	0.25

Formula No. 2

Part A	%
Cetyl Alcohol	0.52
Stearic Acid	0.94
Stearyl Alcohol	0.94
Lanolin	1.04
Mineral Oil, light	26.0
Butyl Paraben	0.01

Part B	%
Methyl Paraben	0.09
Triethanolamine	0.52
Sodium Alginate	0.36
Water	69.33
Perfume	0.25

Formula No. 3

Part A	%
Oleic Acid	3
Lanolin	1.0
Tegin P	6.5
Mineral Oil, light	24
Propyl Paraben	0.15

Part B	
Methyl Paraben	0.15
Triethanolamine	1.50
Water	63.45
Perfume	0.25

Formula No. 4

Part A	%
Stearic Acid	
Isopropyl Palmitate	2
Lanolin	5
Beeswax	8
Polyglycol 400 Monostearate	10
Mineral Oil, light	15
Propyl Paraben	0.15

Part B	
Methyl Paraben	0.15
Propylene Glycol	5.0
Triethanolamine	1.0
Water	51.45
Perfume	0.25

Formula No. 5

Part A	%
Stearic Acid	2.5
Glyceryl Monostearate, pure	2

Amerchol L-101	9
Mineral Oil, light	4.5
Propyl Paraben	0.15

Part B

Methyl Paraben	0.15
Propylene Glycol	4.5
Triethanolamine	1.0
Water	77.95
Perfume	0.25

Formula No. 6

Part A	%
Stearic Acid	2.5
Lanolin	2
Oliec Acid	1.5
Hexachlorophene	1.0
Mineral Oil, light	25
Propyl Paraben	0.15

Part B

Methyl Paraben	0.15
Glycerol	3.5
Triethanolamine	1.3
Water	62.65
Perfume	0.25

Formulas for Baby Lotions Oil/Water Nonionic-Cationic Type

Formula No. 1

Part A	%
Cetyl Alcohol	0.5
Glceryl Monostearate, pure	1.0
Isopropyl Palmitate	3
Lanolin	1
Mineral Oil, light	5

Part B

Methyl Paraben	0.15
Glycerol	3.0
Lactic Acid	0.10
Emcol E-607	0.25
Water	85.90
Perfume	0.10

Formula No. 2

Part A	%
Cetyl Alcohol	0.50
Glceryl Monostearate, pure	1.0
Lanolin	1.0
Amerchol L-101	8

Part B

Methyl Paraben	0.15
Glycerol	3
Lactic Acid	0.10
Hyamine 10-X	0.15
Water	86.0
Perfume	0.10

Formula No. 3

Part A	%
Lanolin	2
Mineral Oil, light	2
Tegin	6.0

Part B

Methyl Paraben	0.15
Sorbitol	2.0
Cetyl Trimethyl Ammonium Bromide	0.16
Water	87.59
Perfume	0.10

Formultions for Baby Creams

These products are used where a greater degree of emollient and lubrication is desired, than is afforded by the baby lotions with thier higher water content. While the lotions are used for cleansing the diaper area and as light lubricants in skin folds, the creams find greatest use in areas requiring more effective skin softening and protection, particularly following the daily bath.

The creams may be formulated both as oil-in-water and water-in-oil emulsions. The former deposit a continuous semipermeable film on the skin. If the water content is relatively high, rapid evaporations of the external aqueous phase from the skin surface may be excessively cooling. Water-in-oil emulsions deposit a continuous, less permeable, hydrophobic film on the skin. The slower evaporation of water from the internal phase characterizes this type as a 'warm' emulsion and may be preferable for younger infants.

Formulations for Baby Creams Oil/Water Nonionic Type

Formula No. 1

Part A	%
Lanolin	3
Atlas G-1702	5
Atlas G-1726	5
Beeswax	5
Hydrogenated Vegetable Oil	25
Mineral Oil, light	20
Propyl Paraben	0.15
Antioxidant	0.05
Part B	
Methyl Paraben	0.15
Water	36.55
Perfume	0.10

Formula No. 2

Part A	%
Beeswax	5
Arlacel 60	3
Tween 60	4
Hydrogenated Vegetable Oil	17.5
Mineral Oil, light	26.0
Propyl Paraben	0.15
Antioxidant	0.05

Part B	%
Methyl Paraben	0.15
Sorbitol	5.0
Citric Acid	0.10
Water	38.95
Perfume	0.10

Formulations for Baby Creams Oil/Water Nonionic Type

Formula No. 1

Part A	%
Lanolin	1.0
Isopropyl Myristate	4.3
Polyglycol 1000 Monostearate	6.0
Stearic Acid	7.20
Glyceryl Monostearate, Pure	4.50
Propyl Paraben	0.15

Part B	
Methyl Paraben	0.15
Propylene Glycol	2.50
Water	74.10
Perfume	0.10

Formula No. 2

Part A	%
Beeswax	3
Spermaceti	3
Glyceryl Monostearate, pure	12
Mineral Oil, light	30
Propyl Paraben	0.15

Part B	%
Methyl Paraben	0.15
Propylene Glycol	8
Water	43.6
Perfume	0.10

Formulations for Baby Creams Water/Oil Nonionic Types

Formula No. 1

Part A	%
Atlas G-1441	1
Atlas G-1425	5
Beeswax	2
Stearic Acid	15
Lanoiln	1.0
Mineral Oil, light	15.0
Propyl Paraben	0.15

Part B	%
Methyl Paraben	0.15
Sorbitol	10
Water	50.6
Perfume	0.10

Formula No. 2

Part A	%
Atlas G-1425	4
Lanolin	1

Arlacel 83	2
Paraffin	10
Mineral Oil,Light	15
Petrolatum	35
Propyl Paraben	0.15

Part B	%
Methyl Paraben	0.15
Sorbitol	2.50
Water	30.10
Perfume	0.10

Formulations for Baby Creams Water/Oil Nonionic Types

Formula No. 1

Part A	%
Glyceryl Monostearate, Pure	5
Petrolatum	5
Mineral Oil, Light	15
Microcrystalline Wax (175 °F)	10
Amerchol L-101	15
Propyl Paraben	0.15

Part B	
Methyl Paraben	0.15
Water	49.60
Perfume	0.10

Formula No. 2

Part A	%
Mineral Oil,Light	25
Microcrystalline Wax (175 °F)	5
Amerchol L-101	10
Lanolin	10
Propyl Paraben	0.15

Part B	%
Methyl Paraben	0.15
Water	49.60
Perfume	0.10

Formula No. 3

Part A	%
Glyceryl Monostearate, Pure	10
Petrolatum	10
Mineral Oil, Light	10
Beeswax	5
Lanolin absoption base	25.0
Propyl Paraben	0.15

Part B	%
Methyl Paraben	0.15
Water	39.60
Perfume	0.10

Other-Formulations for Baby Creams

Part A	%	%
Lanolin	0.9	-
Isopropyl Myristate	4.30	-
Polyglcol 1000 Monostearate	6.1	-
Stearic Acid	7.1	-
Beeswax	-	3.1
Spermaceti	-	3.00
Glyceryl Monostearate, pure	4.6	12.1
Mineral Oil, light	-	29.8
Propyl Paraben	0.15	0.15

Part B	%	%
Methyl Paraben	0.15	0.15
Propylene Glycol	2.6	

Glycerol		7.9
Water	74.0	43.7
Perfume	0.10	0.10

Formulas thus may be formulated as antiseptic baby cream by the incorporation of 0.5 to 1% of a chlorinated bis-phenol (such as hexachlorophene orbithionol), provided such cream meet the standards for antiseptic activity, as described above. Cationic ammonium, pyridinium and morpholinium compounds may be added at concentration of 0.1 to 25% to those formulas which do not contain free fatty acids. The nonionic and nonionic-cationic emulsions offer the advantage of permitting formulations at pH values which conform to the acid mantle of the skin.

Formulations for Baby Powder

The composition of baby powders is not very different from that of ordinary talcum powders, except that they may contain an antiseptic ingredients and are not so highly perfumed. Talc, a natural hydrous magnesium silicate, remains the most important constituent of baby powders. It is used because it has excellent slip characteristics and good adhesion to the skin. Particle size (325-mesh, 44 microns) and shape are important characteristics in the manufacture of an acceptable baby powder. Baby powders are used principally as lubricants in skin folds to prevent chafing, to adsorb perspiration and relieve prickly heat, and to impart a clean, pleasant fragrance to the baby's skin. The incorporation of 3 to 5% zinc or magnesium stearate improves the water-repellent properties of the powder which helps is prevent urine scald.

Formulations for Baby Powders

Formula No. 1

	%
Talc	99.75
Perfume	0.25

Formula No. 2

Talc	97.25
Lithium Stearate	2.5
Perfume	0.25

Formula No. 3

Talc	97.25
Olivfe Oil	2.5
Perfume	0.25

Formula No. 4

Talc	92.25
Lithium Stearate	2.5
Kaolin	5
Perfume	0.25

Formula No. 5

Talc	90.25
Lithium Stearate	2.50
Kaolin	5
Zinc Oxide	2
Perfume	0.25

Formula No. 6

Talc	96.75
Zinc Oxide	3
Perfume	0.25

Formula No. 7

Corn Starch	99.7
Hyamine 10-X	0.05
Perfume	0.25

Formula No. 8

Rice Starch	99.7
Hyamine 10-X	0.05
Perfume	0.25

Formula No. 9

Dry Flo	99.7
Hyamine 10-X	0.05
Perfume	0.25

Formula No. 10

	%
Dry Flo	50
Talc	49.7
Hyamine 10-X	0.05
Perfume	0.25

Formula No. 11

Talc	84.75
Calcium Umdecylenate	15
Perfume	0.25

Formula No. 12

Sterilized Talc	84
Boric Acid	6.0
Perfume	q.s.

Formula No. 13

Sterilized Talc	84.0
Starch	10.0
Boric Acid	6.0

34

HOME-MADE COSMETICS

A tremendous range of herbal cosmetics is available in the market today. In the past, Indian woman made good use of all kinds of everyday items like fruit, vegetables, nuts, cereals in nurturing their beauty. These days even in the most beauty conscious European countries there is a definite tendency towards herbal and natural therapies. The kitchen larder is a store-house of beauty aids. You just have to follow a few recipes, pick the ingredients, mix them in a required ratio and you will soon have a beauty lotion or cream in hand. These home-made herbal preparations help enhance beauty of the skin and complexion and delay ageing without causing harm.

Home-made preparations contain no preservatives. These may be refrigerated for a short time, say for a week. It is advisable to make these preparations in small quantities and bottle them in air-tight jars preferably in china or stainless steel containers which have no chemical reaction. Taking care of your skin is a must in order to remain young. During youth the skin is elastic and smooth but as one grows older, the skin loses its elasticity, natural oils and water content. In days gone by, there were hardly any cosmetics available in the market and home-made preparations were used for skin care. Since ancient times vegetable oils, refined animal fats and the cream of milk have been used for the care of the skin. A number of costly modern creams available in the market today are still based on refined animal fat. These help in keeping the skin smooth.

Making cosmetics at home is as simple as basic cooking. Some beauty consultants frighten people off by making things too complicated. In fact, these are mere fallacies. Making your own creams, tonics and lotions is easy. By learning to make your own cosmetics, you have at your finger-tips not only more luxurious products than you could afford to buy but also those especially suitable for your skin. Most of the recipes mentioned in this book have been tested and are extremely easy to make. Creams and emulsions are all basically a mixture of water and oily substances, waxes and fragrances in varying proportions. A slight change in the preparations change the character of the preparation. Be careful when measuring the ingredients. When measuring the quantity the following rough equivalents should be kept in mind:

60 drops	=	1 teaspoon	=	5 ml
3 teaspoons	=	1 tablespoon		
2 tablespoons	=	1/8 cup	=	1 fl oz
16 tablespoons	=	1 cup	=	8 fl oz

Since volume and weight are different measurements, it is not possible to render the one in terms of the other in a simple table of equivalents because bulk and weight do not correspond for all substances. In case of oil, the same oil of different grades may have different weights as below:

60 drops	=	5ml	= 1 teaspoon
1000ml	=	1 litre	
1 litre	=	1.759 pints	
1 pint	=	20 fl oz	= 0.568 litre

Here are a few more weight measurements which shall help you when preparing a recipe:

15.4 grains	=	1 gm
16 ozs	=	0.453 kilograms
1 kg	=	2.20 lbs

The following Dos and Don'ts should be kept in mind when making a herbal preparation at home:

1. Do not expose oils and waxes to direct heat as these can burn and an intense heat can change the propeties of the preparation.

2. When heating oils and waxes, put them in separate enamel or pyrax bowls, placed in a large pan filled with hot water (not boiling) and continue stirring with either a wooden spoon or a glass rod or a slow speed electric beater. While stirring, add water to the wax or the oils.

3. Add perfume or colouring matter when the preparation is ready and in case of a cream, mix it when it cools and thickens. In case your skin is sensitive or allergy-prone, it is advised to omit the perfume.

4. Ensure that the contents of the prepartation are properly mixed and make sure to continue stirring or beating untill the cream is cool. If

the preparation does not gel, melt it again and repeat the process. Oleic acid is of great help. Add a few drops of this acid to bind together any cream or lotion.

5. Mix all ingredients properly. If these are not dissolved properly, the preparations turn gritty.

6. The herbal ingredients used in preparing the cosmetics mentioned in this book are easily available with either the pansari shops or dispensing chemists. The details of all natural of herbal ingredients have been given in the Glossary.

7. Bees wax, emulsifying wax and cocoa butter can be ordered through a dispensing chemist.

8. Lanolin is readily available with the chemists. These are usually of two types-anhydrous and hydrous. Anhydrous lanolin is commonly used because it has less water content. In case, anhydrous lanolin, but add less water to the preparations as hydrous lanolin has in itself a fairly large water content. The preparation with anhydrous lanolin will be much richer and greasier.

9. Oils, herbs, brans, lentils, Fuller's earth, camphor, etc. can be purchased from a pansari shop.

10. Essential herb oils, perfumed oils, fresh herbs or flowers, thyme, rosemary, basil, lavender, rose petals, tarragon, marigold and jasmine, etc. can be purchased from a good herbalist.

11. Home-made herbal cosmetic preparations have a short life. The life of these preparations can be lengthened by storing them in a refrigerator. It is suggested to make small quantities of the recipe and use them lavishly while still fresh. Keep a small jar in a bathroom and the rest in the refrigerator. NepaginM is an effective preservative. When heating the water contents for your recipe, add a few drops of NepaginM. Stir constantly untill the oily globules disperse. The enhances the shelf life of the home preparation.

35

HERBAL PREPARATIONS FOR BODY

(i) Oatmeal Scrub

Mix together one tablespoon each of finely ground orange peel and grund almonds. This is slightly abrasive and very cleansing. Take roughly a teaspoon in the palm of your hand, mix with a little water and use the paste to scrub the skin, then wash.

(ii) Sugar Scrub

Soap your face well, adding a small handful of sugar to the lather. Massage this in for a couple of minutes, then rinse off with warm water. This scrub is very useful for a spotty and a sluggish looking skin.

(iii) Body Scrub

Ingredients:

Sugar	:	1.5 tablespoons
Rose Water	:	1/2 tablespoon
Lemon Juice	:	1 teaspoon
Egg Yolk	:	One egg

Mix sugar and rose water in a pan over a low heat. When it begins to carmel remove from the heat and add to it beaten yolk of an egg. Replace it on low heat for a minute and mix to it one teaspoon of lemon juice. This recipe is very useful for dry skins.

(iv) Milk Bath

Cleopatra bathed in ass' milk and so also did Poppaca, the wife of Nero. These days, it is not possible for anyone to afford milk for bathing. Here is an alternate process for similar results-add a handful of powdered milk to the bathwater

(v) Soft-water Bath

Use of rainy water is very beneficial. If you cannot get rain water, soften the bath water by simply adding a little sodium sesqui carbonate.

(VI) Vinegar Bath

For itchy skin or dry skin, vinegar bath is very useful. Add a cup of vinegar to the bath water. This will be very effective.

(vii) Oatmeal or Bran Bath

Use one tablespoon of oatmeal in bath. Oatmeal and bran contain oils and vegetable hormones, which soothe and soften the skin.

(viii) Honey Bath

It will not only relieve tiredness and sleeplessness, but will also leave the skin feeling smooth and satiny. Add a teaspoon to honey to your bath water.

(ix) Epsom Salth Bath

Add two handfuls of epsom salt to a bucket of bath water to relieve tiredness.

(x) Starchy Bath

Mix a few tablespoons of laundry starch and a teaspoon of glycerin and add to your bath water. It will leave your skin beautifully smooth, tight and soft.

(xi) Herb Bath

Lavender, hyssop, mint, borage, yarrow, rosemary, balm, or camomile are useful herbs, which can be used in bath water either separately or in a mixture.

(xii) Salth Bath

Mix the following ingredients:

Ordinary Washing Soda	:	Two cups
Potassium carbonate	:	Two tablespoons
Aromatic Essential Oil (lavender or pine)	:	4 to 5 drops

Keep this mixture in a large jar and use about a tablespoon in a bucket of bathwater.

(xiii) Bath Oils

Add any oil, that is almond, olive or sunflower to bath water. Baby oil or mineral oil is not suitable as it cannot be absorbed by the skin and only remains on the skin surface. These basic oils can also be mixed with some of the herbal oils or aromatic oils.

(xiv) Milk and Honey Bath

Ingredients:

Eggs	:	2
Almond oil	:	1/4 cup
Sunflower oil	:	1/4 cup (or corn oil)
Olive oil	:	1/2 cup (or safflower oil)
Honey	:	1 teaspoon
Washing detergent	:	2 teaspoon
Vodka	:	1/4 cup
Milk	:	1/2 cup
Perfume	:	5 to 6 drops

Completely blend the eggs, honey and oils together. Now add to it the detergent which acts as an emulsifer making it thick. Continue beating and add vodka, which makes bath oil to disperse and helps drying skin. Continue beating and add to it the milk which will make the oil slightly thinner and luxurious. Finally, add perfume. This bath oil when mixed to bath water leaves the skin feeling smooth, satiny and thoroughly pampered.

(xv) Bubble Bath

Mix together the following ingredients with an electric beater:

Egg	:	One
Shampoo	:	1/2 cup
Gelatine	:	1 teaspoon

Add the mixture to bath water when the tap is running.

(xvi) Bath Powder

Mix the following ingredients together in a jar and use a little quantity in the bathwater:

Oatmeal flour	:	3 tablespoons
Oatmesal bran	:	1 tablespoon
Ground almonds	:	1 tablespoon
Wheat flour	:	1 tablespoon
Perfume	:	5 to 6 drops

(xvii) Sugar Bath

Collect the following ingredients:

Sugar	:	2 tablespoons
Water	:	2 tablespoons
Egg yolk-beaten	:	One
Lemon juice	:	1 teaspoon

Put sugar and water in a pan, over a low heat. When it begins to caramelise, remove from the heat and add egg yolk. Replace it on the low heat for a minute and mix to it lemon juice. This is very ideal scrub for slightly dry skin or for a spotty and sluggish looking skin. To apply sugar scrub, soap your face well, adding a small handful of sugar to the lather. Massage for a couple of minutes, then rinse off with warm water.

(xviii) Special Massage

Here is a special recipe for brides-to-be used daily at the time of bath for ten days before marriage. Mix the following ingredients to make a paste and rub thoroughly to clense and stimulate the skin leaving it soft and shiny:

Dried, ground and

sieved lemon peel	: 1 tablespoon
Ground almond	: 1 tablespoon
Salt and ground allspice	: a pinch of each
Wheatgerm flour	: 4 tablespoons
Ground thyme	: 1 tablespoon
Almond oil	: sufficient to make a paste
Jasmine oil (to perfume)	: Few drops

Herbal Body Lotions

There are a number of ways to make body lotions yourself which lend a glow to the skin. Here are a few simple recipes to try yourself:

(1) Rose and Lime Lotion

Mix together the following ingredients:

Rose water	: 3 tablespoons
Glycerin	: 1 tablespoon
Lime Juice	: 2 tablespoons

Apply this body lotion after bath, if your have a dry skin. The proportion of this lotion can be changed to suit the skin. This lotion does not feel sticky and mixes into your skin easily. Thef lotion can be stored in a refrigerator.

(2) Blue Satin Body Lotion

Ingredients:

Glycerin	: 1 teaspoon
Water	: 4 tablespoons
Soap flakes	: 3 tablespoons
Witch-hazel	: 1 teaspoon
Olive Oil	: 4 teaspoons
Blue colouring	: few drops
Perfume	: few drops

Put the soap flakes and water in a saucepan and heat. When the soap flakes are dissolved, remove from the heat and add glycerin, olive oil and witch-hazel. Stir until it cools and then add the blue colouring and some perfume. Application of this non-greasy body lotion after a bath leaves the skin glowing like satin.

(3) Lavender Body Lotion

Ingredients:

Borax	: 1 teaspoon
Rose water	: 1 cup
Olive Oil (warm)	: 2 tablespoons
Lavender water	: 1 cup

Lavender water is made by infusing a handful of lavender flowers in two cups of boiling water to make a concentrate of one cup. Now dissolve borax in rose water, then slowly add olive oil, beating constantly. When all the oil has been added to the water and it forms an emulsion, add lavender water. Let this stand for an hour and then strain and use.

(4) Almond body Lotion

Ingredients:

Lanolin	: 3 teaspoons
Almond oil	: 1 teaspoon
Petroleum jelly	: 1 teaspoon
Vegetable lard	: 1 teaspoon
Glycerine	: 2 teaspoon
Water	: 10 tablespoons
Soap flakes	: 1 teaspoon
Cornflower	: 1 teaspoon
Almond essence/perfume	few drops

Heat the oils and water separately. Remove them fron heat and mix them together. Pour the mixture into a bottle and shake vigorousy then add to it the perfume.

(5) Body Massge Cream

Ingredients:

Lanolin	: 4 tablespoons
Sunflower oil	: 4 tablespoons(or safflower oil)
Rose water	: 9 tablespoons

Heat the oils together and then slowly add the heated water. Add a tablespoon of winter green or camphor oil to make a really invigorating massage cream. To make this cream lighter simply add two tablespoons of petroleum jelly.

(6) Body Massage Oil

Mix the following oils together and use:

Camphor Oil	: 1 cup
Almond oil	: 1/2cup
Castor oil	: 1/2cup

Herbal Preparations for Body Odur and Bad Breath

(1) Essential Oil of Rose

Add this oil to the bathwater. This produces a delightful fragrance and softnes the skin.

(2) Flax (linseed)

Boil 50 gms of linseed in one litre of water for 2 to 3 minutes, then strain and use. This is added to the bathwater to soften the skin and act as a tranquiliser.

(3) Wheatgerm and Vitamin E oils

Mix both oils in equal quantity and massage the body. These are now used extensively to heal damaged skin.

(4) Walnut leaves

Use an infusion of 15 gms of fresh leaves to 600 ml water to bathe the affected skin.

(5) Nettle Beer

Ingredients:

Young Nettles	: 900 gms
Lemon	: 2

Water	: 4.5 litre
Damerara sugar	: 450 gms
Cream of tartar	: 25 gms
Brewer's yeast	: 200 gms

Use the tops of the nettles only. Put them in a large enamel saucepan with the thiny pared rinds of the lemons peeled by a potato peeler. Now add water and bring to the boil. Boil for 20 minutes, then strain and use. Mix to it cream of tartar in a plastic bucket. Stir well and add the lemon juice and yeast.

(6) Lavender deodorant

Put 3 drops essetial oil of lavender, 1 tablespoon sugar and 600 ml distilled water in a bottle. Shake well and leave for two weeks. Dab it on with cottonwool or use as a spray.

(7) Witch-hazel

Use it neat (provided, it does not irritate the skin) for a useful antiseptic under-arm or after-shave lotion.

(8) Thyme, rosemary, eau-de-cologne, mint or lavender

Take a large handful of any one of these sweet-smelling, antiseptic herbs and place in a pan. Pour water to the level that herbs are immersed in it. Simmer for five minutes, pour into a jug and let it stand till cold. Strain and bottle.

(9) Essential oils of thyme, marjoram, geranium, verbena, lavender, sandalwood, angelica, cinnamon and cassia

A few drops of any one of these antiseptic oils in warm water bath will reduce body odour and these have delightful effects.

(10) Dandelion leaves or fresh lovage bath bag

Take three handfuls each of dandelion leaves and stinging nettles, two handfuls each of black-currant leaves and scented geraniums. Tie into a muslin drawstring bath bag (or a white cotton handkerchief) and leave under the bath water as it runs. Fresh lovage or any other deliciously fragrant, antiseptic herbs can also be used in the same way.

(11) Seaweed Gel Deodorant

Ingrdients:

Seaweed seeds	: 25 gms
Fresh Irish moss or carrgheen	: 1:25 litres
Water	: 1.5 litres
Scented floral or herb water	: 2 tablespoons

Soak seaweed seeds in fresh water and wash it well. Put it into a large pan with the measured water and bring gently to the boil. Cover and simmer for 30 minutes. Now stir fresh Irish moss or carragheen in the scented water. Mix both contents and pour into the jar when cold and keep in a refrigerator. This deodorising gel should be rubbed all over the body instead of soap, then rinse off in shower or bath.

(12) Powdered Alum Deodorant

Mix 1/2 teaspoon of powdered alum with 300 ml of warm water. This is a very cheap but effective preparation.

(13) Apple Cider Vinegar

Mix together equal quantities of vinegar and water. Apply on cotton wool and leave for a few minutes to allow the smell to disipate before use.

Home-made Mouth Wash

(1) Take the following ingredients, boil them together and use as a mouth wash when it cools:

Vinegar	: 1/4 cup
Wine	: 1/2 cup
Honey	: 1/4 cup
Cloves (powdered)	: 1 teaspoon

(2) Collect the following ingredients and mix together to make a recipe of tooth-powder and also to avoid bad breath:

Soda Bicarbonate	: 3 tablespoons
Sodium chloride (salt)	: 2 tablespoons

When the powder is mixed with warm water, it makes an effective mouth-wash.

(3) The ashes of burnt bread, charcoal, burnt rosemary and a mixture of honey and salt are also effective to clean the teeth. Strawberries, when rubbed over teeth, can also be a good teeth cleanser.

(4) Grind fresh beans with a few cardamom seeds and make a into a reviving cup to be taken without milk in the morning.

(5) One teaspoon hydrogen paroxide added to a cup of warm water with 1 teaspoon of sea salt is very cleansing; gargle and mouthwash. (Remember, avoid swallowing)

(6) Mix the following ingredients together, shake well and bottle to make a refreshing mouth-wash to be used first thing in the morning:

Eucalyptus oil	: 6 drops
Cloves oil	: 2 drops
Tincture of myrrh	: 2 drops
Hot water	: 600 ml

(7) Mix the following ingredients together either separately or combined in vinegar or infusion to make an antiseptic and sweet-smelling herbal preparation:

Lavender, Marjoram, Summer savoury, Thyme and Rosemary.

(8) Mix one teaspoon of syrup of figs in hot water, and use at night to make the breath sweet-smelling.

(9) Simmer the Quine seeds in water until soft, Strain, gargle with and swallow the liquid.

(10) Simmer lemon pipes in honey and spoon down the gooey mixture whilst still warm. This is an old-fashioned remedy to kill worms which cause bad breath.

Remedies for Smelly Feet

(1) Use an influsion of Whit willow bark mixed with a pinch of borax and use as a footh-bath.

(2) Mix 1/2 teaspoon powdered alum with 300 ml of warm water and use as a foot-bath. This reduces sweating and acts as a deodarant.

(3) Massage feet with a mixture of 6 tablespoons of witch-hazel and one teaspoon each of glycerin and tincture of arnica. Avoid using in case of broken skin.

36

SKIN CLEANSING

Cleansing is the first step in caring for your skin. Pespiration, grease, dust, stale make-up, dirt and bacteria-all collect on the skin and must be removed completely, preferably at night before retiring to bed.

As an artist preparesf a canvas, a woman must prepare her skin for good make-up. The first step in make-up is cleansing. Soap and water removes most of the impurities but it does not remove make-up completely, hence cleansing is required. Cleansing should be done with cleansing cream, milk, lotion or just plain cold cream. The cleanser must be massaged into the skin with a light upward and outward movement, paying particular attention to the creases of the nose, under chin area, neck and ear lobes. Use cottonwool for cleaning the face. The heavier the make-up you have been wearing, the more time yor will need to cleanse your skin. If the skin is too greasy or blemished, you may follow your cleansing by washing with soap and clean water. Cleansing cream is also useful for removing stale make-up which has a waxy base which cannot be properly penetrated and cleansed simply by using soap and water. Here are a few cleansing creams which are very easy and quick to make.

(i) Ingredients:

Bees-wax	: 1/2 tablespoon
Emulsifying wax	: 1 tablespoon
Baby oil	: 4 tablespoons
Coconut oil	: 2 tablespoons
Water	: 2 tablespoons
Boraxs	: 1/4 tablespoon
Witch-hazel	: 1 tablespoon
Perfume	: few drops

Mix waxes and oils into an enamel bowl and melt slowly over a pan of boiling water. In a separate bowl, heat the water and borax is completely dissolved. Then add witch-hazel, but do not leave on the heat too long otherwise it will evaporate. When the waxes have melted, remove both the bowls from the heat and mix in water, stirring continuously. When the cream begins to cool, add the prefume. Beat until the mixture thickens and cools. Use of baby oil (mineral oil), does not penetrate the skin and spreads easily and melts easily.

(ii) Ingrdients:

Bees-wax or white paraffin wax	: 1.5 tablespoons
Emulsifying wax	: 1 tablespoon
Mineral oil	: 4 tablespoons
Rose water	: 6 tablespoons
Borax	: 1/2 teaspoon
Rose oil (perfume)	: a few drops

Melt the waxes and oil together, and at the same time heat the water and borax and make sure that the borax is completely dissolved. Remove both bowls from heat and pour water into the oil. Continue stirring until a white cream begins to form. Add a few drops of rose oil when the mixture begins to cool. Carry on beating until the mixture thickens.

iii) Ingredients:

Bees-wax	: 3 teaspoons
Coconut oil	: 4 teaspoons
Olive/mineral oil	: 5 teaspoons
Cucumber juice	: 4 tablespoons
Glycerine	: 1 teaspoon
Borax	: a pinch
Green colouring	: 1 drop

Melt oils and wax in the usual way over a plan of boiling water. Simultaneously, heat the cucumber juice, glycerine, colouring and borax in a separate bowl. Ensure that the borax dissolves thoroughly. When the contents of both the bowls are melted and warm, add water drop by drop to the oil stirring continuously. Now remove it from heat and beat until the mixture thickens and cools. Keep the cream in the refrigerator as cucumber juice rots quickly. Make the cream in a small quantity.

(iv) Ingredients:

Lanolin	: 1/2 tablespoon
Petroleum Jelly	: 1 tablespoon
Mineral oil	: 4 tablespoons
Water	: 10 tablespoons
Violet extract	: 5 drops

(v) Here is a very quick-to-make cleansing cream. Melt two tablespoons vegetable lard and mix it to the mixture of two tablespoons corn oil and four tablespoons sunflower oil, stirring constantly. When it is cool, mix to it few drops of perfume. Store half a cup of this pale gold cream in the refrigerator.

These are special creams not only to lift the dirt and grime from the skin, but also to remove make-up. Make-up has a waxy base which cannot be properly penetrated and cleansed by simply using soap and water, and a cleansing cream or lotion is essential for this. Remember, cleansers should be applied with an upward movement and kept on the skin for atleast 30 seconds.

MOISTURISING FOR ALL SKINS

Almost all skins need a moisturiser-even the oily types. But for a dry skin a moisturiser is vita. The drier your skin, the more lavish you should be with the use of moisturiser. Moisturisers are available either in the form of creams or lotions. Moisturiser is applied after cleansing and toning, and always before applying make-up. A thin layer of moisturiser is helpful under a face pack for a very dry skin, which gives moistures to the skin cells. During sleep, the skin is usually busy replacing dead skin cells with fresh ones. That is why sleep is very important for beauty because there are no outside influences to bother the skin. Every night application of a nourishing cream relaxes tight muscles and accelerates circulatio. If the skin is too dry, use a second application of moisturiser. Here are a few easy-to-make simple moisturisers:

(1) Almond Oil Moisturizing Cream

Ingredients:

Beeswax	: 3 teaspoons
Emulsifyinng wax	: 1 teaspoons
Almond oil	: 5 teaspoons
Lavender oil	: a few drops

Melt over water both bees-wax and emulsifying wax in a bowl. When melted, mix almond oil to it. In another bowl heat water over the same water so that the two bowls are at the same temperature. Now slowly add water to the melted waxes and oils, stirring all the time. Remove mixture from the heat and continue stirring. When cool, add a few drops of lavender oil.

(2) Herb Cream

Ingredients :

Lanolin	: 1 tablespoon
Emulsifying wax	: 2 teaspoons
Beeswax	: 6 tablesspoons
Almond oil	6 tablesspoons (or herb lotion)

Put the oil and waxes together in a small container. Place the container in a bigger on with hot water and keep till the wax melts. Cool and store in a refrigerator. Take a couple of teaspoons of this, melt it and add a teaspoon of any herb lotion or infusion. Comfrey is a healing herb ideal for sensitive skins or if the skin has irritation or spots. Take a handful of comfrey, liquidize it, then strain it and use.

(3) *Avocado and almond Cream*

Ingredients

Beeswax	: 3 teaspoons
Emulsifying wax	: 3 teaspoons
Almond oil	: 1/2 cup
Avocado oil	: 1/4 cup
Rose water	: 3 tablespoons

Melt the waxes in an enamel pan over a water bath, then add the avocado and almond oils. Now add the heated rose water drop by drop, stirring constantly. Remove from heat and continue stirring till it cools. Now add a few drops of perfume. Both almond and avocado oils are rich for the skin.

(4) Sunflower Cream

Lanolin	: 4 teaspoons
Emulsifying wax	: 2 teaspoons
Beeswax	: 2 teaspoons
Sunflower oil	: 5 tablespoons
Water	: 6 tablespoons
Glycerine	: 2 teaspoons
Borax	: 1/2 teaspoon

Melt the waxes, oil and lanolin over a water bath. Separately heat water, glycerin and borax making sure the borax is completely dissolved. While the melted oils and waxes are still on the heat, slowly add water to it drop by drop and continue beating with a wooden spoon till you get a whitish, thick and creamy textured rich cream. It leaves the skin looking moist and soft.

(5) Jasmine Moisturising Cream

Ingredients:

Emulsifying wax	: 2 tablespoons
Almond or sunflower oil	: 2 tablespoons
Lanolin	: 1 teaspoon
Borax	: 1/2 teaspoon
Witch-hazel	: 1 teaspoon
Glycerine	: 1.5 teaspoons
Water	: 8 tablespoons
Jasmine oil	: a few drops

Melt the waxes, oil and lanolin together over a water bath. In a separate bowl heat water, glycerine and borax. Make sure the borax is completely dissolved. Then add witch-hazel. Now slowly add water to the oils, stirring constantly until it cools. Then add a few drops of jasmine oil. The non-gresy cream thus formed is suitable for normal and greasy skins.

6) Ingredients:

Lanolin	: 3 tablespoons
Honey	: 1/2 tablespoon
Lecithin	: 1 teaspoon
Warm water	: 4 tablespoons
Perfume	: a few drops

Heat lanolin, honey and lecithin in a bowl. Now mix to it warm water, stirring constantly. This is one of the creams you don't need to refrigerate.

NOURISHING CREAM

Nourishing preparations include all the skin foods whether they are oil-based or of the moisturising type, whether they are light and immediatel absorbed or heavy and sticky, needing to be massaged into the skin. Hormone creams and lotions, vitamin products, serum ampules, anti-wrinkle creams and lotions, biologically active preparations all come into the nourishing group. Some of the easy-to-make nourishing recipes are given below:

(1) Cocoa Butter Cream: Heat the following ingredients together over a water bath, stirring them thoroughly:

Cocoa butter	: 2 tablespoons
Emulsfing wax	: 2 tablespoons
Bees-wax	: 1 tablespoon
Sesame oil	: 4 tablespoons
Almond oil	: 1 tablespoon

When the ingredients are completely melted, remove from the heat and stir until the cream is cool, adding a few drops of perfume. This cream leaves the skin smooth without being greasy.

(2) Lanolin Cream: Mix 2 tablespoons lanolin with 8 tablespoons almond oil over a water bath. It is good for dry skins and neglected are as of the body such aselbows, knees, feet and neck. In case the cream has

to be applied on oily skin, add 2 tablespoons rosewater or ordinary soft water (in case rose-water is not available).

(3) Elder Flower Cream:

Ingredients:

Almond oil	: 3 tablespoons
Elder flower blossoms	: 4 tablespoons
Lanolin	: 2 tablespoons

Mix together all the above ingredients in ad bowl over a water bath. Let it simmer together for an hour, strain and then add warm water slowly, stirring.

(4) Honey Cream: Honey is very useful for a dry, coarse and sensitive skin. To make a nourishing honey cream for sallow skin, mix 3 tablespoons lanolin, 1/2 tablespoon honey and 1 teaspoon lecithin in a bowl and melt over a water bath. Now, slowly add 4 tablespoons warm water to it, beating continuously until it cools.

(5) Vitamin Cream:

Ingredients:

Bees-wax	: 1 tablespoon
Emulsifying wax	: 1 tablespoon
Lanolin	: 1 tablespoon
Wheat-germ oil	: 3 tablespoons
or	
Vitamin E	: 2 capsules
Carrot oil	: 3 tablespoons
or	
Vitamin A	: 2 capsules
Distilled water	: 6 tablespoons
Borax	: 1/2 teaspoon
Tincture of benzoin	: 2 drops
Orange flower oil	: a few drops

Melt waxes and oils over a water bath. At the same time, in a separate bowl dissolve borax in warm water. Add water to the oils and beat until it cools. Add tincture of benzoin and continue beating until you get a thick nourishing cream. When mixing vitamin capsules, simply prick open the capsules and add contents to the mixture.

(6) Wheat-Germ Cream:

Ingredients:

Bees-wax	: 1 teaspoon
Emulsifying wax	: 1 teaspoon
Lanolin	: 5 tablespoons
Sesame oil	: 3 tablespoons
Wheat-germ oil	: 2 tablespoons
Water	: 5 tablespoons
Witch-hazel	: 1 tablespoon
Borax	: 1/2 teaspoon
Perfume	: a few drops

Melt the waxes and oils over a water bath. Heat water and borax and make sure that the borax has completely dissolved. Now slowly add water to the melted oils and waxes. Stir until a thick, glossy nourishing cream is ready. Lanolin and wheat-germ oil contain Vitamin E.

(7) Vegetable Cream:

Ingredients:

Bees-wax	: 2 tablespoons
Emulsifying wax	: 4 tablespoons
Lanolin	: 3 teaspoons
Almond oil	: 4 tablespoons
Sesame oil	: 4 tablespoons
Avocado oil	: 2 tablespoons
Safflower oil	: 2 tablespoons
Sunflower oil	: 2 tablespoons
Water	: 5 tablespoons
Borax	: 1/2 teaspoon
Amber oil	: a few drops

Mix and melt the waxes and oils together over a water bath. In a separate bowl dissolve borax in warm water. Add water to the oils and beat until the cream cools. It leaves no sign of grease but gives the skin a satiny sheen

(8) Strawberry Cream: Mix 250 gms strawberries and 100 gms sugar in a pan and bring to boil. Cool and boil again. Allow strawberry juice to cool and store in the refrigerator. This lotion is very useful for oily skins. Now melt 2 tablespoons each of lanolin and sunflower oil together over a water bath and mix to it strawberry juice. Remove from the heat and stir thoroughly till it thickens to a creamy consistency.

(9) Oily Nourishing Cream: Melt the following ingredients together over a water bath:

Coconut oil	: 3 tablespoons
Olive oil	: 2 tablespoons
Almond oil	: 1 tablespoon
Bees-wax	: 1/2 tablespoon

Now in a separate bowl dissolve 1/2 teaspoon borax in 3 tablespoons of heated water, and mix it to melted oils slowly, stirring until a cool cream is ready.

(10) Orange Flower Skin Tonic

Ingredients:

Bees-wax	: 2 teaspoons
Emulsifying	: 2 teaspoons
Almond oil	: 8 teaspoons
Lanolin	: 4 teaspoons
Coconut oil	: 4 teaspoons
Orange flower water	: 6 teaspoons
Tincture of benzoin	: a few drops
Orange oil	: a few drops

Melt the waxes and oils together and add to it heated orange flower water and drops of tincture of benozin and orange oil, stirring continuously. Besides nourishing, this cream helps to clear lines and wrinkles alnes and wrinkles.

Here is another very effective herbal remedy for the skin. Mix and shake the following ingredients in a glass jar with a tightly fitting lid. Let it keep for a week, shaking it twice daily:

Honey	2 tablespoons
Coriander seeds (dhania)	2 teaspoons
Nutmeg (jai-phal)	2 teaspoons
Cloves	1 teaspoon
Lemon peel (grated)	4 teaspoons
Orange flower water	4 teaspoons
Alcohol	8 teaspoons
Rose-water	4 teaspoons
Benzoin	1/2 teaspoon
Borax	1/2 teaspoon

Toning the Skin by Herbal Ways

Skin toning is always followed after the cleansing routine with a mild skin freshner or with a medium strength skin tonic. Toning removes greasiness remaining from cleansing preparations, closed pores, refines the skin and if you intend to apply make-up, it leaves a smooth clean texture which will hold the foundation and powder for long. Basically, skin tonic freshens the skin. The cheapest toner is simply to splash the face with cold water.

Skin tonics are generally composed of infusions of herbs, flowers, vinegar, rose water and witch-hazel. Stronger skin tonics or astringents dry the skin removing all traces of oil on the skin. These are suitable for greasy skins. Avoid using very storng astringents for any type of skin, as the harsh action of the alcohol toughens and coarsens the skin and prevents it from functioning normally. Apply tonic or astringent with a piece of cotton wool, but if the skin is looking sluggish, pat it on with a brisk slapping movement. Toning stimulates the blood supply to the skin. Moisten folded cotton wool with your skin tonic and pat on the cheeks, the neck and chin. Avoid any areas with broken veins.

HERBAL SKIN TONICS

(1) Rose Water: It is one of the oldest skin freshners which was discovered by an Arabian dermatologist in the tenth century. Rose water is available at a chemist shop, but it is very easy to make on your own too. Mix rose essence in pure water and shake thoroughly. Two

tablespoons essence of roses is sufficient for four litres purified water.

(2) Gypsy Rose Water: Put 2 handfuls of dark, scented rose petals into a jar or a wide-topped bottle containing 1 litre of water and 200 gms of sugar. Keep the mixture for two hours, shake thoroughlt, then strain and store in a cool place.

(3) Rose Water and Witch-hazel Tonic: Mix 1 cup of rose water and 1/4 cup witch-hazel. (In case the skin is very greasy, you can use equal proportion of rose water and witch-hazel).

(4) Flower and Herb Tonic: Flower and herb water of all kinds make deliciously scented, highly effective skin tonics. Mix two tablespoons of dried herbs or flowers to a pint of boiling water and cover the pan to prevent steam from being lost. Let the herbs steep for a couple of hours. Strain and bottle.

(5) Marigold Skin Tonic: Marigolds are known for their healing properties. Mix two dried or three fresh marigold flowers to a pint of water and keep for 10 to 12 hours. Now mix to it two tablespoons of witch-hazel. It is especially for greasy, spotty skins

(6) Hollyhock Skin Tonic: Put three tablespoons of hollyhock leaves into a half pint of boiling water. Cover and simmer gently for 5 minutes. Leave for half an hour, then strain and it is ready for use. Similarly, many other flowers and leaves such as lilac, geranium, honey-suckle, lime flowers, lavender and landelions can also be used in the same way, to freshen and cure sallowness of the skin.

(7) Elder Flower Tonic: Wash a handful of elder flower and mix to it six tablespoons of boiling water in a large jar; let them steep overnight, and strain next morning.

(8) Vinegar Skin Tonic: Mix the following ingredients and leave for seven days, shaking the bottle twice daily.

Cider vinegar (or wine)	: 1/2 cup
Cloves	: 1/2 teaspoon
Lavender	: 1 tablespoon
Rose petals	: 1 tablespoon

Rosemary	: 1 tablespoon
Rose/orange flower water	: 2 tablespoon

Vinegar is ideal for the skin. The skin has an acid mantle and vinegar being acidic, restores this. Always use vinegar diluted in the ratio one part to eight parts of water.

(10) Cucumber Tonic: Wash and liquidize half-peeled cucumber. Put the juice in a saucepan, bring it to boil and simmer it for five minutes. Cool and strain it, then add one tablespoon of witch-hazel to every two tablespoons of cooked cucumber juice. Store the juice in a refrigerator. Mint can also be used in it. Add four tablespoons mint in the cucumber tonic.

(11) Orange and Lemon Tonic: Put one slice of orange, half lemon and two tablespoons of castor sugar into a pan with a cup of milk. Heat the mixture to near boiling point. When it is cool, it is ready for use. Store the tonic in a refrigerator.

(12) Apple Tree Bark Tonic: Infuse 4 tablespoons of apple tree bark in 2 cups of boiling water. Add about 1 tablespoon of sage and apply this to the face. Other herbs that can be used for skin tonic are yarrow, camomile, rosemary, parsley, tansy, mint, fennel and comfrey. Yarrow is ideal for greasy skin. Camomile helps to eliminate wrinkles. Rosemary is healing and firming. Mint is stimulating, Parsley contains Vitamin C and is very useful for spotty and patchy skins. Tansy helps to get rid of freckles. Comfrey is good for clearing up spooty skins.

(13) Mix together the following ingredients in a bottle and shake thoroughly before use:

Elder flower water	: 3 tablespoons
Rose water	: 3 tablespoons
Witch-hazel	: 3 tablespoons
Boric Acid	: 1 tablespoon

(14) Mix the following ingredients together in a large bottle:

Elder flower water	: 10 tablespoons
Cucumber juice	: 5 tablespoons
Eau-de-cologne	: 4 tablespoons
Tincture of benzoin	: 1 tablespoon

Keep above mixture for 24 hours, then filter. This is a useful recipe for open pores.

(15) Collect the following ingredients:

Elder flower water	: half cup
Tincture of benzoin	: 4 tablespoons
Tincture of myrrh	: 6 drops

Slowly add tincture of bezoin to elder flower water . Then mix to it myrrh and let it remain for 24 hours, then filter. This recipe can also be used as after-shave lotion by men.

(16) Collect the following ingredients:

Butter milk or plain milk	: 1/2 cup
Elder flower water	: 6 tablespoon
Honey	: 1 tablespoon

Heat milk and elder flower water together on a very low heat for about 30 minutes. Remove from the heat and let it stand for three hours. Now re-heat and strain, then add honey. This recipe is very useful for a hard and itchy skin.

(17) Mix 4 teaspoons each almond oil, lanolin and coconut oil. Now melt 2 teaspoons each bees-wax and emulsifying wax on low heat and mix together, stirring. Now melt tablespoon 6 teaspoons of orange flower water and continue stirring till the mixture becomes thick adding 3 drops tincture benzoin. When the mixture gets cold, store in a bottle.

HOME-MADE ASTRINGENTS AND SKIN TONICS

Making your own beauty preparations is as simple as basic cooking-sometimes even simpler. Some people never try making their own cosmetics because they think that commercial products must be better. Learning to make your own cosmetics is wonderful and very interesting provided you have interest in it.

Astingents

Astringent lotion is used to tone the skin and is necessary to remove the last traces of grease and closed pores. Never choose a harsh astringent lotion. Strong astringent lotions usually contain alcohol (Vodka is the nearst equivalent), surgical spirit (but this smells too much and is extremely harsh) and witch-hazel (which is good, but not as strong). Strong astringents over-dry the skin, leaving it feeling tight, paper-like and dehydrated. It is advisable to use a mild skin tonic as far as possible. Astringent is applied to the oily parts on the face such as the sides of the nose, chin and forhead. This helps to close the skin pores and discourage the gresy excretions from building up too rapidly underneath your make-up. Here are a few home-made astringent preparations:

(1) Honey Water Astringent: Honey water has been in vogue since 286 BC for caring of the skin invented by Theophrastus. Mix the following ingredients together in a jar which should be air-tight and keep for two weeks, shaking it daily:

Sandalwood oil	: 8 tablespoons
Musk or sandal-wood chips	: a pinch
Bergamot oil	: 1 teaspoon
Lavender oil	: 1/4 teaspoon
Clove oil	: 1/8 teaspoon
Rose water	: 4 tablespoons
Orange flower water	: 4 tablespoons
Honey	: 1 tablespoon

(2) Rosemary Water Astringent: Mix the following ingredients together in a large air-tight bottle and let it stand for 48 to 72 hours, shaking frequently:

Rosemary	: 2 tablespoons
Rose water	: 1/2 cup
Alcohol or witch-hazel	: 1/4 cup
Orange peel and pitch	: 1/4 cup
Lemon peel and pith	: 1/2 cup
Mint	: 4 sprigs

(3) Lemon Astringent: Mix the following ingredients together in a large bottle for 24 hours, then strain and use for greasy skin:

Lemon juice	: 4 tablespoons
Peppermint extract	: 1/2 teaspoon

Witch-hazel	: 8 tablespoons
Alcohol	: 2 tablespoons

(4) Camphor Astringent: Mix the following ingredients in a large bottle:

Rose water	: 1/2 cup
Witch-hazel	: 1/2 cup
Distilled water	: 1/2 cup
Camphor spirit	: 1 tablespoon
Blue colouring	: 2 drops

To make the lotion stronger, add a pinch of alum. Now strain and use to tighten and tone the skin. The recipe is especially good if you suffer from large pores and spots. This lotion can also be used as an after-shave lotion by men.

Home-made Skin Tonics

Camphor, sulphur, onions, garlic, curds, yeast, Fuller's earth, herbs and vegetable juices are all useful in treating a blemished and pimply skin. Here are a few easy-to-make skin foods:

(1) Orange Flower Skin Tonic

Beeswax	2 teaspoons
Emulsifying wax	2 teaspoons
Almond oil	8 teaspoons
Lanolin oil	4 teaspoons
Coconut oil	4 teaspoons
Orange flower	a few drops
Tincture of benzoin	a few drops

Melt bees-wax and emulsifying wax. Add to it almond oil and lanolin and coconut oil and continue heating, adding to it orange flower water and drops of tincture of benzoin, stirring continuously. Besides nourishing, this cream helps to clear lines and wrinkles.

(2) Oily Nourishing Cream

Coconut oil	4 tablespoons
Olive oil	2 tablespoons
Almond oil	1 tablespoon

Beeswax	1/2 tablespoon
Borax	1/2 tablespoon

Heat over a water bath coconut oil, olive oil, almond oil and beeswax. In a separate bowl, dissolve borax in 3 tablespoons of heated water. Then slowly add heated water to oils and stir until a cool cream is ready.

(3) Garlic Skin Tonic: Beat one egg white. Add to it the following ingredients.

Kaolin	: 1 teaspoon
Honey	: 1 teaspoon
Carrot juice	: 1 teaspoon
Garlic	: 1 clove

(4) Onion Skin Tonic

Onion	1
Fuller's Earth	1 teaspoon
or	
Kaolin	1 teaspoon
Honey	1 teaspoon

Mash and sieve the onion, and mix onion juice into paste with one tablespoon Fuller's earth or Kaolin and one teaspoon of honey. This tonic prevents blemishes and wrinkles.

(5) Sulphur Skin Tonic

Sulphur powder	1 teaspoon
Fuller's Earth	2 tablespoons
Egg white	1 (egg)

Make a paste of one teaspoon pure sulphur powder, two tablespoons Fuller's earth and one egg white. This pack cures skin.

37

HERBAL PREPARATIONS FOR FEET AND HANDS

(1) Astringent Foot Freshener

Ingredients:

Rose water	: 1/4 cup
Witch-hazel	: 1/4 cup
Distilled water	: 1/4 cup
Spirit of Camphor B.P.	: 1 tablespoon
Alum	: a pinch

Mix all the ingredients into a large bottle and shake well. Dab on with a wad of cottonwool to cool hot, tired feet. Cucumber juice will also cool aching feet, especially in summer.

(2) Balm for corns

Ingredients:

Coconut oil or lard	: 50 gms
Oil of camphor	: 30 ml
Turpentine oil	: 15 ml

Melt oil or fats in a bowl over boiling water. Beat in the remaining ingredients and continue beating until the mixture cools. Pot and seal. Rub corns with this balm daily in the morning and at night.

(3) Thyme and Rosemary Lotion

Add a few drops of the essential oil of either herb to an egg-cupful of olive oil and rub into the affected area.

(4) Rosemary Jelly

Ingredints:

Rosemary water	: 8 tablespoons
Glycerine	: 1 tablespoon
Arrowroot	: 2 tablespoons

Heat rosemary water and glycerine in two separate bowls over water-bath. Stir the arrowroot into glycerine to make a smooth paste, then add the rosemary water. Continue to heat over simmering water, stirring all the time, until the mixture becomes like jelly.

38

HAIR SHAMPOOS AND SETTING

Over and above the daily brushing and combing, it is necessary to remove from the hair dirt and all the secretions of sebaceous glands which accumulate on the scalp. Women are advised to shampoo once every 8 to 10 days for normal hair, once every fortnight for dry hair and once every 5 to 6 days in case of oily hair. Too frequent washing of hair, however good the quality of shampoo used, can in the long run cause damage to the hair. There are a variety of shampoos available in the market and these synthetic detergents clean the hair more thoroughly due to their greater lathering and emulsifying power, but are gradually being replaced with herbal shampoos. There are a number of medicated shampoos available in the market used to correct any disorder of secretion in the scalp. In case of dry hair, choose a shampoo containing sulphur or essence of cedar is best.

HOME-MADE SHAMPOOS

(i) An Energy Recipe

If you are short of time and your hair badly needs a shampoo, there is a dry cleaning method. It take only a few minutes. Take an old stocking and cover the brush bristles with it. Spray some hair freshner or conditioner on the bristles and brush hair.

(ii) Panama Wood Shampoo

Boil 50 gms Panama wood in two pints of water. Let it soak for an hour. Strain off the liquid and use. This is a good preparation for normal and oily hair.

(iii) Rum Shampoo

Combine two egg-yolks with two tablespoons of odourless linseed oil and two tablespoons of rum. Soak the hair and scalp. Keep it on for an hour, then rinse off with warm water. This is especially good for dandruff and dry hair.

(iv) Egg Shampoo

This is one of the oldest beauty recipes. Eggs are full of protein. Beat two egg yolks in a glass of hot water. Strain, soak hair and scalp and scalp. Keep this on for an hour, then rinse off with water.

(v) Conditioning Shampoo

Mix together 1-2 tablespoons cheap shampoo, one egg and one tablespoon unflavoured gelatine powder. Beat slowly in order to avoid lumps. This is an effective conditioning shampoo as egg and gelatine are both proteins and make hair lovely and thick.

(vi) Herb Shampoo

Wash 200 gms each of dried olives and shikakai beans in cold water. Then soak overnight in an iron pot, keep for 10 to 12 hours, boil in the morning for 10 to 15 minutes and strain. Liquidize the pulp that remains and use the paste to wash your hair. This shampoo leaves you hair soft and shiny.

(vii) Tonic Shampoo

Put 130 gms each dried reetha, shikakai and amla into one litre water. Keep it for 24 hours. Boil, then allow to cool, strain and use as a shampoo.

(viii) Soapwort and Camomile Shampoo

Ingredients:

Dried Camomile	: 1 tablespoon
Soapwort root (powder)	
Flower	: approximate quantity
Boiling water	: 275 ml

Soak the herbs in water overnight, then strain before using. Soapwort makes a soapy liquid which whilst it does not lather will thoroughly cleanse the hair. Camomile will strengthen weak hair but other herbs may be used to meet specific problems.

Hair Styling and Setting Lotions

(1) Lemon Juice: Squeeze a lemon and use the strained juice for setting the hair. It makes the hair softy and shiny. Lemon juice dries very fast and can be used as an affective hair lacquer. To make a lemon hair laquer, cut the lemon into pieces and boil it with a cup of water until it shrinks to only half a cup. Strain and use. A few drops of alcohol (or vodka) may be added to preserve it.

(2) Gelatine is a protein agent, and is excellent as a setting lotion, giving body to limp hair. Dissolve 2 tablespoons gelatine in 2 cups of boiling water, and use it as final rinse.

(3) Add 1 tablespoon sugar to a glass of boiling water and when it has dissolved use it as a setting lotion by putting it into a spray bottle.

(4) Wood shavings are soaked in water overnight and the translucent sticky fluid rising to the water surface can be well used as lacquer. It should be applied with a brush.

(5) Collect the following ingredients:

Gum tragacanth	: 1 tablespoon
Water	: 8 tablespoons
Alcohol	: 1 tablespoon
Glycerin	: 1/2 teaspoon

Crush the gum tragacanth with a pestle and mortar. Now add water to it and stir until the gum dissolves and you have a smooth solution. Now add alcohol and glycerin. After a couple of hours the lotion will thicken.

(6) Brilliantine: Melt together in a bowl over pan of hot water 1 tablespoon each castor oil, coconut oil, petroleum jelly (or vaseline) and emulsifying wax. Remove from heat and add perfume, beating till you have made brilliantine. To make preparation more useful, you can add 2 teaspoons of lanolin to the mixture while melting. When removed from heat, just mix 1 teaspoon of water. This brilliantine holds the most unruly hair.

(7) Hair Perfume: It is pleasant to perfume the hair after washing it when the hair is half dry. Collect the following ingredients:

Powdered Charcoal	:	6 tablespoons
Powdered myrrh	:	5 tablespoons
Powdered benzoin	:	1 tablespoon
Potassium nitrate	:	1 tablespoon
Sandalwood oil	:	2-3 drops
Bergamot oil	:	2-3 drops
Mucilage tragacanth		

Mix the powders together and sieve, and then add the oils. Now add potassium nitrate and mucilage tragacanth to make a stiff paste. Heat the mixture in a bowl held over a pan of hot water and allow it to dry.

39

HOW TO LAY OUT A COSMETIC FACTORY

THE BEST quality cosmetic are usually manufactured in wellequipped, neatly arranged plants. Good equipment, well arranged, is conducive to cleanliness, and low production costs. Arrangement or layout is of most importance because a poor layout reduces the efficieny of even the best equipment, while a good layout will increase the efficiency, not only of good equipment, but also of poor equipment.

It is much easier to lay out a new cosmetic plant than it is to re-arrange an old one, for the reason that no partitions have to be torn down; no piping and wiring have to be replaced, and when a new factory is being established, the type of building or floor space can be selected with the requirements of cosmetic manufacture in mind. But the problem of organizing a new plant does not occur often. Most factories have been established for some time, and, whether the building is suitable or not, the prodution manager of the plant must make the best of it. Regardless of how suitable for cosmetic purposes the space may be, the ingenious superintendent can always arrange his equipment to suit the building and to secure the utmost economy in operating costs.

Many cosmetic plants are inefficiently arranged and poorly equipped. This situation arises from the fact that profits have been sufficiently large to enable manufacturers to ignore production costs. At this time owing to increasing competition, besides a number of other factors, this condition does not generally prevail and as a result keen attention is being devoted to reducing costs by means of better layout and the use of improved equipment.

For the purpose of arranging manufacturing equipment, cosmetic products may be divided into three main classes: powders, creams, lotions. From a study of the formulas of these products, it is obivious that there are several stages in their manufacture, and whenever manufacturing and packaging processes are subdivided it is necessary to handle the product from one operation to another. Considering the character of the materials, we perceive at once that since all will flow, we may either arrange the various units of equipment on different floors or levels, or we can use pumps or otherwise convey them between processing operations. This brings us, then, to a consideration of the type of building available. This may consist of either a single floor or a number of floors. Creams require a three stage layout: melting, mixing, filling. Lotions require three: mixing, filtering, filling. Powders require three: sifting, mixing, filling. This being the case, it is best to provide for transportation between operations in the cheapest possible manner, which is by means of gravity. To utilize gravity flow the various units of equipment can be arranged above each other so that the product will drop from one machine to the next. This arrangement requires several floors or else a single floor with sufficient head room so that mezzanines or "set backs" can be constructed. It has been said that the economical manufacture of cosmetics requires a multi-storyed building. With this opinion we do not agree entirely. Manufactures located in cities have to use multi-story buildings because land values are too great to permit spreading out. Space must be increased by building up into the air. In rural towns, where land is cheap, a factory may cover as much space as is necessary. But whether we have several floors or only one, we can always arrange for gravity flow within certain limits.

An excellent arrangement for a cosmetic plant of the mult-story type. The fourth floor is devoted mainly to the laboratories and the office with a small portion reserved at the rear of the building for the storage of powder materials and the sifting room. A similar space for the storage of cream materials and melting tanks is provided. Because of the weight of oil and petrolatum drums, melting tanks should be set into and not on the floor. This arrangement enables the operator to dump barrels directly into them.

On the floor below, the third floor, the mixing equipment for powders is located on one side, directly under the sifters, while on the opposit side directly under the melting tanks, the cream mixers are located. In the center of the building between the powder mixing room and the cream mixing room the lotion manufacturing department is situated. At the rear of the same floor packaging materials are stored. Conveyors and chutes connect this department with the heads of the packaging lines and also with the ends of the lines. By such an arrangement cases of bottles or boxes can be sent directly to the point where they are used on the floor below. Or, as an alternative, they may be transported on trucks by means of the elevators.

On the finishing floor, the second floor, the packaging machines are located. These are arranged so that the filling machines for powder, lotions, and creams are directly under the mixing machines on the floor above. The rest of the packaging equiment, cappers, labelers, cartoners, etc., are arranged in order in rows pointing toward the freight elevators. On the first floor, street level, the finished stock room and shipping rooms are located.

Such an arrangement is efficient because gravity flow is utilized to the fullest extent and the laboratories and offices are located on the top floor, above the noise inevitably made by processing equipment.

This layout is unsatisfactory only that the storage space for packaging materials should be located at the head of the packaging lines and the finished stock storage at the end of the lines, as such an arrangement saves rehandling finishing materials and finished stock.

A single floor arrangement in which a mezzanine or high platform has been constructed so as to secure gravity flow for cream materials. A mezzanine can be erected on single floor as most industrial buildings have at least twelve feet of head room. When fifteen feet of head room are available a "set back" or staggered arrangement can be made. In such a case, the melting tanks shown in Figure 2 do not have such long legs but are lowered and set back untill the discharge valves are flush with the top of the mixing tank. Under the mixing tank above the filler are the additional equipment. For instance, let us assume that we wish to run the cream through a colloid mill after it has been mixed. In this case the colloid mill should be located where the mixer is shown. The mixer should be on the mezzanine and the melting kettles, instead of being directly above it, should be set back to one side. In such an arrangement, bowl type melting kettles with side discharge valves should be used in order to reduce overall height and to obviate the need for lifting raw materials very high.

A one floor layout in which provision is made to secure the advantges of gravity flow to the fullest possible extent.

But it is not necessary to erect a mezzanine on a single floor layout. A single floor layout in which all the equipment is located on the same level. Here are shown a powder mixer, a sifter and a filler. The powder is loaded into the mixer and mixed for the required length of time, after which the discharge gate is opened and the powder dropped into a conveyor. This takes it up to a point above the sifter into which it is dropped. After passing through the sifter the material drops into another conveyor which carries it up and drops it into the hopper of the filling machine. A similar arrangement may be made for lotions and for creams, in which case, of course, it is necessary to pump the liquid materials during the successive stages of manufacture.

Gravity flow can be secured for all types of materials by still another means. An overhead track and trolley system and a series of portable hoppers and tanks can be provided so that semi processed and finished materials may be hoisted up and moved into position above the various machines. Track and trolley systems are inexpensive, flexible and efficent.

It is important to arrange packaging equipment efficiently because more people are employed in handling packaged materials, and packages are fragile and cannot be handled in bulk. Even the least logical arrangement will provide for placing the packaging equipment in order,i.e., filling machines, cappers, labelers, cartoners, wrappers. Many cosmetic layouts are not logical because packaging equipment is not arranged in logical sequence. This condition necessitates stacking filled containers on trays and transporting them to the point at which the next operation will be performed. In addition to arranging the equipment in logical sequence, it is essential to connect the various units by means of conveyors so that packages will travel from one machine to another without being rehandled.

Although a "straight line is the shortest distance between two points," it really does not matter as we stated already whether the packaging equipment is arranged in a straight line or in the form of a U, an L or even a Z. In this case a U type layout will be more efficient and will save space because packaging operations will begin and end at a point near the elevator, thus saving trucking and eliminating congestion. When incoming and outgoing freight elevators are located at opposite ends of the building the straight line or 1 type of layout is best. This type is also suitable when the finished stock room is located on the same floor at the end of the packaging lines.

Progressive people like to visualize the flow of production like a river, following the line of least resistance and proceeding along swiftly and without interruption to its destination. When they come to the problem of arranging a cosmetic factory, they attempt to secure this ideal, but in so doing sometimes overlook the fact that cosmetic production is an intermittent process and not a continuous one. They forget to provide interim storage facilities between processes. For example, they may connect the fillers directly to the mixers without realizing that such an arrangement puts the mixers out of action untill the batch has been filled. Then, when it has been filled, it is necessary to shut the bottling lines down untill another batch can be made up. Intermittent or batch production requires accumulating hoppers or tanks between the last manufacturing operation and the filling operation, and may also require interim storage facilities between various manufacturing processes

40

PROJECT PROFILES

PLANT ECONOMICS OF AFTER SHAVE LOTION

Rated Plant Capacity = 380.00 LITRES./day

LAND & BUILDING

(Total land area required 500 sq.mts) Rs. 11,00,000.00

FIXED CAPITAL

1. LAND & BUILDING	Rs.	11,00,000.00
2. PLANT & MACHINERY	Rs.	8,40,000.00
3. OTHER FIXED ASSETS	Rs.	3,90,000.00
TOTAL	Rs.	23,30,000.00

TOTAL WORKING CAPITAL/MONTH

1. RAW MATERIAL	Rs.	7,85,500.00
2. SALARY & WAGES	Rs.	53,375.00
3. UTILITIES & OVERHEADS	Rs.	1,46,500.00
TOTAL	Rs.	9,85,375.00

TOTAL CAPITAL INVESTMENT

TOTAL FIXED CAPITAL	Rs.	23,30,000.00
TOTAL WORKING CAPITAL FOR 3 MONTHS	Rs.	29,56,125.00
TOTAL	Rs.	52,86,125.00

TURN OVER/ANNUM

Cash receipt by sale of 1,14,000 - litre of Antiseptic Solution in 100 ml. & 200 ml.bottles	Rs. 1,71,00,000.00

PROFIT SALES RATIO = Profit / Sales x 100 = 23.66 %

RATE OF RETURN = Operating profit / T.C.I x 100 = 76.53 %

BREAK EVEN POINT (B.E.P) = 35.12 %

FACE CREAM AND BODY CREAM

PLANT ECONOMICS

Rated Plant Capacity = 50.00 KGS./day

CAP : 50 KGS/DAY
PACKING IN 1,000 BOTTLES OF
50 GMS. EACH.

LAND & BUILDING

(Total land required 400 sq.mts.)	Rs.	8,90,000.00

FIXED CAPITAL

1. LAND & BUILDING	Rs.	8,90,000.00
2. PLANT & MACHINERY	Rs.	5,08,000.00
3. OTHER FIXED ASSETS	Rs.	1,75,000.00
TOTAL	Rs.	15,73,000.00

TOTAL WORKING CAPITAL/MONTH

1. RAW MATERIAL	Rs.	16,015.00
2. SALARY & WAGES	Rs.	34,320.00
3. UTILITIES & OVERHEADS	Rs.	1,34,750.00
TOTAL	Rs.	1,85,085.00

TOTAL CAPITAL INVESTMENT

TOTAL FIXED CAPITAL	Rs.	15,73,000.00
TOTAL WORKING CAPITAL FOR 3 MONTHS	Rs.	5,55,255.00
TOTAL	Rs.	21,28,255.00

TURN OVER/ANNUM

By sale of 3,00,000 bottles of Vanishing Cream & Cold Cream (50gms each)(15MT/Year)	Rs.	60,00,000.00

PROFIT SALES RATIO = Profit / Sales x 100 = 53.71 %

RATE OF RETURN = Operating profit / T.C.I x 100 = 151.42 %

BREAK EVEN POINT (B.E.P) = 29.80 %

PLANT ECONOMICS OF HERBAL COSMETICS

Rated Plant capacity = 305.00 Kgs/day
HERBAL COSMETICS

LAND & BUILDING
(Land 2000 sqmt.) Rs. 26,50,000.00

FIXED CAPITAL

1. LAND & BUILDING	Rs.	26,50,000.00
2. PLANT & MACHINERY	Rs.	12,35,000.00
3. OTHER FIXED ASSETS	Rs.	3,20,000.00
TOTAL	Rs.	42,05,000.00

TOTAL WORKING CAPITAL/MONTH

1. RAW MATERIAL	Rs.	4,60,644.45
2. SALARY & WAGES	Rs.	63,000.00
3. UTILITIES & OVERHEADS	Rs.	41,500.00
TOTAL	Rs.	5,65,144.45

TOTAL CAPITAL INVESTMENT

TOTAL FIXED CAPITAL	Rs.	42,05,000.00
TOTAL WORKING CAPITAL FOR 3 MONTHS	Rs.	16,95,433.35
TOTAL	Rs.	59,00,433.35

TURN OVER/ANNUM
Herbal Hair Oil 15,000 litres
(30,000 Nos. bottles 500 ml each)
Herbal Hair Shampoo 30000 litre
(150000 Nos.bottles 200 ml each)
Herbal Tooth Paste 15000 kgs
(75,000 Nos Herbal Tooth Paste,
200 gm each tube)
Herbal Tooth Powder 1500 kgs
(1,50,000 Nos Tooth Powder, 100gms each)
Herbal cleansing cream 1500 kgs
(30,000 Nos cleansing cream, 50gm each tube)
Herbal Henna 15000 kg(100000 Nos
Herbal Henna, 150 gms each)
TOTAL Rs. 1,08,75,000.00

PROFIT SALES RATIO = Profit / Sales x 100 = 23.47 %

RATE OF RETURN = Operating profit / T.C.I x 100 = 43.25 %

BREAK EVEN POINT (B.E.P) = 44.46 %

PLANT ECONOMICS OF HAIR STYLING GEL

Rated Plant capacity = 500.00 KGS/day

LAND & BUILDING
(Land area 250 Sq.Mts.) Rs. 7,50,000.00

FIXED CAPITAL

1. LAND & BUILDING	Rs.	7,50,000.00
2. PLANT & MACHINERY	Rs.	16,10,000.00
3. OTHER FIXED ASSETS	Rs.	4,00,000.00
TOTAL	Rs.	27,60,000.00

TOTAL WORKING CAPITAL/MONTH

1. RAW MATERIAL	Rs.	4,00,540.00
2. SALARY & WAGES	Rs.	85,120.00
3. UTILITIES & OVERHEADS	Rs.	1,42,500.00
TOTAL	Rs.	6,28,160.00

TOTAL CAPITAL INVESTMENT

TOTAL FIXED CAPITAL	Rs.	27,60,000.00
TOTAL WORKING CAPITAL FOR 3 MONTHS	Rs.	18,84,480.00
TOTAL	Rs.	46,44,480.00

TURN OVER/ANNUM

By sale of 600000 Nos (250 gms)
hair styling gel

Rs. 1,50,00,000.00

PROFIT SALES RATIO = Profit / Sales x 100 = 41.62 %

RATE OF RETURN = Operating profit / T.C.I x 100 = 134.41 %

BREAK EVEN POINT (B.E.P) = 27.03 %

PLANT ECONOMICS OF Herbal Oil (Banphool Oil)

Rated Plant capacity = 14700.00 Bottles/day

LAND & BUILDING
(Total land required 3000 Sq.Mtrs.) Rs. 12,75,000.00

FIXED CAPITAL

1. LAND & BUILDING	Rs.	12,75,000.00
2. PLANT & MACHINERY	Rs.	9,30,000.00
3. OTHER FIXED ASSETS	Rs.	2,23,000.00
TOTAL	Rs.	24,28,000.00

TOTAL WORKING CAPITAL/MONTH

1. RAW MATERIAL	Rs.	53,43,609.90
2. SALARY & WAGES	Rs.	77,750.00
3. UTILITIES & OVERHEADS	Rs.	67,000.00
TOTAL	Rs.	54,88,359.90

TOTAL CAPITAL INVESTMENT

TOTAL FIXED CAPITAL	Rs. 24,28,000.00
TOTAL WORKING CAPITAL FOR 3 MONTHS	Rs. 1,64,65,079.70
TOTAL	Rs. 1,88,93,079.70

TURN OVER/ANNUM

By sale of 44,10,000 bottles (100 ml each) of herbal oil (ayurvedic) like banphool oil	Rs. 7,93,80,000.00

PROFIT SALES RATIO = Profit / Sales x 100 = 12.35 %

RATE OF RETURN = Operating profit / T.C.I x 100 = 51.90 %

BREAK EVEN POINT (B.E.P) = 31.01 %

PLANT ECONOMICS OF HAIR FIXER

Rated Plant capacity = 100.00 LITRES./day

(500000 NOS. BOTTLES/ANNUM
(60 ML EACH BOTTLE)

LAND & BUILDING

(Land area 500 sq.mtrs.)	Rs.	9,07,500.00

FIXED CAPITAL

1. LAND & BUILDING	Rs.	9,07,500.00
2. PLANT & MACHINERY	Rs.	3,56,000.00
3. OTHER FIXED ASSETS	Rs.	1,35,000.00
TOTAL	Rs.	13,98,500.00

TOTAL WORKING CAPITAL/MONTH

1. RAW MATERIAL	Rs.	1,34,234.00
2. SALARY & WAGES	Rs.	47,500.00
3. UTILITIES & OVERHEADS	Rs.	49,000.00
TOTAL	Rs.	2,30,734.00

TOTAL CAPITAL INVESTMENT

TOTAL FIXED CAPITAL	Rs. 13,98,500.00
TOTAL WORKING CAPITAL FOR 3 MONTHS	Rs. 6,92,202.00
TOTAL	Rs. 20,90,702.00

TURN OVER/ANNUM

By sale of 5,00,000 Nos. Bottles (60 ml each) of Hair Fixer (Hair Gel for Afro Hair)	Rs. 40,00,000.00

PROFIT SALES RATIO = Profit / Sales x 100 = 17.77 %

RATE OF RETURN = Operating profit / T.C.I x 100 = 33.99 %

BREAK EVEN POINT (B.E.P) = 58.06 %

PLANT ECONOMICS OF HAIR DYE IN CREAM FORM

Rated Plant capacity = 25.00 KGS/day

LAND & BUILDING
(Land area required 500 Sq.mt.) Rs. 1,50,000.00

FIXED CAPITAL

1. LAND & BUILDING	Rs.	1,50,000.00
2. PLANT & MACHINERY	Rs.	2,85,000.00
3. OTHER FIXED ASSETS	Rs.	35,000.00
TOTAL	Rs.	4,70,000.00

TOTAL WORKING CAPITAL/MONTH

1. RAW MATERIAL	Rs.	26,407.60
2. SALARY & WAGES	Rs.	27,500.00
3. UTILITIES & OVERHEADS	Rs.	23,900.00
TOTAL	Rs.	77,807.60

TOTAL CAPITAL INVESTMENT

TOTAL FIXED CAPITAL	Rs.	4,70,000.00
TOTAL WORKING CAPITAL FOR 3 MONTHS		
	Rs.	2,33,422.80
TOTAL	Rs.	7,03,422.80

TURN OVER/ANNUM

By sale of 75000 Packs Hair dye cream Rs. 15,00,000.00

PROFIT SALES RATIO = Profit / Sales x 100 = 21.79 %

RATE OF RETURN = Operating profit / T.C.I x 100 = 46.46 %

BREAK EVEN POINT (B.E.P) = 59.80 %

PLANT ECONOMICS OF LIPSTICKS OF VARIOUS COLOURS

Rated Plant capacity = 1000.00 PCS./day

LAND & BUILDING
(Total land area in 500 sq.mts.) Rs. 6,05,000.00

FIXED CAPITAL

1. LAND & BUILDING	Rs.	6,05,000.00
2. PLANT & MACHINERY	Rs.	85,000.00
3. OTHER FIXED ASSETS	Rs.	50,000.00
TOTAL	Rs.	7,40,000.00

TOTAL WORKING CAPITAL/MONTH

1. RAW MATERIAL	Rs.	54,480.00
2. SALARY & WAGES	Rs.	17,000.00
3. UTILITIES & OVERHEADS	Rs.	17,650.00
TOTAL	Rs.	89,130.00

TOTAL CAPITAL INVESTMENT

TOTAL FIXED CAPITAL	Rs. 7,40,000.00
TOTAL WORKING CAPITAL FOR 3 MONTHS	Rs. 2,67,390.00
TOTAL	Rs. 10,07,390.00

TURN OVER/ANNUM

By sale of 3,00,000 pieces of lipsticks

Rs. 18,00,000.00

PROFIT SALES RATIO = Profit / Sales x 100 = 27.77 %

RATE OF RETURN = Operating profit / T.C.I x 100 = 49.61 %

BREAK EVEN POINT (B.E.P) = 44.27 %

PLANT ECONOMICS OF NAIL ENAMEL

Rated Plant capacity = 4000.00 NOS/day

LAND & BUILDING		
(Land area 500 sq mts.)	Rs.	8,90,000.00

FIXED CAPITAL

1. LAND & BUILDING	Rs.	8,90,000.00
2. PLANT & MACHINERY	Rs.	1,84,000.00
3. OTHER FIXED ASSETS	Rs.	1,05,000.00
TOTAL	Rs.	11,79,000.00

TOTAL WORKING CAPITAL/MONTH

1. RAW MATERIAL	Rs.	46,775.00
2. SALARY & WAGES	Rs.	34,250.00
3. UTILITIES & OVERHEADS	Rs.	1,64,200.00
TOTAL	Rs.	2,45,225.00

TOTAL CAPITAL INVESTMENT

TOTAL FIXED CAPITAL	Rs.	11,79,000.00
TOTAL WORKING CAPITAL FOR 3 MONTHS	Rs.	7,35,675.00
TOTAL	Rs.	19,14,675.00

TURN OVER/ANNUM

Revenue by sales of 12,00,000 Nail
Enamel containers of each containin g 10cc of enamel

Rs. 48,00,000.00

PROFIT SALES RATIO = Profit / Sales x 100 = 28.15 %

RATE OF RETURN = Operating profit / T.C.I x 100 = 70.56 %

BREAK EVEN POINT (B.E.P) = 51.92 %

PLANT ECONOMICS OF PETROLEUM JELLY

Rated Plant capacity = 500.00 KGS./day
PETROLEUM JELLY

LAND & BUILDING (Land 300 Sq. Mt.)

	Rs.	3,25,000.00

1. LAND & BUILDING	Rs.	3,25,000.00
2. PLANT & MACHINERY	Rs.	1,90,000.00
3. OTHER FIXED ASSETS	Rs.	24,000.00

TOTAL WORKING CAPITAL/MONTH

1. RAW MATERIAL	Rs.	3,53,750.00
2. SALARY & WAGES	Rs.	34,125.00
3. UTILITIES & OVERHEADS	Rs.	53,800.00
TOTAL	Rs.	4,41,675.00

TOTAL CAPITAL INVESTMENT

TOTAL FIXED CAPITAL	Rs.	5,39,000.00
TOTAL WORKING CAPITAL FOR 3 MONTHS	Rs.	13,25,025.00
TOTAL	Rs.	18,64,025.00

TURN OVER/ANNUM

1. Sales of 150 M.T of jelly	Rs.	75,00,000.00

PROFIT = 17,21,264.50

PROFIT SALES RATIO = Profit / Sales x 100 = 22.95 %

RATE OF RETURN = Operating profit / T.C.I x 100 = 92.34 %

BREAK EVEN POINT (B.E.P) = 34.35 %

PLANT ECONOMICS OF SHAVING CREAM

Rated Plant capacity = 100.00 KG/day
SHAVING CREAM

LAND & BUILDING (Land area 500 sq.mts) Rs. 5,30,000.00

FIXED CAPITAL

1. LAND & BUILDING	Rs.	5,30,000.00
2. PLANT & MACHINERY	Rs.	4,25,000.00
3. OTHER FIXED ASSETS	Rs.	1,75,000.00
TOTAL	Rs.	11,30,000.00

TOTAL WORKING CAPITAL/MONTH

1. RAW MATERIAL	Rs.	65,250.00
2. SALARY & WAGES	Rs.	37,375.00
3. UTILITIES & OVERHEADS	Rs.	94,800.00
TOTAL	Rs.	1,97,425.00

TOTAL CAPITAL INVESTMENT

TOTAL FIXED CAPITAL	Rs.	11,30,000.00
TOTAL WORKING CAPITAL FOR 3 MONTHS	Rs.	5,92,275.00
TOTAL	Rs.	17,22,275.00

TURN OVER/ANNUM

1. By sale of 15,000 kg of Shaving cream

2. By Sale of 15,000 kg of Shaving Soap

TOTAL Rs. 34,50,000.0(

PROFIT SALES RATIO = Profit / Sales x 100 = 16.28 %

RATE OF RETURN = Operating profit / T.C.I x 100 = 32.62 %

BREAK EVEN POINT (B.E.P) = 67.25 %

SUPPLIERS OF PLANT & MACHINERIES

SUPPLIERS OF COSMETICS PRODUCTS MACHINERY

Yash Pharma Machineries

Mr. Bhupendra Panchal (CEO)
No. 16,
Abhinadan Industrial Estate,
Girnar Scooter Compound,
Behind Bank Of India,
Odhav - Kathwada Ring Road,
Odhav, Ahmedabad - 382415,
Gujarat, India
Mobile: +(91)-9376148872,
+(91)-9426040661

Global Project Consultants

Mr. Afzal Khan
No. 176/ 21, Zakir Nagar
New Delhi - 110025, Delhi, India
Mobile: +(91)-9313165720,
+(91)-8307590890
Phone: +(91)-(11)-64711921
Fax: +(91)-(11)-26984272
Email:
globalproject99@yahoo.com

Sehgal Industrial Works

Mr. Vikas Sehgal (Manager)
T-1698, Malka Ganj Road,
Subzi Mandi
New Delhi - 110007, Delhi, India
Mobile: +(91)-9811706010
+(91)-9711706010
+(91)-9810136096
Phone: +(91)-(11)-23857381,
+(91)-(11)-23850636,
+(91)-(11)-32988722
Fax: +(91)-(11)-23857381

Emkay Engineering Works

Mr. M. Hasan (Partner)
B-33, DDA Shed,
Okhla Industrial Area, Phase - II
New Delhi - 110020, Delhi, India
Mobile: +(91)-9811301650
+(91)-9873231650
+(91)-9873241650
Phone: +(91)-(11)-41610110
+(91)-(11)-26388489
+(91)-(11)-26830350
Fax: +(91)-(11)-26388489
+(91)-(11)-41610110

Parth Enterprise

Mr. Roopesh Dave (Proprietor)
3, Jivan Vihar Society,
Opp. Bank Of Bikaner & Jaipur,
Maninagar (East),

Ahmedabad - 380008,
Gujarat, India
Mobile: +(91)-9909018406
Email:
roopesh_dave2000@yahoo. com,
parthenter@gmail.com

Apex Industries Thane

Mr. Salil Pradhan
No. 27, Gupta Despande Industrial Estate,
Pokran Road No. 1,
Upavan
Thane - 400 606,
Maharashtra, India
Mobile: +(91)-9892522986
Phone: +(91)-(22)-25856039

Raj Engineering

Mr. Arvind Tripathi
Mr. Bablu Tripathi (Owner)
Plot No. 3103/3,
4th Phase,
Opposite Bank Of Baroda,
GIDC Vapi - 396195,
Gujarat, India
Mobile: +(91)-9998242011
+(91)-9173521303
+(91)-9974889361
+(91)-9662734333

Kashi Machine Tools

Mr. Kashi Ram Sharma
C - 131, Sector - 10
Noida - 201 301,
Uttar Pradesh, India
Mobile: +(91)-9312223649
Phone: +(91)-(120)-4346836

SHAMPOO MAKING AND FILLING MACHINE

Sakun Engineers

Mr. Hiten Bhavsar
Mr. Bharat Bhavsar (Proprietor)
33/a New Arbuda Estate,
Near G.s.t Crossing Road,
Ranip, Ahmedabad - 382 470,
Gujarat, India
Mobile: +(91)-9825339820
Phone: +(91)-(79)-27523886

Neelam Industries

Mr. Nilesh Patel
Plot No. 3735, Behind New Nirma,
Phase - 4, G. I. D. C., Vatva,
Ahmedabad, Gujarat - 382 445, (India)
Mobile +(91)-9925170468/
9824314469
Phone: +(91)-(79)-25840049/
25842653 / 55237536
Fax: +(91)-(79)-25842894
Email:
neelam@neelampharmamech.com

Unitek Packaging Systems Private Limited

Mr. Diwakar Sharma (Director)
S - 23, G. F. Okhla Industrial Area,
Phase - 2
New Delhi - 110020, Delhi, India
Mobile: +(91)-9560992709
+(91)-9810014265
Phone: +(91)-(11)-41045551,
+(91)-(11)-41045552
Fax: +(91)-(11)-40503166
Email: info@unitek.in,
ds@unitek.in

The Bombay Engineering Works

Mr. Mayur Joshi
1 Unit Nos. 12, Navyug Industrial Estate,
Tokersey Jivraj Road, Sewree West
Mumbai - 400 015,
Maharashtra (India)
Phone: +(91)-(22)-24137094/ 24135959
Fax: +(91)-(22)-24135828
Mobile : +(91)-9821042408/ 9820026383
E-Mail: bomeng@vsnl.com
bombayengg@yahoo.co.in

Shree Bhagwati Machtech India Ltd.

Mr. Arjun Rao (Director)
No. 9, Bhagyoday Estate,
Ajod Dairy Road, Rakhial
Ahmedabad - 380023,
Gujarat, India
Mobile: +(91)-9898070475
(91)-9099940861
+(91)-9099935530
Phone: +(91)-(79)-22770475
+(91)-(79)-22730075
Fax: +(91)-(79)-22770475
+(91)-(79)-22762466

Bro Engineers

Mr. Paresh Langalia (CEO)
No. 10, Ashok Industrial Estate,
Plot No. 6,
Udyog Nagar, Near Flyover,
Goregaon West
Mumbai - 400 001,
Maharashtra, India
Call Us: 08447552995
Mobile: +(91)-9324509325,
+(91)-9699480805
Phone: +(91)-(22)-28741761,
+(91)-(22)-28765694,
+(91)-(22)-28738724
Fax: +(91)-(22)-28738724
Email:
contact@bhagwatipharma.co.in,
contact@bhagwatipharma.com,
info@filling.in

CREAM GEL AND LOTION PLANT

Bectochem Consultants & Enggs Private Limited

Mr. Mayur S. Hedaoo (Manager)
Building 5, C /204, Mittal Estate,
Andheri - Kurla Road, Andheri East,
Mumbai - 400 059, Maharashtra, India
Mobile: +(91)-9167390040,
+(91)-9970922799
Phone: +(91)-(22)-28502400,
+(91)-(22)-28500057,
+(91)-(22)-28500008
Fax: +(91)-(22)-28506785
Email:
mayur@bectochem.com,
sales@bectochem.com

Prism Pharma Machinery

Mr. Dilip Patidar (Partner)
Plot No. 3713, Phase - 4, G. I. D. C., Vatva
Ahmedabad - 382445, Gujarat, India
Mobile: +(91)-9825044789,
+(91)-9375044789

Phone: +(91)-(79)-29095204
Fax: +(91)-(79)-25841623
Email:
sales@prismpharmamachinery.com
mkt@prismpharmamachinery.com

Yoga Industries

Mr. Rajesh B. Panchal
A - 1/1 & 2, G. I. D. C.,
National Highway,
District- Gandhi Nagar,
Kalol - 382725, Gujarat , India
Mobile: +(91)-9825712535
Phone: +(91)-(2764)-224261
Website:
www.pharmamachineries. co.in

OINTMENT PLANT FOR COSMETIC INDUSTRY

Shiddhi Engineering

Mr. R. N. Panchal (CEO)
No.174, Shubh Industrial Estate,
Near Zaveri Farm, Singarva Road,
Kathwada, Ahmedabad - 382430,
Gujarat, India
Mobile: +(91)-9998367678
Email:
shiddhiengineering@hotmail.com

Parth Enterprise

Mr. Roopesh Dave (Proprietor)
3, Jivan Vihar Society,
Opp. Bank Of Bikaner & Jaipur,
Maninagar (East),
Ahmedabad - 380008,
Gujarat, India
Mobile: +(91)-9909018406
Email:
roopesh_dave2000@yahoo.com
parthenter@gmail.com

Prism Pharma Machinery

Mr. Dilip Patidar (Partner)
Plot No. 3713, Phase - 4,
G. I. D. C., Vatva
Ahmedabad - 382445,
Gujarat, India
Mobile: +(91)-9825044789,
+(91)-9375044789
Phone: +(91)-(79)-29095204
Fax: +(91)-(79)-25841623
Email:
sales@prismpharmamachinery.com,
mkt@prismpharmamachinery.com

Jicon Industries

Mr. Chetan Hemani (CEO)
No. 37 - D, Sarita Estate, Jarimari,
Opposite St. Judes High School
Mumbai - 400072, Maharashtra, India
Phone: +(91)-(22)-28510398,
+(91)-(22)-28525135
Fax: +(91)-(22)-28516488

Ravi Kiran Industries

Mr. Samir Sampat
(Managing Partner)
No. 213, Mittal Estate, No. 2,
Marol Naka, Andheri East,
Mumbai - 400 059,
Maharashtra, India
Mobile: +(91)-9820478893
Phone: +(91)-(22)-28506569,
+(91)-(22)-28506135
Fax: +(91)-(22)-28506135
Email:
ravikiran@vsnl.com,
sales.ravikiran@gmail.com

Shree Shakti Pharma Equipment

Mr. Manik Panchal (CEO)
Plot No. 406, Road No. 28,
Ramnagar, Ramwadi,
Near Spearige Company,
Wagle Estate
Thane - 400604,
Maharashtra, India
Mobile: +(91)-9892809768
Phone: +(91)-(22)-25838454

AEROSOL PLANTS

Twin Tech India Pvt. Ltd.

Mr. P. K. Sharma (CEO)
No. H - 75 - A, Sector - 12,
Pratap Vihar, Near Santosh Medical College
Ghaziabad - 201009,
Uttar Pradesh, India
Mobile: +(91)-9310052700,
+(91)-9310052701
Phone: +(91)-(120)-2840276
+(91)-(120)-2841949
+(91)-(120)-6545141
Fax: +(91)-(120)-2840723
Email: sales@twinindia.com,
info@twinindia.com

BLENDERS

Prism Pharma Machinery

Plot No. 3713, Phase 4, G.I.D.C.
Vatva, Ahmedabad - 382445,
Gujarat, India
Phone: 08376805843

Shiv Shakti Process Equipment Private Limited

Shiv Shakti, No. 407,
Shivam Chambers,
S. V. Road, Goregoan West,
Mumbai - 400104,
Maharashtra, India
Website: www.shivshaktiequip.in

Hexamide Agro Tech LLP

Plot No.-11, Aditya Industrial Estate,
At Post Kumbiwali,
Taluka Khalapur,
District- Raigad,
Navi Mumbai - 410210,
Maharashtra, India
Phone: 08447556832
Website:
www.usedchemicalreactor.com

Namdhari Industrial Works

D - 26, Focal Point,
Khanna - 141 401, Punjab, India
Phone: 08377804783
Sanskruti Engineers
Gate No. 7, Chimbali,
Tal- Khed, Pune - 410501,
Maharashtra, India
Phone: 09953363082

Surya Techno Chem

Opposite Radha Swami Satsang,
Village Morta, Meerut Road,
Ghaziabad - 201003,
Uttar Pradesh, India
Phone: 09953354911

The Bombay Engineering Works

Unit Nos. 12,
Navyug Industrial Estate,
Tokersey Jivraj Road,
Sewree West,
Mumbai - 400 015,

Maharashtra, India
Phone: 08447572988
Website:
www.pharma-machinery.co.in

Om Engineering

No. 242, Pushkar Industrial Estate,
Phase 1, GIDC, Vatva,
Near Torrent Power,
Opposite Macon Zone,
Ahmedabad - 380016,
Gujarat, India
Phone: 09953355936
Website:
www.om-engineering.com

Harshika Industries

No. 5, Near Dwarka Industrial Estate,
Naikpada, Valiv Road, Vasai East,
Thane - 401208, Maharashtra, India
Phone: 08447508563
Website:
www.filling-machinemanufacturer.com

Siddhi Pharma Equipment

Plot No. L - 2901/4, 4th Phase,
G.I.D.C., Vapi, Valsad - 396195,
Gujarat, India
Phone: 09953356072
Website:
www.siddhipharmaequipments.com

Ram Tech, Chennai

3/914, Kundrathur Road,
Madanandapuram,
Porur, Chennai - 600125,
Tamil Nadu, India
Website: www.ramtech.org

Khodiyar Engineering Works

B - 1, Shanti Nagar,
Industrial Estate,
Shanti Nagar Road No. 27,
Wagle Estate,
Thane - 400604,
Maharashtra, India
Phone: 08376808428
Website: www.khodiyarind.com

Shiv Pharma Engineers

34-36, Tejandra Industrial Estate,
Opposite C. M. C., Odhav Road,
Ahmedabad - 382 415,
Gujarat, India
Phone: 08373904427
Website: www.gmpmachines.com

Excel Plants & Equipment Private Limited

Gat No. 611, Mouje Kuruli,
Chakan M. I. D. C., Tal- Khed,
Pune - 410501, Maharashtra, India
Website:
www.excelspraydryers.com

Rikon Pharma

Gala No. 1/1,
Sagar Signature Complex,
Samkit Building, Near Ipol,
Waliv Phata, Waliv,
Vasai East, Thane - 401208,
Maharashtra, India
Phone: 08377800131

Ghaziabad Polymers Private Limited

C- 136, Site- 1, Buland Shahar Road Industrial Area,
Ghaziabad - 201 009,

Uttar Pradesh, India
Phone: 09953353149
Website:
www.ghaziabadpolymers.com

SS Enterprises

Plot No. 99, Khasra No. 101/24, Vijay Nagar Colony,
Opposite Bharat Dharam Kanta,
Narela Road,
Bawana - 110039,
Delhi, India
Phone: 09953357524

FILTER PRESS

Merit Industries Limited

No. 112/3D, Madhapur Road,
Kaniyur Village, Karumathampatti Via,
Coimbatore - 641659,
Tamil Nadu, India
Phone: 08447570276
Website:
www.meritindustriesltd.com

Ace Industries

113, Alpine Industrial Estate,
Marol Military Road,
Andheri East,
Mumbai - 400059,
Maharashtra, India
Phone: 08373903188
Website: www.acecentrifuges.co.in

Mech Static Hydraulics

No. 43/A, Srinivasa Nagar,
Third Street, Uppilipalayam,
Coimbatore - 641015,
Tamil Nadu, India
Phone: 08588874078

The Adarsh Engineering Works

Ghat Road, Near Union Bank,
Nagpur - 440018,
Maharashtra, India
Phone: 08447569191
Website:
www.theadarshengineering.com

Energy Equipment

No. 9 - A, Zackaria Colony,
Main Road,
Choolaimedu, Chennai - 600094,
Tamil Nadu, India
Phone: 08447507985
Website: www.aquaflex.in

Charul Polymer Products

Plot No. 3235/3236, GIDC,
Phase- 3, T A, Kalol, Chhatral,
Gandhinagar,
Ahmedabad - 382729,
Gujarat, India
Phone: 09953358163

BDS Hydro Treat Consultants Private Limited

G - 42, Ground Floor,
Dilshad Colony,
New Delhi - 110095, India
Phone: 08376808134
Delite Filter Press

Delite Ceramic Machinery Equipment,

Plot No. - 228, Road No. 2, GIDC,
Kathwada,
Odhav, Ahmedabad - 382430,
Gujarat, India
Phone: 09953353221
Website: www.delitefilterpress.com

Bipin Pharma Equipment

Off. 19,C Floor, Holly Hock Bldg, Cosmos Lounge,
Near Neelkanth Green,
Mulla Baug, Opp. G. B. Road, Mumbai,
Thane - 400 610,
Maharashtra, India
Phone: 08447499213
Website:
www.sparklertypefilterpress.com

Filter Machines Private Limited

Behind Nirbhay Auto, N. H. 8,
Vapi - 396 191, Gujarat, India
Phone: 08447514084
Website: www.filtermachines.in

Metal Craft Technologies Co.

Shivneri Apartments, 2nd Floor,
Gala No- 305, Nardas Nagar,
Bhandup West,
Mumbai - 400 078,
Maharashtra, India
Phone: 08588874754
Website: www.metalcraftech.com

G. P. Filtech Engineers

Gala No. 26, R. J. Compound,
Alvin Nagar, Jama Masjid Lane,
Kherani Road,
Saki Naka, Mumbai - 400072,
Maharashtra, India
Phone: 08447502381

Shri Ram Engineering Co.

Patel Marg, Ghaziabad - 201 001,
Uttar Pradesh, India
Phone: 08588873144

S. S. Pharma Equipments

No. 103, Veena Industrial Estate,
L. B. S. Marg, Vikhroli West,
Mumbai - 400083,
Maharashtra, India
Phone: 08447557403
Website: www.sspharma.net

Amar Plastic

No. 3220 - 21, Phase 3, GIDC,
Chattral, Gandhinagar - 382 729,
Gujarat, India
Phone: 08447541248

MacLean Equipments

B- 39, Sector- 57, Noida - 201301,
Uttar Pradesh, India
Website:
www.macleanequipments.com

Goyum Screw Press

Plot No. 324/2, Industrial Area - A,
Ludhiana - 141003,
Punjab, India
Website: www.oilexpellerindia.com

Deveshi Engineering

B- 5, Maruti Estate,
Near Choksi Tube,
G. I. D. C., Phase - 1, Vatva,
Ahmedabad - 382345,
Gujarat, India
Phone: 09953364202

Krishnaja Engineering

Plot No-31, Door No-26, 5th Street,
Officer's Colony, Adambakkam,
Chennai - 600088,
Tamil Nadu, India
Phone: 08588802004

DRYERS AND DRYING OVENS

Metal Press Industries

A- 17, Pushpak Estate,
Gujarat Bottaling, Char Rasta,
Rakhial, Ahmedabad - 380023,
Gujarat, India
Phone: 08377806497

Shiv Pharma Engineers

34-36, Tejandra Industrial Estate,
Opposite C. M. C., Odhav Road,
Ahmedabad - 382 415,
Gujarat, India
Phone: 08373904427
Website: www.gmpmachines.com

Richard Engineering Bom Private Limited

First Floor, Brij Complex,
K. B. Road,
Railway Flyover Junction,
Ambarnath (W), Thane - 421 501,
MS, India
Phone: 08447558651
Website: www.chemicalpharmaequipment.com

Krishna Scientific Works

D - 23, Site - C,
Surajpur Industrial Area,
Dadri Road,
Greater Noida - 201306,
Uttar Pradesh, India
Phone: 08377805857

Ahlada Industries Private Ltd.

Sy. No. 66- 68, Bahadurpally,
Qutbullapur Mandal,
Ranga Reddy District,
Hyderabad - 500043, A. P. India
Phone: 08376808108
Website: www.ahladaindustries.net

Biomate India Pvt Ltd

436, Shahabad Daulatpur,
Near Sec -17,
Rohini, New Delhi - 110042,
Delhi, India
Phone: 08376805941
Website: www.fermentor.co.in

Balaji Enterprises Krishna & Co.

Paper Box, Near Hotel White House,
Mahakali Caves Road,
Andheri East,
Mumbai - 400093,
Maharashtra, India
Phone: 09953362138

Shreeji Instruments

Shop No. 8/9 G,
Karnavati Shopping Center,
Near Bhurhani Society,
Behind Smruti Mandir,
Ghodasar, Opposite Pushpkunj Bungalows,
Ahmedabad - 380050,
Gujarat, India
Phone: 08377805971

Rajyog Industries

Plot No. 5209,
Near Seven Water Tank,
G. I. D. C., Ankleshwar - 393 002,
Gujarat, India
Phone: 09099021320

Shrink Wrap Machinery

S. No. 96, Opposite Hotel Savoy,
Off. Sakivihar Road, Sakinaka,
Andheri East,
Mumbai - 400072,
Maharashtra, India
Phone: 09869044686

Aarathi Engineers

No. 2, Cross Street - 1, Main Road,
G. K. Industrial Estate, Porur,
Chennai - 600116,
Tamil Nadu, India
Phone: 09655056922

Perfect Industries

B/4/1, Ambica Industrial Estate,
Nagarwell Hanuman Road,
Sukhramnagar,
Ahmedabad - 380 023,
Gujarat, India
Phone: 09714058877

Leela Pharma Machineries

Jivdhani Industrial Estate,
Unit No. C-10,
Dhumal Nagar, Behind Rashmi Bungalow,
Vasai Fata East, Vasai - 401208, Maharashtra, India
Phone: 08447496414

Chitra Machineries Pvt Limited

Plot No. 202 & 226, Road No. 3,
G. I. D. C., Kathwada,
Near Odhav,
Ahmedabad - 382 430,
Gujarat, India
Phone: 09953355329

PLANETARY MIXERS

Kwality Process Equipments Private Limited

Plot No. 198, Sector - 1,
Vasai Taluka,
I. E. Gauraipada,
Thane - 401208,
Maharashtra, India
Phone: 08447520194
Website:
www.kwalityengineeringcorporation.com

Maharashtra Enterprises

Rani Residency, Shop No. 7,
Ground Floor,
Chirag Nagar, Ghatkopar West,
Mumbai - 400086,
Maharashtra, India
Phone: 09953360621

Vinayak Industries

D-3, Sheetal Industrial Estate,
Behind Tirupti Gas Godown,
Meera Bhayandar Phatak Road,
Bhayandar East, Thane - 401105,
Maharashtra, India
Phone: 08447525218
Website: www.resinplants.com

Gangaa Machines

No. 13/ 62 - C, Trichy Main Road,
Chinthamani Pudur Post,
Coimbatore - 641103,
Tamil Nadu, India
Phone: 08447501162
Website:
www.gangaamachines.com

Haifa Engineering

5, BR Nath Pai Marg,
Pine Building,
Opp. Hajee Cassum Compound,
Mazgaon, Mumbai - 400010,
Maharashtra, India
Phone: 09953358657

Traxit Engineers Pvt. Ltd.

406, Solaris- 2, Opposite L & T Gate No. 6
Saki Vihar Road, Powai,
Mumbai - 400072,
Maharashtra, India
Phone: 08377809843
Website: www.traxiteng.co.in

East India Trading Co.

No. 71/ B, Netaji Subhash Road, 2nd Floor,
Room No. 118, Gooptu Mansion,
Kolkata - 700001,
West Bengal, India
Phone: 09953360763

Prism Pharma Machinery

Plot No. 3713, Phase - 4
G. I. D. C., Vatva,
Ahmedabad - 382445,
Gujarat, India
Phone: 08376805843

Excel Plants & Equipment Pvt Ltd

Gat No. 611, Mouje Kuruli,
Chakan M. I. D. C., Tal- Khed,
Pune - 410 501,
Maharashtra, India
Website: www.excelplants.com

Conveying Machines Manufacturing Co.

No. 106, Ashok Service Industrial Estate,
L. B. S. Marg, Bhandup West,
Mumbai - 400 078,
Maharashtra, India
Phone: 08376806177

Sahyog Enterprise, Mumbai

No. 5, Tarun Plastic Industrial Estate,
Mogra Village Road, Andheri East,
Off Nagardas Cross Road,
Mumbai - 400 069,
Maharashtra, India
Phone: 08373902911
Website: www.agitatorsindia.net

Imochem Engineers

No. 411, Janabai House,
Kurla West,
Mumbai - 400070,
Maharashtra, India
Phone: 08373903857
Website: www.imochemengineers.com

Wang Professionals

Flat No. C, First Floor,
Plot No. 106/1A,
Kishan Garh, Near
MCD School, Vasant Kunj,
New Delhi - 110070, Delhi, India
Phone: 09953360718

Victor Engineering Enterprises

B - 09, Bharat Market, 2nd Lane,
Subhash Nagar,
J. M. Road, Asalfa,

Ghatkopar West,
Mumbai - 400084,
Maharashtra, India
Phone: 08447550269

Pratham Engineering

A - 04/05, Bharat Compound,
Opposite Dhodiya Petrol Off W. E. Highway,
Kashimira, Mira Road East,
Thane - 401 104,
Maharashtra, India
Website: www.paintindustrymachines.com

Prakash Engineering Works

Plot No. 5175,
Near Paras Industries,.
G. I. D. C., Ankleshwar - 393002,
Gujarat, India
Phone: 08588873519

Pharma Chem Machineries

No. 311/2484, Motilal Nagar No. 2,
M. G. Road, Goregaon West,
Mumbai - 400 104,
Maharashtra, India
Phone: 08447570288
Website: www.ipharmashop.com

Pledge International

AF- 4, Soham Complex,
Soni Ni Chawl,
Ahmedabad - 382415,
Gujarat, India
Phone: 08377808655

Mars Technologies

No. 44, 13th Cross, MTS Layout,
Kengeri Satellite, Town-60,
Bengaluru - 560060,
Karnataka, India
Phone: 09686467653

PASTE FILLING EQUIPMENTS

Bharat Sales Corporation

No. 45, G. B. Road,
Delhi - 110006, Delhi, India
Website: www.bharatsales.co.in

Raman Industries

W. Z. - 40/3, Sant Garh,
Street No. 30, Tilak Nagar,
Delhi - 110018, Delhi, India
Phone: 09953353079

Om Chamunda Enterprises

123, Diamond Industrial Estate,
Near Tolnaka,
Ketki Pada Road,
Dahisar East,
Mumbai - 400068,
Maharashtra, India
Phone: 08447496851
Website: www.omchamundaindia.com

Ad Industries

No. 29, Dhanlaxmi Industrial Estate
Near Police Commissioner Office,
Shahibuag,
Ahmedabad - 380004,
Gujarat, India
Phone: 08376805975
Website: www.adpackagingmachine.com

Manilal Pack Plast Pvt Limited

Chandanmani,
Opposite Kalupur Chakla Post Office,
Tankshal Road,
Kalupur, Ahmedabad - 380001,
Gujarat, India
Phone: 08373902742
Website:
www.manilalpackplast.com

S. S. Pharma Tech

PX 65, Azad Lane,
Ambhedkar Chowk,
ITT Bhatti,
Western Express Highway,
Goregoan East,
Mumbai - 400063,
Maharashtra, India
Website:
www.creamfillingmachine.com

Komal Enterprises

Shop- 5, Opposite NMC Mini Market,
Near Ambad Police Station,
Nashik - 422009,
Maharashtra, India
Phone: 08377806967

Indian Packaging Machineries

I - 15, Phase - 1,
D. L. F. Industrial Area,
Faridabad - 121 003,
Haryana, India
Website:
www.packagingmachinary.com

Harshika Industries

No. 5, Near Dwarka Industrial Estate,
Naikpada, Valiv Road, Vasai East,
Thane - 401208,
Maharashtra, India
Phone: 08447508563
Website:
www.filling-machinemanufacturer.com

Genius Engineering

Plot No. 27/47- 48, Laxmi Ratan Industrial Complex,
Opp. Government of India Press,
Near Hardware Chowk,
N. I. T., Faridabad - 121001,
Haryana, India
Phone: 08377801730
Website:
www.geniuspackaging.com

Pack - Well Engineers

No. 13, Manhar Plot,
Opp. Delhi-Rajasthan Transport Co.,
Godown Road, Rajkot - 360002,
Gujarat, India
Phone: 09953356411

Bhavani Engineering Works

A- 32, Akshardham Industrial Estate,
Near Panchratna Industrial Estate,
Phase - 4,
G. I. D. C., Vatva,
Ahmedabad - 382 445,
Gujarat, India
Phone: 08587079996

Koyka Electronics Pvt. Ltd.

F 121, Tirkha Colony,
Tigaon Road, Ballabhgarh,
Faridabad - 121 006, Haryana, India
Website: www.koykagroup.co.in

Delight Fabricators

A-45, Bileshwar Estate,
Opposite G.V.M.M, GIDC,
Kathwada Roao,
Odhav, Ahmedabad - 382415,
Gujarat, India
Phone: 09953360273
Website: www.delightfabricators.com

42

Suppliers of Raw Materials

Shankar Dyes & Chemicals

No. 1209, Shankar Building,
Gali No. 11, Sadar Bazar,
New Delhi - 110 006,
Delhi, India
Phone: 08447498163
Website: www.shankardyes.com

Cosmetics of India

Plot No - 221, Pocket-C, D sidc,
Sector-5, Bawana Industrial Area,
Delhi - 110039, Delhi, India
Phone: 09811230720

Dev International

No. 301, 3rd Floor,
Solitaire Complex,
Opposite Bombay Garage,
Shahibaug,
Ahmedabad - 380004,
Gujarat, India
Phone: 08377800758

Chemical Corporation

No. 2, Rajputpara No. 4,
Amardeep Complex,
Near Khodiyar Chamber,
Rajkot - 360 001, Gujarat, India
Phone: 09427209556

Microtrol Sterilisation Services Private Limited

No. 355-65-3, Sarjapur Road,
Agara, Near Hsr Layout,
Bengaluru - 560 102,
Karnataka, India
Phone: 09902366779

HERBAL COSMETIC RAW MATERIALS

Vasavi India

No. 122, Varadhamuthiappan Street, Geroge Town,
Chennai - 600 001,
Tamil Nadu, India
Phone: 09840123444

Indian Commercial Co.Pvt. Ltd.

Oriental House, 5th Floor, No. 7,
Jamshedji Tata Road, Churchgate,
Mumbai - 400020,
Maharashtra, India
Phone: 08588802838

Kirpal Export Overseas

BP- 130, Shalimar Bagh West,
New Delhi - 110 088, Delhi, India
Phone: 08447557523
Website: www.henna-manufacturers.com

Hennex India
Unit- II, No. 489, Link Road,
Delhi Gate,
Old Faridabad,
Faridabad - 121002,
Haryana, India
Phone: 08376807668

Nathubhai Cooverji & Sons
No. 417, Vasant Nivas, 3rd Floor,
Bhaudaji Cross Road,
No. 10, Matunga,
Mumbai - 400019,
Maharashtra, India
Phone: 08447523788
Website: www.ncsons.com

Aadi Enterprises
F-25, Bhram Tower,
Harimarg, Bajaj Nagar,
Jaipur - 302006,
Rajasthan, India
Phone: 09460587905

COSMETICS PACKAGING MATERIALS

Global Print & Pack
A-110, Okhla Industrial Area,
Phase-2, New Delhi - 110020,
Delhi, India
Phone: 08588873511

Akar Shrink Packs
C- 40, MIDC, Sinnar,
Nashik-Pune Highway,
Nashik - 422113,
Maharashtra, India
Phone: 08377801577

Sudham Packaging
Unit No. 101,
Dewan & Shah Industrial Estate No. 1,
Navghar Road,
Vasai, Thane - 401210,
Maharashtra, India
Phone: 09953354927

Excell Plastics
Shailesh Industrial Estate No. 3,
Unit No 24/ 25/ 26,
Vasai East,
Thane - 400 601,
Maharashtra, India
Phone: 08447526256
Website: www.excellplastics.com

Abhinav Enterprises
A - 67, D. D. A. Shed
Okhla Industrial Area,
Phase - 2, New Delhi - 110 020,
Delhi, India

Krishna Packaging
401- 421- B,
Jheel Khuranja,
Near Bank Of Baroda,
Tanga Stand,
Near Gandhi Nagar,
Delhi - 110 051, Delhi, India
Phone: 09953363051

Creative Plastics
No. 74, Mistry Industrial Complex
MIDC Cross Road- A, M. I. D. C.,
Andheri (E), Mumbai - 400093,
Maharashtra, India
Phone: 08447501418
Website: www.creativeplastics.in

Vee Dee Enterprises

No. 802,
Gold Crest Business Center,
Opp.manubhai Jewellers,
L. T. Road, Borivali West,
Mumbai - 400 092,
Maharashtra, India
Phone: 08373902801
Website:
www.pouchepackaging.com

Khushi Handicraft

No. 1- 10885,
Gali No -4,
Subhash Park,
Shahdara,
Delhi - 110032,
Delhi, India
Phone: 09999531783

Purity Flexpack Limited

Vanseti, PO-Tajpura,
Near Halol,
District Panchmahal,
Halol - 389350,
Gujarat, India
Phone: 09953354370
Website:
www.packaging-pouches.com

Silvertone Gravu Flex Pvt. Ltd.

No. 27, DLF Industrial Area,
Opposite Metro Pillar No. 311,
Moti Nagar,
New Delhi - 110015,
Delhi, India
Phone: 08377801826

Ask Enterprises

Gate No. 63, Jyotiba Nagar,
Sonawane Wasti,
Talawade,
Pune - 412114,
Maharashtra, India
Phone: 08376806769
Website: www.ask-pack.com

Star Industrial Corporation

No. 79 / 81,
Bora Bazar Street,
Narayandas Wadi Building,
1st Floor,
Fort, Mumbai - 400 001,
Maharashtra, India
Phone: 09953364077

Venkatesh Gifts, Indore

No. 207, Mamta Tower,
Manormaganj,
Near Mayank Hospital,
Indore - 452001,
Madhya Pradesh, India
Phone: 08588874473

Ayush Flexipack Private Limited

B - 5, Sector - 57,
Noida - 201301,
Uttar Pradesh, India
Phone: 09953358609

COSMETIC BOTTLES

Aadeshwar Corporation

No. 29, Haribhai Market,
Revdi Bazar, Kalupur,
Ahmedabad - 380002, Gujarat, India
Phone: 09953356727

Millennium Polymers

Plot No. 22/22A,
Shop No. 105, 1st Floor,
Valbah Sadan,
Prashanthi Nagar I.E.,
Kukatpally,
Hyderabad - 500072,
Andhra Pradesh, India
Phone: 09953353188
Website:
www.millenniumpolymers.in

Maharashtra Metal Works Pvt. Ltd.

Pramod Woolen,
Next To Kamani Oil Mill,
Chandivali Farm Road,
Chandivali,
Mumbai - 400072,
Maharashtra, India
Phone: 08376807526
Website: www.mmw.co.in

Rohan Industries

H - 119, Mega Center,
Hadapsar, Pune - 411028,
Maharashtra, India
Phone: 08376806277
Website: www.bottlesindia.com

Priyanka Polypack

No. 408/1,
Aggarwal Compound,
Near Khatipura Link Road,
Near Gori Nagar,
Indore - 455 115,
Madhya Pradesh, India
Phone: 08377802449

Dura Plast

No. 1108, G. I. D. C. Estate,
4th Phase,
Vitthal Udyognagar,
Anand - 388121,
Gujarat, India
Phone: 08377802370

Shreeji Bottle Trading Company

No. 179/5,
Ashirwad Industrial Estate,
Ram Mandir Road,
Goregaon West,
Mumbai - 400 104,
Maharashtra, India
Phone: 09953362268

Durga Agencies

F - 797, B, Road No. 14,
V. K. I. Area,
Jaipur - 302013,
Rajasthan, India
Phone: 08377802131

Laxmi Plastic Industries

Dabhoi Road Vill. Kelanpur,
Vadodara - 390016,
Gujarat, India
Phone: 09953358437

Janki Polymers

X-259, Gali No. 13,
Samaypur Industrial Area,
Near Samaypur Railway Station,
Badli, Delhi - 110042,
Delhi, India
Phone: 09953359627

SVM Enterprises

C - 401/402, Bhaveshwar Plaza,
L. B. S. Marg,
Near Shreyas Cinema,
Ghatkopar West,
Mumbai - 400 086,
Maharashtra, India
Phone: 09953354955

Alpha Group

No. 505, Union Trade Center,
Udhana Darwaja,
Surat - 395003,
Gujarat, India
Phone: 08377803192

Jyoti Chemicals

B - 43, M. I. D. C., Ambad,
Nashik - 422 010,
Maharashtra, India
Phone: 08447558017
Website: www.jyoti-chemical.com

Hary Pack Pharma Pvt. Ltd.

No. 19, Prakash Estate,
Ritanagar Road,
Vastral Road,
Near Rabari Colony,
Charrasta,
Amraiwadi,
Ahmedabad - 380026,
Gujarat, India
Phone: 09426511776

Master Pet Industries

K1 - 26/1, G.I.D.C. Kadi,
Near Somani Ceramic,
Kadi - 382 715, Gujarat, India
Phone: 08588873504

Medosha Plast

No. 210,
Hiranandani Industrial Estate,
Opposite Kanjurmarg Railway Station,
Kanjur Marg West,
Mumbai - 400 078,
Maharashtra, India
Phone: 09953362236

Plastopack Industries

No. 26 - 29,
Sheetal Shagun Industrial Estate,
1st Floor,
Sativali Road,
Near Waliv Phata,
Opposite Mahindra Showroom,
Vasai East,
Mumbai - 401208,
Maharashtra, India
Phone: 08588802564

PAPS Electronics

W. Z. - 49, Khampur,
West Patel Nagar,
New Delhi - 110 008,
Delhi, India
Phone: 08588874520

PMD Enterprises

No. 4, Aban's Pravesh,
Aban Park,
Kolshet Road,
Dhokali,
Thane - 400607,
Maharashtra, India
Phone: 08586982595

Sri Maruthy Marketing Company

No. 1596, New No. 26,
2nd Cross,
Nagappa Block,
Srirampuram,
Bengaluru - 560021,
Karnataka, India
Phone: 09953362747

HERBS AND HERBS EXTRACTS

Mother Herbs (P) Ltd

C - 39, 2nd & 4th Floor, 13 - Street,
Madhu Vihar, Patpadganj,
New Delhi - 110092, Delhi, India
Website: www.motherherbs.com

Impressions Cosmetics

R - 7 - A, 2nd Floor, Green Park Main,
New Delhi - 110 016, Delhi, India
Phone: 09953353197
Website: www.impressionhenna.com

Hennex India

489, Link Road, Delhi Gate,
Old Faridabad,
Faridabad - 121 002,
Haryana, India
Phone: 09953357163
Website: www.henna-india.com

Surajbala Exports Private Limited

39, Aaya Nagar,
Opp. Govt High School,
Near Arjan Garh Metro Station,
New Delhi - 110 047,
Delhi, India
Phone: 08376808352
Website: www.ayurveda-herbal.com

AADI ENTERPRISES

F-25, Bhram Tower, Harimarg,
Bajaj Nagar, Jaipur - 302006,
Rajasthan, India
Phone: 09460587905

Ustadji & Co.

WP-13 C, Near City Park Hotel,
Pitam Pura,
New Delhi - 110 088, Delhi, India
Phone: 09810880855

Neelam Phyto-extracts

No. 106-107.
Kanara Business Center,
Behind Everest Garden
Near Laxmi Nagar,
Ghatkopar East,
Mumbai - 400 077,
Maharashtra, India
Phone: 08373903567
Website: www.naturalextracts.in

A. E. S. Boys Hostel Campus,

Near University Library,
Navrangapura,
Ahmedabad - 380 009,
Gujarat, India
Phone: 09953356815
Website: www.sristiinnovation.com

Nathubhai Cooverji & Sons

No. 417, Vasant Nivas, 3rd Floor,
Bhaudaji Cross Road,

No. 10, Matunga,
Mumbai - 400019,
Maharashtra, India
Phone: 08447523788
Website: www.ncsons.com

Hennex India

Unit - II, No. 489, Link Road,
Delhi Gate,
Old Faridabad,
Faridabad - 121002,
Haryana, India
Phone: 08376807668

Reddy International

No.270, Valluvar Kottam High Road,
Nungambakkam, Chennai - 600034,
Tamil Nadu, India
Phone: 08377801761

COSMETIC PRODUCTS PERFUMES

Link International

No. 257/ 5, Darvesh, Behind Gandhi Market,
Old Flank Road, Sion East, Mumbai - 400022,
Maharashtra, India
Phone: 08586982109

Planters International Company

No.466, 3 A Main, 2nd Stage,
Indiranagar, Bengaluru - 560 038,
Karnataka, India
Website:
www.plantersinternational.com

Balaji Aromatics

No. 2317/19, 1st Floor,
Nanak Market,
Gali Hinga Beg, Tilak Bazar,
Khari Baoli,
Delhi - 110 006, Delhi, India
Phone: 09810394961

Etosha Pan, (India) P. Limited

209, Munish Plaza, 20,
Ansari Road,
New Delhi - 110002, Delhi, India
Phone: 08377802447

Makhulal Ayodhya Prasad & Grandson

4/B, Madan Mohan Burman Street,
Kolkata - 700007,
West Bengal, India
Phone: 08447547908

Aromatik Bangalore Pvt Ltd.

No. 5, Chikkasandra Hesaraghatta Road,
Dasarahalli Post,
Bengaluru - 560 057,
Karnataka, India
Phone: 09953353982

Creative Aromatics Private Limited6

7/3, Industrial Suburb,
Yeshwanthpur,
Bengaluru - 560022,
Karnataka, India
Phone: 08447528328
Website:
www.flavorsandfragrances.co.in

Darussalam India
No. 324, Triplicane High Road,
Triplicane,
Chennai - 600 005,
Tamil Nadu, India
Phone: 08377800043

Patsons
No. 6, SSA-1, 2nd Floor,
Rutika Chamber,
Pathardi Phata,
Shrawan Sector, Ashwin Nagar,
Nashik - 422009,
Maharashtra, India
Phone: 08588800131

Ador Multiproducts Limited
5th Floor, Ador House,
6 K Dubhash Marg Fort,
Mumbai - 400001,
Maharashtra, India
Phone: 09967031184

Dynasty Aromas
709 Crystal Paradise,
Off. Veera Desai Road,
Andheri (West),
Mumbai - 400 053,
Maharashtra, India
Phone: 09820375117

Winmark Trading Corporation
No. 255, 5th Cross,
3rd Main Road,
Chennammana Kere
Achukattu Banashankari,
3rd Stage, Bengaluru - 560 085,
Karnataka, India
Phone: 09953355381

S. K. Flavours & Fragrances
J-138/1, MIDC, Tarapur, Boisar,
Thane - 401506,
Maharashtra, India
Phone: 09953359978

Janak Perfumers
Para Bazar,
Near Raiya Naka Tower,
Rajkot - 360001, Gujarat, India
Phone: 09953364945

Ansan Chemical Company
No. 2404, Next To Post Office,
Goverdhan Behari Colony,
Shahdara,
Delhi - 110 032, Delhi, India
Phone: 09953354604

Shiv Sales Corporation
252, Kotla, Mayur Vihar, Phase-1,
Near Gujjar Bhavan,
Delhi - 110091, India
Phone: 08447566062
Website: www.shivorganics.com

Ban Labs Limited
Ban House, Gondal Road South.,
Rajkot - 360004, Gujarat, India
Phone: 08447529106
Website:
www.banpersonalcare.com

Jagsan Cosgo Pvt Ltd.
Sanjeevani Distributors,
Shop No. 7,
Chidhanand Building, Ram Nagar,
Old Ayere Road, Dombivali East,
Thane - 421201, Maharashtra, India
Phone: 09702665777

Sepr Refractories India Limited

Post Box No 1 Kanjikode West,
Palakkad - 678623, Kerala, India
Phone: +(91)-(491)-2568655

Honey Money Top

No. 9 - A & B, Main Road,
Taimoor Nagar,
N. Friends Colony,
Delhi - 110065, Delhi, India
Phone: 09953364885

Moksha Lifestyle Products

Address: No. 24/157, Shakti Nagar,
G. T. Karnal Road, Delhi - 110007, India
Phone: 08377802094
Website: www.indiaessentialoil.com

Gift House

Shop No. 482, LBS College Road,
Opp. Kaju Wala, Raja Park,
Jaipur - 302004, Rajasthan, India
Phone: 08588851370

Ronak Flavours & Fragrances

No. J - 74 , M. I. D. C. Boisar,
Thane - 401 506,
Maharashtra, India
Phone: 09321717975

PERFUMERY CHEMICALS

Aspire Speciality Chemicals

Jay House, Plot No. 731,
Phase - 2,
G. I. D. C. Industrial Estate,
Vapi - 396195,
Gujarat, India
Website: www.aspirespeciality.com

Aman Enterprises

No. 901,
G. D. I. T. L. Tower - B - 08,
Netaji Subhash Place, Pitampura,
Delhi - 110034, Delhi, India
Phone: 08447565337

Premier Chem Corporation

No. 203, Himalaya House,
2nd Floor,
No. 79, Palton Road,
Mumbai - 400 001,
Maharashtra, India
Phone: 09953355184

Kumar Trading Company

No. 80, Gandhi Street,
Tilak Bazaar Chowk,
Khari Baoli, Delhi - 110 006,
Delhi, India
Phone: 08376805280

Rohit Marketing

No. 101, Abhivishwa Complex,
Bohlegoan Phata,
Ahmadnagar - 414111,
Maharashtra, India
Phone: 09527886003

Flower Synth

G - 9 & 10, Industrial Estate,
Behind Administrative Block,
Yadavagirii, Mysore - 570 020,
Karnataka, India
Phone: 09845115120

Dattani Book Agency
No. 349 - A A.,
Mangaldas Building No. 5,
Kitchen Garden Lane,
Mumbai - 400002,
Maharashtra, India
Phone: 08377809710
Website:
www.dattanibookagency.com

Neptune Chem India Pvt. Ltd.
111, Atlanta Estate,
Hanuman Tekdi Road,
Goregaon East,
Mumbai - 400 063,
Maharashtra, India
Phone: 09821075695

Shri Sai Trading Company
1/2249, 3rd Fioor-2,
Street No. 12 & 13,
Near Shanti Opticals,
Subhash Road,
Ramnagar, Shahdara,
Delhi - 110 032,
Phone: 08447518302
Website:
www.shrisaitradingcompany.com

Ujjwal Mentha Products
Near Gauri Sahai Mandir
Kote East,
Sambhal, Moradabad - 244302,
Uttar Pradesh, India
Phone: 09760004405

Karnataka Aromas
K. C. I. Chambers, No. 160,
3rd Floor, 5th Main Road,
Chamrajpet,
Bengaluru - 560 053,
Karnataka, India
Phone: 08447564523
Website: www.karnatakaaromas.in

Ronak Flavours & Fragrances
No. J - 74 , M. I. D. C. Boisar,
Thane - 401 506,
Maharashtra, India
Phone: 09321717975

Prakash Chemicals
Anaj Mandi, Budaun - 243 601,
Uttar Pradesh, India
Phone: 09412295642

Maschmeijer Aromatics (India) Pvt. Ltd.
P. B. No. 3,
Great Southern Trunk Road,
Chromepet, Chennai - 600044,
Tamil Nadu, India
Phone: 08377807568

Suyash Herbs Export Pvt. Ltd.
No. 4311/3, GIDC, Sachin,
Road No. 4, Near Sagar Hotel,
Behind Laxmi Atta
Near Priya Gold Biscuit Factory,
Sachin,
Surat - 394230, Gujarat, India
Phone: 09376012345

Zen Intratrade Pvt. Limted
G-2, Leela Apartment,
(Opp. Gtc Inds. Ltd.)
355, S.V.Road, Vile Parle(West),
Mumbai - 400056,
Maharashtra, India
Phone: 09223306873

ALCOHOL

Akhil Healthcare Pvt. Ltd.

No. 205/206, B. B. C. Tower,
Opposite World Trade Center,
Sayajigunj, Vadodara - 390020,
Gujarat, India
Phone: 08377805714

Triveni Aromatics And Perfumery Pvt. Ltd.

No. 134, Pancharatna Char Rasta,
G. I. D. C., Vapi - 386195,
Gujarat, India
Phone: 08376808198
Website:
www.trivenichemicals.com

Alpha Chemicals Pvt. Ltd.

Flat No. A-004, Janvi Building,
Plot No.58/2,
Behind New Prant Office,
Panvel - 410206,
Maharashtra, India
Phone: 08447565119
Website:
www.alphachemicalsindia.com

Rubsol Enterprises

Gala No. 20,
Cresent Industrial Premises,
Co- Operative Society Ltd.,
A. K. Estate,
Loyalka Street, Kherani Road,
Saki Naka,
Mumbai - 400 072,
Maharashtra, India
Phone: 08373903316
Website: www.rubsol.com

Sai Organics

B - 117, Rajeev Nagar, Mandoli,
Delhi - 110093,
Delhi, India
Phone: 08588873897

Thurs Organics Pvt. Ltd.

Udyog Mandir No. 1,
Unit No. 19,
Pitamber Lane, Mahim West,
Mumbai - 400016,
Maharashtra, India
Phone: 08376808471
Website: www.thursorganics.com

Triveni Chemicals

No. 135, Pancharatna Char Rasta,
G. I. D. C.,
Vapi - 396 195,
Gujarat, India
Phone: 08447574103
Website: www.trivenichemical.com

Prakash Chemicals Pvt. Ltd.

Induchacha House,
Opposite Chhani Octroi,
Naka, Vadodara - 390002,
Gujarat, India
Phone: 08588802567

Shreeji Fine Chem

78/80, V. V. Chandan Street,
Mogi Niwas,
Ground Floor,
Masjid West,
Mumbai - 400003,
Maharashtra, India
Phone: 08373903526
Website: www.shreejifinechem.net

Niram Chemicals

No. 8, Ground Floor,
Vireshverdhara,
Bajaj Road, Vile Parle West, Mumbai - 400 056,
Maharashtra, India
Phone: 08376809629

COSMETIC GRADE CLAY

Selekta International

PO Box N- 18, Bouhsina,
Sousse - 40 48, Tunisia
Phone: 098208134

Hind Enterprises

No. 10/ 12, Narayan Niwas,
Office No. 10,
3rd Floor,
Opposite Edward Cinema,
Jamboolwadi,
Kalbadevi Road,
Mumbai - 400002,
Maharashtra, India
Phone: 08376805858
Website: www.hindenterprises.net

Sri Ramamaruti Vermiculite Mines

310, SIDCO AIEMA Tower,
1st Main Road,
Ambattur Industrial Estate,
Chennai - 600058,
Tamil Nadu, India
Phone: 08447573603
Website: www.vermiculitemanufacturers.com

Ecosense Lab India Pvt. Ltd.

B. P. T. Plot No. 225,
Boathard Road,
Darukhana Reay Road,
Mazgoan,
Mumbai - 400010,
Maharashtra, India
Phone: 08377801258

Fire & Safety House

No. 12,
Umesh Commercial Complex,
Ground Floor,
Near Chaudhary High School,
Rajkot - 360001, Gujarat, India
Phone: 08377806675

Sanjay Chemical Industries

A-8, Vishal Industrial Estate,
Goddev Fatak Road,
Opposite Panchal Estate,
Near Sai Temple,
Bhayander - East,
District Thane, Mumbai - 401 105,
Maharashtra, India
Phone: 08447496453

Dev International

No. 301, 3rd Floor,
Solitaire Complex,
Opposite Bombay Garage,
Shahibaug,
Ahmedabad - 380004,
Gujarat, India
Phone: 08377800758

Caltron Clays & Chemicals Pvt. Ltd.
Office No. B - 37,
Ashoka Super Market,
S. V. Road, Goregaon West,
Mumbai - 400104,
Maharashtra, India
Phone: 08376808427
Website: www.caltron-clays.com

Golden Micro Chemicals
Ambewadi No. 2, Sangam Society,
Opposite H.C.C.,
L.B.S. Marg, Vikhroli- West,
Mumbai - 400083,
Maharashtra, India
Phone: 09953354945

Royal Mineral
Hasan Peer Bazar, Mundra,
Kutch - 370421, Gujarat, India
Phone: 08586923446

Labdhi Chemicals
No. A - 503, Nirman Complex,
Opposite Havmor Restaurant,
Behind Navrangpura Bus Stop,
Navrangpura,
Ahmedabad - 380009,
Gujarat, India
Phone: 08377804454

MENTHOL

Abdullabhai Abdul Kader
4 A, 2nd Floor, Shalimar Complex,
Mahalaxmi Five Cross Road,
Paldi, Ahmedabad - 380007,
Gujarat, India
Phone: 08377808093

Bhagat Aromatics Ltd
A - 76, Sector - 57,
Noida - 201301,
Uttar Pradesh, India
Phone: 08586975053

Katyani Exports
No. 325, 3rd Floor, Plot No. 12,
Vardhman Big 'V' Plaza,
Near M2K,
Road No. 44, Rani Bagh,
Pitampura,
New Delhi - 110034, Delhi, India
Phone: 08447573725
Website: www.katyaniexport.com

Akhil Healthcare Pvt. Ltd.
No. 205/206, B. B. C. Tower,
Opposite World Trade Center,
Sayajigunj, Vadodara - 390020,
Gujarat, India
Phone: 08377805714

Akshar Exim Company Pvt. Ltd.
No. 32, Baranasi Ghosh Street,
Near Girish Park Metro,
Kolkata - 700007,
West Bengal, India
Website: www.akesharexim.com

Atreyee Impex
D-11, Dronacharya Apartment,
Mayur Vihar Extension,
Phase 1,
Noida - 110091,
Uttar Pradesh, India
Phone: 08373903436
Website: www.atreyeeimpex.com

Tirupati Organics
No. 101, Civil Line, Near Budaun Club,
Budaun - 243 601, Uttar Pradesh, India
Phone: 09412295328

Suyash Herbs Export Pvt. Ltd.
No. 4311/3, GIDC, Sachin,
Road No. 4,
Near Sagar Hotel,
Behind Laxmi Atta
Near Priya Gold Biscuit Factory,
Sachin,
Surat - 394230, Gujarat, India
Phone: 09376012345

Planters International Company
No.466, 3 A Main,
2nd Stage, Indiranagar,
Bengaluru - 560 038,
Karnataka, India
Website: www.plantersinternational.com

AOS Products Pvt. Ltd.
S - 33, South Side Of G. T. Road,
Industrial Area, Near Vijay Nagar,
Ghaziabad - 201009,
Uttar Pradesh, India
Phone: 08447514892

AL - Mamoon Overseas
Room No. 108, 1st Floor,
Parshvnath Plaza - 1, Delhi Road,
Moradabad - 244 001,
Uttar Pradesh, India
Phone: 08373905702

Swastik Industries
Bisuali Gate, Chanduasi,
Moradabad - 202412,
Uttar Pradesh, India
Phone: 09927042730

Mint & Herb
D1- D2 - Ajeetpur Industrial Estate.
Rampur - 244901,
Uttar Pradesh, India
Phone: 09837050756

Royce Trading Company
E- No. 109, Pandav Nagar,
Delhi - 110092, Delhi, India
Phone: 09717682356

K.V. Aromatics Pvt. Ltd.
D - 212 - 215, E. P. I. P. Site - 5,
Surajpur.Industrial Area, Kasna,
Greater Noida - 201306,
Uttar Pradesh, India
Phone: 08447550367
Website: www.kvaromatics.com

Northern Trade Corporation
No. 17- A., Vishawkarma Colony,
Mirzapur Road, Hisar - 125001,
Haryana, India
Phone: 09215600133

Kalawati Laboratories Pvt. Ltd.
S. C. F. 272, 1st Floor,
Mansa Devi Road,
Mani Majra,
Chandigarh - 160101,
Chandigarh, India
Phone: 09356420206

Quality Flavours Export
Mora Industrial Estate,
Prem Nagar,
Export Zone,
Moradabad - 244 001,
Uttar Pradesh, India
Phone: 09761096000

Arora Aromatics Pvt. Ltd.
2 KM Stone,
Moradabad Road, Sambhal,
District Moradabad,
Sambhal - 244 302,
Uttar Pradesh, India
Phone: 09837006477

Reko Industries
No. 14, Satnampark,
Street No. 3,
Bhagat Singh Road,
Delhi - 110 051,
Delhi, India
Phone: 09810175858

ESSENTIAL OILS

Xena Bio Herbals Pvt. Ltd.
No. 3-6-294, Hyderguda,
Hyderabad - 500029,
Andhra Pradesh, India
Phone: 08376808102

Kelkar Foods & Fragrance
No. 1866, Sripati Apartments,
Sadashiv Peth
Opp. Datewada Vande Mataram Chowk,
Pune - 411030, Maharashtra, India
Phone: 08376809198

L. D. G. International
A/43, Badli Extension,
Village Badli,
Near Rohini Jail,
New Delhi - 110042,
Delhi, India
Phone: 08373902853
Website: www.ldginternational.in

M. S. International
No. 166/3, Shastri Nagar,
Kanpur - 208 005,
Uttar Pradesh, India
Phone: 09795396447

Shiv Sales Corporation
252, Kotla, Mayur Vihar, Phase-1,
Near Gujjar Bhavan,
Delhi - 110091, Delhi, India
Phone: 08447566062
Website: www.shivorganics.com

Sagar Aromatics
Off No. 9, Building No. 162,
Udhyan Darshan,
Near Samta Nagar Bus Depot,
Kandivali East,
Mumbai - 400101,
Maharashtra, India
Phone: 08447501270
Website:
www.naturalaromaoilsofindia.com

Etosha Pan, (India) Pvt. Ltd.
209, Munish Plaza, 20,
Ansari Road,
New Delhi - 110002, Delhi, India
Phone: 08377802447

S. K Expo, New Delhi

No. 1115, Main Bazar,
Pahar Ganj,
New Delhi - 110055, Delhi, India
Phone: 08586968853

Ultra International Ltd.

No. 64/1, Site - 4,
Sahibabad Industrial Area,
Ghaziabad - 201 010,
Uttar Pradesh, India
Phone: 09953359268

Scientific International

1590, Madarsa Road,
Kashmere Gate,
Delhi - 110006, Delhi, India
Phone: 08447499614
Website: www.laboratory-testing-instruments.com

Shri Sai Trading Company

1/2249, 3rd Floor-2,
Street No. 12 & 13,
Near Shanti Opticals,
Subhash Road,
Ramnagar, Shahdara,
Delhi - 110 032,
Phone: 08447518302
Website: www.shrisaitradingcompany.com

Prisha Herbals

Plot No. 576/ 203, Sai Residency,
Shiv City,
Indore - 452012,
Madhya Pradesh, India
Phone: 08586924829

Harish C. Khosla & Co. Pvt. Ltd.

No. 1954, Zinat Mahal,
Lal Kuan Bazar,
Delhi - 110006, Delhi, India
Phone: 08377805347

Moksha Lifestyle Products

No. 24/157, Shakti Nagar,
G. T. Karnal Road,
Delhi - 110007, India
Phone: 08377802094
Website: www.indiaessentialoil.com

Veera Fragrances Pvt. Ltd.

No. 86, F. I. E., Patparganj,
Delhi - 110 092, India
Phone: 08376807904

K. K. Enterprise

U-22, Mahalaxmi Market,
Near Old Udhna Petrol Pump,
Udhna, Surat - 394210,
Gujarat, India
Phone: 08447516138
Website: www.kkaromatic.in

Shiv Sales Corporation

No. 252, Kotla, Mayur Vihar,
Phase-1,
Near Gujjar Bhavan,
Delhi - 110091, India
Phone: 08447576304
Website: www.essentialaromaoils.com

Sms Traders

Address: Adda Chabawal,
Hoshiarpur - 146102, Punjab, India
Phone: 09316086724

Munna Lal Sons & Company Perfumers Pvt. Ltd.

Hina Building, P. O. Box No. 16,
Kannauj - 209 725,
Uttar Pradesh, India
Phone: 09839702952

Shree Botanicals

25, Pratima Colony,
Opp. Palm Fuel Petrol Pump Pipeline Road,
Ahmadnagar - 414111,
Maharashtra, India
Phone: 09527886003

Centaur Exports

No. 3059, Sector - E,
Sudama Nagar,
Indore - 452009,
Madhya Pradesh, India
Phone: 08377804375

Green Field Exports

No. 20, New Fruit Mandi,
Bhadwasiya,
Jodhpur - 342006,
Rajasthan, India
Phone: 08373904642
Website: www.spicesexporter.com

Shakti Oils & Fats

Guru Kripa, No. 62/5,
Atindra Mukherjee Lane,
Shibpur, Howrah - 711102,
West Bengal, India
Phone: 08376806695
Website: www.shaktioilsfats.com

Jugal Kishore Perfumery

H. No.- 2108, Chandra Mahal,
Shadual Singh Ki Naal,
Jaipur - 302 001,
Rajasthan, India
Phone: 09953360240

Suyash Herbs Export Pvt. Ltd.

No. 4311/3, GIDC, Sachin,
Road No. 4,
Near Sagar Hotel,
Behind Laxmi Atta
Near Priya Gold Biscuit Factory,
Sachin,
Surat - 394230, Gujarat, India
Phone: 09376012345

Shri Aromas

No. 50, Kathayani Niliya,
2nd Cross,
Obaiah Lane, Akkipet Cross,
Bengaluru - 560053,
Karnataka, India
Phone: 09953361638

Quality Products Lab Pvt. Ltd.

C- 78, Near Sector- 83,
Hosiery Complex,
Phase- 2 Extn., Noida - 201301,
Uttar Pradesh, India
Phone: 09868124165
Website: www.qualityproductslab.in

Indian Spice Oils Industries

R 9/53, Rajnagar,
Ghaziabad - 201 002,
Uttar Pradesh, India
Phone: 08377805034

43

PACKAGING CRITERIA FOR COSMETICS AND TOILETRIES

Packaging is an integral part of the consumer products merchandising. Cosmetics industry whether it is soaps, detergents, toiletries, cosmetics, packaged foods or beverages, healthcare products or consumer durables all owe their success to the packaging industry.

The following table gives an idea of the present size of the cosmetics market.

PRODUCTS	QUANTITY	VALUE (Rs. Mn)
Talcum Powder	12,700 Mt	2300
Soaps	44,000 Mt	5000
Creams	2,000 Kl	1330
Lotion	1,150 Kl	447
Shampoo	13,700 Mt	3200
Toothpaste	50,000 Mt	6000
Antiseptic Liquids	1,590 Kl	200

Packaging development is a multi-functional involvement with marketing/sales, research, engineering, materials and manufacturing having prominent role in successful packaging development.

EVOLUTION OF PACKAGING

The role of packaging development can be traced to early days of industrialisation with emphasis on productivity and convenience to customers. A few decades ago it was a common sight to see consumers depending for their requirements for bulk dispensing. Packaged goods have changed this scenario altogether. Today even products like salt are packed in small, convenient packs.

With the setting up of cosmetics and toiletry manufacturing units in the early 60s, packaging got a tremendous impetus when several home made products were replaced by manufactured and packed products. Early packaging consisted of mostly tin containers or glass bottles in simple shapes and sizes with emphasis on utility rather than aesthetics. With consumers becoming more and more educated and influenced by media explosion, demand for aesthetically attractive and functionally superior packaging has been exponentially increasing. Manufactures of cosmetics and toiletry products have fully realised the importance of attractive and efficient packing system conveying quality and brand image.

FUNCTIONAL REQUIREMENTS OF PACKAGING

Functional requirements of packaging can be classified into :

* Technical
* Aesthetics
* Cost

Technical : Under technical consideration, the factors to be examined are chemicals and physical compatibility of the product with the packaging material).

Aesthetic : Presentability/appearance, technicalities and practicability in packaging design and abiding SWAMPAC Rules.
Cost : Cost-effectiveness of package is an important consideration.

CHEMICAL COMPATIBILITY :

The primary container (package) and the auxiliaries coming in contact with the product (e.g. plug, wadliner, etc.) should not react with the product or any of its ingredients. The material from which the container is made should be impermeable to the product. If the product is liable to deterioration/discoloration in sunlight, then the container must have UV absorbers. To meet this requirement, one has to be very familiar with the chemical properties of the product as well as the chemical properties of packaging material components.

Chemical compatibility may be ascertained by checking product stability. Stability of the product over the period for which it is expected to lie on the shelf is done by conducting accelerated ageing studies (at 38 deg. C temperature and 90% R.H.) Stability study will also confirm whether the colour of the container (in case of coloured packaging materials) leaches out and affects the colour of the product of vice-a-versa.

Some plastic materials impart their own smell or modify the perfume. The perfume notes have to be checked after ageing the product in the container in the case of perfumed products.

PHYSICAL COMPATIBILITY

1. Retention of Volatiles : Many health care products have a high percentage of volatiles such as water or alcohol, loss of volatiles would affect the quality of product, perfume is usually more volatile and hence its retention is very important. The volatiles should neither escape in vapour form from the closure system nor permeate through container walls.

2. Leak proof caps : No container, however, perfect is of any value unless it has an efficient closure system. Idealy the closure should be easy to remove and replace, but should give a seal that prevents the diffusion of gases and vapours and of liquids. Most bottle and tube closures consist of a screw cap containing compressible wad, although wadless caps are coming into wider use of late. Leak-proof property of the cap along with the container must be checked with the intended product and not with water. As water may not leak but through many closure systems but products like shampoo, oil can find a way to come out as each of them has got peculiar characteristics.

There is increasing trend for making the closure not only leak-proof, but also tamper-indicating. This is a very desirable development.

3. Tamper-proof Seal : Most of the consumer products in the category of cosmetics/toiletries attract very high duties which make them expensive. A customer who is willing to pay a high price for such a product will naturally expect an intact product. A product pack having tamper-proof seal will automatically assure its intactnes to the customer. Most manufacturers are in the process of developing pilfer-proof seal for

their products wherever it is not there. A few examples are - many plastic containers now are seen with PVC heat-shrinkable pilfer-proof sleeves ; Glass and plastic bottles with ROPP caps ; Cartons are either closed with cellotape or glued, if not, the product inside is packed in a sealed polybag. Aluminium collapsible tubes have metallic membrane seals on the nozzles.

4. Transport Hazards : Tertiary packaging materials (shippers) are designed to take care of the product damaged during transit. If the shipper is made of corrugated box, then grammage, type of paper, flute, number of primary packs to be packed are considered. Even the type of glue to be used while manufacturing corrugated box has to be specified. Cushioning material also plays an important role in taking care of this factor.

AESTHETIC FACTORS

(i) Presentability/Appearance - The aesthetic side of package design is basically a marketing responsibility, but a very close liaison between marketing and packaging experts is essential to ensure that a design is aesthetically functional and technically feasible. This applies not only to the container itself but also to the labelling and printing, and to the design of the display holders too.

In packaging of cosmetic products probably the package is ten times more important than the product. Esoteric shapes of crystal clear glass bottles, fancy spray systems, oversize decorative caps, glossy sophisticated lables and eye-catching cartons made from laminated boards combine to make a pack of cosmetic product a piece of art. Its designing requires the imagination of creative artist rather than scientific knowledge of a package engineer.

An attractive pack appeals to the consumer and contributes substantially to the initial sales of the product. An average product with appealing package can succeed. On the other hand even an excellent product with defective packaging is bound to fail. Good packaging is, therefore, very important for the success of a product.

(ii) Packaging Design - Technicalities - As far as technicalities of the package design are concerned, in general, the final pack must be sufficiently strong to survive the normal treatment it is liable to receive during manufacturing process, distribution, sale and actual use at customer's end. There is bound to be a certain failure of packs, largely due to accidents, but it is essential that this failure rate is very low, if the product has to be a commercial success. Typical possible problems we look for in package design are :

a) Thin areas in containers - glass or plastic ;
b) Highly stressed areas-when polyolefins are used ;
c) Very small radius convex areas on the outside of focusing UV radiation, and so concentrate its harmful effects on to small areas of a product ; and
d) Stability of the container - especially plastic containers with unstable bases can give rise to troubles on a mechanical filling line.

Apart from all the technical and aesthetic parameters of a pack, it must also dispense the product easily and be convenient for the customer to handle. There is nothing more infuriating to a customer than a lotion that will not come out of a container because the orifice of the nozzle is too small, or a deodorant squeeze pack that squirts a direct jet of liquid rather than the expected fine spray. Problem of a badly judged orifice size in the first example and incorrect orifice dimensions and design in the second example can stop the growth of the respective products. These two problems can easily be overcome if proper attention is paid while designing the pack. One of the solutions to avoid these problems is to do technical survey of similar packs used for similar products. Any shortcomings in the competitor's pack can be a lesson to overcome similar problems while designing the pack.

iii) Packaging Design - Pratically - The practicability includes easy availability of the material, presence of alternative suppliers, supplier's capacity, limitations as far as their machines are concerned and cost considerations.

Whenever any new packaging material has to be introduced its availability must be checked, we must check the expertise, technical know-how and capabilities of the existing supplier. It is always advisable to go for indigenously available packaging material where availability is not a problem. Packaging expert must visit the supplier's premises and check under what conditions the supplier is going to manufacture the material. It is also better to check whether more than one suppliers are available. Manufacturing capacity must also be critically evaluated.

COST-EFFECTIVENESS OF PACK

The last but not the least factor to be considered is cost. Selection of design, material shape, weight, etc. must be appropriate. Every paise saved in packaging is the real profit.

Secondly, cost economy can be achieved by minimising the handling of the packaging material, e.g. corrugated boxes can be delivered to the plastic container manufacturer who in turn will pack them in the desired manner and despatch them to the factory. In this process we can avoid loading-unloading, opening-closing of the shippers. Moreover containers packed uniformly will help to make on-line operations (i.e. stamping conveying) easier.

Another example we can take is that of printing. One can go for four colour off-set printing or settle with two colours. As three colour off-set printing machines are not available in our country. Either we can print on four colour machine or print twice on two colour machine.

It is true that cost holds the balance between aesthetic and functional considerations. When this equilibrium is attained, then we can say the pack is cost-effective.

PACKAGING MATERIALS

A wide range of materials are used in packing cosmetics and soaps. These can be broadly classified into the following :

* Glass
* Metal - Tin and Aluminium
* Plastics
* Paper

Glass : Glass is still one of the oldest materials known for packaging goods right from the Bronze Age. It is believed that Egyptians were using glass as early as 3000 B.C. Commercial manufacturing of glass commenced in early 1900. Glass is impervious to virtually all common liquids and gases. Glass is most suitable for products which must not change for a long time.

Glass is highly attractive with characteristic sparkle due to high refractive index. Glass is highly resistant to corrosion and not attacked by the contents of most toiletries and cosmetic products.

With all the goodness as primary packaging material, glass is heavy, having more weight per unit volume packed ; it is fragile, breakable and breaks in sharp edges, Being clear, it offers little protection to the contents from harmful UV irradiation. Sodium ions can leach from glass causing emulsion destabliisation.

Glass is rigid and cannot be used for easy-to-dispense squeezable products. Over 80% of the glass containers are used in packing food and beverages. Only 10% are used in pharmaceutical products. In cosmetics, glass is used for packing colognes, sprays, perfumes, etc., which reflect better value for money to the customer.

Glass containers can be made scratchproof by applying suitable lacquer.

Metal : Metal containers are most suited for packing powder and cream either in tins, collapsible tubes or shallow tins. By and large, metal containers are mainly used for packing beer, fruits, processed food and to a lesser extent for packing cosmetics products.

Most commonly packed products in collapsible tubes are different types of creams apart from tooth pastes.

Collapsible tubes and shallow tins are made from high purity aluminium which is readily deformable, light and does not puncture under normal usage conditions. It is totally impermeable to liquids and gases.

While packing in aluminium tube, careful attention must be paid to the problem of corrosion which can be caused due to acidity or alkalinity or by galvanic reaction. Highly attractive products such as depilatories and acidic such as hydroquinone skin bleaches cannot be packed in aluminium tubes. Galvanic corrosion of aluminium is very common and tubes placed under slightly acidic or alkaline condition or even under neutral conditions if electrolytic is present. Interior of aluminium tubes is generally coated with chemical resistant epoxy lacquers.

Plasticss : Plastic materials overcome a number of shortcomings of glass as they are light-weight, tough, unbreakable, and can be flexible. Whereas glass offers a high degree of clarity and impervious, plastics are generally somewhat inferior in this respect and barrier properties depend on the type of plastics used.

A wide range of plastic materials are used in packaging. Large toonage plastics used are :

* HDPE
* Polypropylene
* Polyvinyl chloride
* Polystyrene
* Polyethlene terpthalate
* PETG (Glycol modified)

Table 1 gives comparative properties of different plastics.

Plastic materials being organic in nature are susceptible to attack by a variety of agents such as oil, plasticizer, alcohol, water, etc. Products packed should be compatible with the plastic container. There should be no migration of the product through the packaging material nor there should be leaching of plastic additives into the product which may interfere with perfume and colour.

Paper : Different types of papers are used as secondary of tertiary packing, but to a less extent primary packing except for soaps.

Glassine, pulp board laminated with polythylene, and printed and laminated maplitho paper are used in wrapping soaps.

As secondary packing, various types of boards, viz., duplex, chromo board or Eurocote are used in making cartons.

Tertiary packing, viz., shippers or outers are made from different grades of kraft paper with different types of flutings.

PRODUCT EVALUATION :

Before deciding on any packaging material or whenever there is change of packaging material or source, it is necessary to carry out product packaging compatibility study. Compatibility study is generally carried out by keeping filed containers at 38 deg and 49 deg C at 90% relative humidity for a period upto 3 months. There is no hard and fast rule on protocol and accelerated compatibility studies. Generally following observations are made :

- Exudation of contents, if any

- Perfume retention/deterioration

- Weight loss/drying of product

- Emulsion stability

- Preservative stability

- Colour migration/retention

Compatibility study is best carried out alongwith current packaging material control. If there is no undersirable effects, the packaging material is released for use.

TRANSIT TRIALS

The importance of transit trials cannot be overemphasised. Though there are transit simulators, which give results in a short time, the best results are obtained by sending experimental packages through different modes of transit and assessing the condition of the packages for breakage, leakage, bursting, tear, etc. It is advisable to send packages as part load consignment which undergoes multiple handling and hence more susceptible to damage.

PRODUCT CHARACTERISTICS & PACKAGING MATERIALS

Each type of cosmetic product will require a different type of packaging material, depending upon the properties of the packaging material and the contents.

Table-II gives a brief summary of different types of cosmetic products, their characteristics, packaging requirements and suitable packaging matrials.

LEGAL REQUIREMENTS

All packaged goods in India are governed under The Standards of Weights and Measures (Packaged Commodities) Rules 1977 (SWAMPAC) and subsequent amendments from time to time. These rules prescribe the manner in which the product can be packed in specified quantities, statutory declarations, price, date of manufacturing, address of manufacture, etc. These rules also specify the pack sizes in which a product cannot be marketed, the letter size of the text matter on the label, requirements of principal display panels, etc.

SWAMPAC rules are quite comprehensive and cover all aspects of packaged goods. These rules are covered under eleven schedules. They are :

SCHEDULE	CONTENTS
First	Maximum permissible error with respect to quantity (some items)
Second	Maximum permissible error with respect to quantity (all items)
Third	Commodities can be packed in specified quantities only
Fourth	Quantity to be qualified by words "When Packed", etc.
Fifth	Commodities to be sold by weight, measure and number only.
Sixth	Commodities to be sold in specified quantity when sold by number
Seventh	Declaration of the unit sale price
Eighth	Commodities for sale in smaller quantities from a packed unit
Ninth	Selection of samples for testing
Tenth	Determination of net quantity
Eleventh	Weight checking data sheet

Besides the above mentioned schedules, major emphasis is on minimum information to be provided on the principal display panel in the prescribed manner. Principal display panel (PDP) should carry the relevant information which will enable the consumer to make decision in respect of price, quantity, date of manufacture, manufactureres ' name, etc. The information displayed should be such that the consumer can read it easily and hence there are requirements of minimum letter height depending upon the area of the pack. These rules also place restrictions on the certain expressions which are ambiguous like Jumbo, Economy, King, Queen, Giant, etc. Such expressions tend to distort the information related to the product and create some false impressions.

CLOSING

Packaging is a vast and a rapidly changing field giving tremendous scope for an individual to design a cost effective, most attractive and easy to use packaging system. For a satisfactory packaging design, it is essential to have in-depth knowledge of product characteristics and packaging material.

Products/packaging compatibility is the single most important factor deciding the suitability of a particular packaging material and this requires a very careful evaluation as the product packed has to remain on the shelf for a number of years. With a proper selection of material and judicious choice of container shape, manufacturing machinery, cost effective and elegant packaging can be designed. Besides packaging designing, we need to pay special attention to the legal requirements.

TABLE-I PERMEABILITY OF PLASTICS

Plastic	Clarity	WVT	Gas Permeability			Chemical Resistance		
			Oxygen	Nitrogen	Carbon Dioxide	Acid	Alkali	Solvent
HDPE	Translucent	0.3	600	70	450	E	E	E
LDPE	Translucent	1.3	550	180	290	G	G	G
PP	Translucent	0.7	240	60	800	E	E	E
PVC	Transparent	4	150	-	970	E	E	E
PET	Transparent	2-4	10	-	20	E	E	E

WVT :
gloss/24hr./100 sq inch/mil at 95 deg F, 90% RH
Gas Permeability :
cc/24hr./100 sq inch/mil at 77 deg F, 50% RH

TABLE-II
PRODUCT CHARACTERISTICS & PACKAGING MATERIALS

Product	Characterstics	Packaging Requirments	Suitable Packaging Material
Talcum Powder	Inert, perfumed	Retain perfume, easy to apply, should not discolour the product	Metal container, HDPE, PP
Soap	Alkaline, pH 9.5-10 Tendency to dry. Perfume retention	Paper should not discolor, impervious to moisture loss, retain perfume	Glassine, polycoated board BOOP/PET laminated paper. poli pouch, cartons
Shampoo	Mild acidic to alkaline, pH 5.5-9.0 contains surfactants	Should not undergo stress cracking, plasticiser /additives. Should not leach into product	Glass, HDPE PVC, PET, PETG
Oils	Mineral oil/Vegetable oil inert	Can migrate through plastics	Glass, HDPE, PVC, PET PETG
Creams	O/W or W/O emulsion. Contain surfactants, tendency to dry, perfume retention	Air tight packing, should not exude /leak	Aluminium tin, collapsible tube, laminated tube, LDPE tube, HDPE ceramic.
Cologne/After Shave	Volatile, contains alcohol.	Withstand pressure, not affected by alcohol.	Glass, HDPE, Aluminium Aerosal container.
Shaving Cream Foam	Soap based alkaline	Should not affect container	Aluminium tube. Aerosal container

AUTOMATIC CARTON OVERWRAPPING MACHINE

Automatic wrapping machine for over wrapping rectangular cartons like tooth brush carton, blade carton & cassettes with B.O.P.P./ Cellophane.

* Output upto 120 cartons/min.
* Power input 2 KW

POWDER DOZING MACHINE

Dozing unit for accurate filling of powders like tooth powder, talcum powder, baby powder, dry syrups, coffee, etc. in pouches or containers.

* Output upto 2000 fills/hr.
* Power input 0.75 KW

CREAM FILLER

Filling machine for creams, grease, adhesives, lotions, balms, gums, etc. in pouches or containers.

* Output upto 2000 containers/hr.
* Power input 0.75 KW

AUTOMATIC ROTARY CAPPING MACHINE

Rotary capper for automatic capping of pre-threaded plastic caps on to bottles of different shapes & sizes.

* Output upto 120 bottles/min.
* Power input 2 KW

FLOW WRAPPING MACHINE

Suitable for single/multiple products as feeding is directly on to the film can be used for wide range of product sizes. Accommodates variety of heat sealable films and laminates.

* Output upto 7200 Pkts/Hr.
* Power input : 2.5 KW
* Pillow type packing

4449 Nai Sarak, Main Road, Delhi - 110006 (INDIA)
Ph : 91- 11- 23916431, 23918117, 45120361, 64727385, 23947058
E-Mail : eiriprojects@gmail.com Website: www.eiriindia.org